1982

Characters in the Twilight

HARDY

ZOLA

and

CHEKHOV

CHARACTERS IN THE TWILIGHT

Hardy, Zola, and Chekhov

Anthony Winner

UNIVERSITY PRESS OF VIRGINIA
Charlottesville

THE UNIVERSITY PRESS OF VIRGINIA
Copyright © 1981 by the Rector and Visitors
of the University of Virginia

First published 1981

ISBN 0-8139-0894-9

Library of Congress Cataloging in Publication Data

Winner, Anthony.
    Characters in the twilight.

    Contents: Balzac's Le père Goriot: the character
of society—Hardy's moderns: the ache of uncertain
character—Zola: characters in the fields of
force—[etc.]
    1. Characters and characteristics in literature.
2. Fiction—19th century—History and criticism.
I. Title.
PN3411.W56   809.3'927   81-10355
ISBN 0-8139-0894-9   AACR2

Printed in the United States of America

DARIO SORIA

1912–1980

Uncle, Counselor, Friend

CONTENTS

Acknowledgments

This book exists as the result of support and concern so extensive as to be beyond specific acknowledgment. Loved ones, friends, colleagues, and students have all contributed. For their encouraging advice on various stages of my progress I should like to mention Janice Carlisle, Gay Clifford, Hoyt Duggan, and Austin Quigley. Without the generous arrangement for research time worked out by Robert Kellogg, I could not have proceeded. A research grant from the University of Virginia helped defray the cost of typing.

INTRODUCTION

The creation of character is the glory of the novelistic traditions that Hardy, Zola, and Chekhov inherit. In their different ways, they all subscribe to the idea of character dominant in nineteenth-century representational fiction. The disparity between this model and the seemingly unprecedented conditions of contemporary actuality accounts in large part for the bafflement, contradiction, and human pain they so persistently narrate. For each author, what E. M. Forster terms roundedness or multidimensionality is not an interpretative category but the moral imperative of novelistic art. For each author, the creation of character conflates ethical and rhetorical aspirations; cultural ideals and narrative ambitions, the proper conduct of life and the genuine achievement of art, are as one. Recent semiotic and structuralist as well as Marxist and psychophilosophical criticism questions the premises of this desired union. "Character" and "realism" are now subject to intense, often valuably skeptical, scrutiny. The very nature of this kind of investigation, however, sets aside the historical configurations that shape Hardy's Wessex, Zola's Second Empire, and Chekhov's Twilight Russia.[1] Yet the

---

[1] See, for example, J. Hillis Miller's Preface to his *Thomas Hardy: Distance and Desire*: "Literary criticism is language about language, or, to put it another way, a re-creating in the mind of the critic of the consciousness in the texts studied, generated there by the words. To say this is to put in question certain habitual metaphors for what happens in the act of criticism. . . . Illicit also are the metaphors for criticism which propose to explain the text by something extralinguistic which precedes it and which is its generative source—

radical disjunction between tradition and reality experienced by these three writers, and the rethinking of purpose and technique it necessitates, constitutes the threshold to modern fiction and the clearest point of departure for subsequent inquiries into the meaning and legitimacy of fiction itself. From the vantage of recent speculation, the aims, quandries, and responses I study may appear to be ingenuous, even unnecessary or ill-founded. The commitment to create realistic characters may seem a dubious effort on an uncertain ground. But our doubts originate in the beleaguered structure of late-century fiction. And to reproduce the tone and temper of the questioning this fiction contains we must suspend as anachronistic the judgments of recent inquiry.

In the traditions Hardy, Zola, and Chekhov would reform, character—as distinguished from personality—is a synthesis of inner energies, the factual circumstances of the sociohistorical moment, and the often concealed but all-important purposes of moral culture. Character is formed through a dynamic interaction between the private demands of innate notions or desires and the ordering goals provided by what the professor in Chekhov's *A Dull Story* calls "a general idea, or the god of a living man."[2] The synthesis represented by achieved character requires that the thesis of personal aspiration be alchemized by the antithesis of real things. During the last third of the century, the realities that previously functioned as a crucible for the development and cultural mediation of individual energy come to seem in absolute opposition both to subjective needs and to moral

---

the life or psychology of the author, historical conditions at a certain time . . ." (Cambridge, Mass.: Harvard Univ. Press, 1970, p. vii).

[2] Anton Chekhov, *Ward Six and Other Stories*, trans. Ann Dunnigan, (New York: Signet Classics, 1965), p. 216.

truths. The period is well evoked by the word once used to describe the baffled energies and blurred perspectives of late-century Russia: the Twilight. For many writers and thinkers, not just in Russia but in the West as well, the clarity of prior definitions and assumptions becomes dim or uncertain. The doubtful atmosphere beclouds inherited models: in the novel, traditional stories often appear to be inappropriate and traditional techniques of discourse to be inapplicable. Rather like Pirandello's six characters a generation later, the figures I discuss are in search of an author—or more exactly, they, as well as the psychic and public worlds they inhabit, have been cast loose from the authority of aspiration and judgment that so many midcentury writers brought to their characterization.

Underlying the manifold uncertainties besetting Twilight fiction is the perception that prior notions about the inner nature of man are inadequate. Whether sympathetically or satirically, novelists of the previous generation had deemed this nature to be an unavoidable but unstable point of departure in the work of character. The truths of inwardness are viewed as incomplete. Those who attempt to create wholeness using only the materials of the private and personal are presented as unrealistic: sometimes otherworldly, more often childish, egocentric, or enthusiastically naive. The experience of worldly things and the support of public frameworks must temper potentiality into character. The difficult development Balzac plots for Rastignac, George Eliot for Dorothea, and Tolstoy for Pierre rings changes on the basic covenant of education that Scott had dramatized in *Waverley* years before. At the conclusion of the young man's story he "felt himself entitled to say firmly, though perhaps with a sigh, that the romance of his life was ended, and that its real history had now commenced."[3] However circuitous the roads from private romance to real history, the trip is a precondition for "real" character. Those who do not wish to travel and those who turn back remain outside the realistic pale. They may be idealists, their pure natures may be of infinite value, but their existence lies on the far side of the Rubicon that Balzac in *Père Goriot* sees as dividing pristine solitude from the dramatic battlefield of actuality.[4] The pure self is without historical form; souls, as Dostoevsky implies in the epilogue to *Crime and Punishment*, are not subjects for novels.

To the large extent that they believe character to require external form and validation, Hardy, Zola, and Chekhov accept the premises of the earlier idea. At the same time, however, they participate in the turn taken by late-century thought toward a more analytic conception of selfhood. They are confronted by intimations of the phenomenon that will preoccupy figures such as Rilke's Malte Laurids Brigge. "I am learning to see," Brigge writes near the beginning of his *Notebooks*. "I don't know why it is, but everything penetrates more deeply into me and doesn't stop at the place where until now it always used to finish. I have an inner self of which I was ignorant. Everything goes thither now. What happens there I do not know."[5] Brigge stands on the verge

[3] Sir Walter Scott, *Waverley* (London: Everyman's Library, 1973), p. 406. The passage occurs at the end of Chapter 60.

[4] Eugène "was not yet even completely free of the fresh, sweet notions that twine like leaves around a country-bred childhood. He had continually hesitated to cross the Paris Rubicon." *Pere Goriot*, trans. Henry Reed (New York: Signet Classics, 1962), p. 217.

[5] Rainer Maria Rilke, *The Notebooks of Malte Laurids Brigge*, trans. M. D. Herter Norton (New York: Capricorn Books, 1958), pp. 14–15.

of a future that will transform the fascinations and complex materials of the psyche into a heroic career of self-creation. Character will develop out of itself, will be absolved of the need for cultural definition. Such absolution is granted by neither Hardy, Zola, nor Chekhov. Yet the fiction of these writers is often challenged by suggestions that "the mysteries of identity," in Robert Langbaum's phrase,[6] may offer a brave new novelistic world; the possibility that the inner life may be in itself a metaphysical unity undercuts the traditional philosophy of character. Part of the sense of contradiction we receive from Hardy's account of the mayor of Casterbridge and Chekhov's of Doctor Ragin in *Ward Six* originates in a division of attention between compelling private realities and moribund public truths.

In the work of Huysmans and several other novelists of the period, character becomes an artifice to be invented; selfhood and art enter into a partnership that will ultimately take over from selfhood and education. Believing as they do in the moral and cultural necessity of the latter collaboration, Hardy, Zola, and Chekhov refuse any version of the former. And this principled refusal leads directly to the melodrama of incompletion and thwarted need that lies at the core of their fiction. The self must learn its true form in the world outside. But this world is sick; its values are devalued or inauthentic. The situation of character in each of the three authors anticipates Thomas Mann's diagnosis of Hans Castorp's state at the beginning of *The Magic Mountain*. "A man lives not only his personal life, as an individual, but also, consciously or unconsciously, the life of his epoch. . . . Now, if the life about him, if his own time seem . . . to be at bottom

---

[6] Robert Langbaum, *The Mysteries of Identity: A Theme in Modern Literature* (New York: Oxford Univ. Press, 1977).

empty of such food for his aspirations; if he privately recognizes it to be hopeless, viewless, helpless, opposing only a hollow silence to all the questions man puts . . . as to the final, absolute, and abstract meaning in all his efforts and activities; then, in such a case, a certain laming of the personality is bound to occur."[7]

Not only is there a laming; the failure of the late-century environment to provide sustenance simultaneously cuts away the sheltering, cultivated terrain of familial or communal realities that once had been marked off for the fulfillment of individual potential. Weakened as they are, characters must endure the elemental, usually alien forces often equated with Schopenhauer's "Will." Instead of the intermediate drama outlined by social conventions—the displacement or transposition of primal passion into marriage stories, of tyranny into politics or finance, of life and death into the stages of sociohistory—private persons must play cosmic parts. The vast schemes of legend, myth, and archetype that later writers will frequently bring to their characters' support emerge in late-century lives as nemeses. Behind the social structures that fail Hardy's men and women lie forces beyond society's ken: energies that prompt to extreme acts and that demand precultural settings such as Egdon Heath and Stonehenge. Hardy at times wants to suggest that the somber realities revealed by the disappearance of social gods and doctrines may prod into being a new strength of character, but his best fiction cleaves to the tragic estrangement of the old. Zola too wants to see in the corruption, self-seeking, and falsity of contemporary social nurture a necessary precondition for renewal. The past must be cauterized, its bad faith gutted

[7] Thomas Mann, *The Magic Mountain*, trans. H. T. Lowe-Porter (New York: Alfred A. Knopf, 1966), p. 32.

out, so that a purged, elemental, national, and communal character can grow. But the radical disfranchisement of social order leads to a reign of terror in which nihilistic lust and mythic murderousness hold sway. The dramatic ground of Zola's fiction is the victimization of traditional individuality at the hands of depredating extremity. Nostalgia and melodramatic pathos usually obscure the intended vision of the dawning of a better mankind. By contrast, Chekhov refuses any omniscient highlighting of meaning. His own inability to believe in the traditional prescriptions of his culture is realized in his fiction through the pained objectivity that immerses itself in the characters' distress but can portray no satisfactory alternatives. Nonetheless, the lives and actions Chekhov so empathically draws create a picture much like that Hardy and Zola paint on their bolder canvases. The shortsightedness of middle-class protagonists is intensified into purblindness by the cruel nature of things. Peasants suffer not only social but cosmic injustice. Conventions no longer shelter character.

The psychological and moral integrity that these writers desire for their characters has no plausible foundation in the real world they describe. Greyness, exhaustion, and insincerity mark the historical moment and conspire to blight the most intimate of affections, the most private of stories. The symptoms vary as does the art that expresses them. But each author equates the revalidation of character with the fundamental purposes of his art. Each wants to restore the sustaining meaning his human figures have lost. Hardy, Zola, and Chekhov all work to adapt and renovate what I describe in my first chapter as the Balzacian idea of character: a collaboration of private energy with public form that is accepted by European novelists as the nucleus of realistic characterization. But acceptable form can no longer be extrapolated from present circumstances; the models provided by the epoch are inauthentic and inappropriate. The descriptive overviews and detailed explications in the studies that follow investigate three different responses to the destitution of realistic character. The writers are traditionalists who see themselves cast out of their traditions. In order to repossess their birthright, they must improvise. But improvisation threatens the continuity they would affirm. Perhaps for this reason, the need for innovation is enacted in created lives that are usually presented through a markedly conservative narrative art. Subsequent generations of novelists and critics have applauded and learned from the technical and thematic departures to be found in this fiction. But even in Zola's *La Faute de l'abbé Mouret*, the most clearly experimental of the works I analyze at length, artistic originality mirrors an existential innovation that the author condemns. In Zola's novel, as in Hardy's *The Mayor of Casterbridge* and Chekhov's *Ward Six*, the tension between an enforced and often uncomfortable experiment to extend the traditional possibilities of the novel and a commitment to the moral standards implicit in these possibilities shapes a lamed but impressive achievement. And although altered so extensively as to be nearly unrecognizable, this tension enters definitively into the questions, speculations, and experiments that dominate present attitudes toward narrative art.

I

BALZAC'S *LE PERE GORIOT:*

The Character of Society

Lecturing on Dostoevsky in 1922, André Gide proclaimed the Russian's drama of randomness and inconsistency to be a conclusive refutation of the "Balzacian ideal" dominant in Western fiction.

> I can say with respect not only to the *Comédie Humaine*, but also to the comedy of everyday life as we live it, that the *dramatis personae* ... are after a Balzacian ideal. The inconsequences [inconsistencies] of our nature, should such exist, seem to us awkward and ridiculous. We deny them. We try to ignore them, to palliate them. ... We consistently behave as the character we are—or fancy we are—ought to behave. The majority of our actions are dictated, not by the pleasure we take in doing them, but by the need of imitating ourselves and projecting our past into the future. We sacrifice truth (that is to say, sincerity) to purity and continuity of line.

Dostoevsky's characters, who "without any thought for consistency, yield with facility to every contradiction and negation of which their particular constitution is capable,"[1] are true; the characters of the Balzacian ideal are not.

For Gide, the consistency of action that the characters of Western fiction absorb from their culture is as illusory as

[1] André Gide, *Dostoevsky*, trans. anon. (London: Secker & Warburg, 1949), pp. 101–2.

the purposes of that culture. Gide exalts a unique identity resistant to the falsities of sociohistory. He and many other early modern novelists would transcend the confusion of the Twilight by fashioning heroes who, pursuing their private ideas and sensations, construct selves that are proof against inauthenticity. The kind of perversity Dostoevsky places on exhibit in *Notes from Underground* becomes a method for tearing out the social emphases and values that the Balzacian ideal internalizes in its idea of character.

In Balzac's major fiction it is precisely the framework provided by internalized social realities that structures the historical validity and mundane effectiveness of character. Unlike the writers of the Twilight, who cannot conceive viable character without social dimension and yet cannot believe this dimension capable of insuring existential meaning, Balzac consistently depicts social processes, roles, and aspirations as inseparable from meaningful individuality. Even the moral, quasi-allegorical types with which, for example, *La Cousine Bette* abounds are realized dramatically through their involvement in a social setting whose motives and cues for action include class ideology, the economics of love and lust, and the expectations of mundane power. As Georg Lukács has argued, the dynamics of individual psychology are usually particularized versions of general social processes.[2] Balzac appoints himself secretary to a world in which neither ideal sentiments nor principles can be staged. Both the earthly drama and its dramatis personae act out a realistic pragmatism akin to that advocated by the diabolic empiricist Vautrin. This drama, of course, is intended to demonstrate truths outside itself: to be a vehicle for Balzac's conservative,

[2] See Georg Lukács, *Studies in European Realism*, trans. Edith Bone (London: Hillway Publishing Co., 1950), pp. 47–64.

if sentimental, Catholic and Royalist beliefs. But these beliefs rarely possess dramatic force; their message is often segregated into moralistic asides, and their truth risks becoming an abstract premise rather than a source of compelling action.

Given Balzac's intense concern with social drama, the interplay between good and evil is forced to adopt the often ambiguous parts provided by economic and political issues. In a sense the blurring of moral distinctions is the price exacted by the narrative patterns social life grants the writer. Rephrasing absolute definitions within the empirical data of manners and history, Balzac protects his plots and characters against the alternations that so often turned the fiction of his parent generation into a set of vertiginous gyrations between absolutism and dailiness. *La Comédie humaine* grows out of and well beyond the grubstreet Gothicism and historical-sentimental romances that were the popular fare of Balzac's youth and that he himself helped turn out: a fiction prone to see human action as always teetering upon the brink of sensationalistic extremity, only weakly attached to the mediations and complex stabilities of social existence. Responding to the exceptional stimuli with which their authors bombarded them, the characters in such fiction were repeatedly cast out of earthly time and place into uncharted realms. Development, community, and even the type of particularized exemplary behavior common to *Clarissa* and *La Nouvelle Héloïse* were carried away in the rebound of many late eighteenth- and early nineteenth-century romantic fables into sheer emotion or action. Such figures as Werther and Victor Frankenstein—at the beginning and the end of the period—unable to integrate their desires with the circumstantial limits of probable social life, sought their truths elsewhere: the feeling heart, and with it the possibility of domestic loving, reacted to commonplace frustrations by passionate rebellion; the curious mind, and with it the possibility of temporal education, veered off from conventional curricula to confront primal mystery.

Balzac retains much of the melodrama of these plots, but he desires to bring it within the pale of his society. "All is true," as the epigraph to *Le Père Goriot* announces, but at the same time home truths are truer. What is wrong with Gothic romances and their like is not the implausibility of their basic action but the implausible implications fostered by their ahistorical, asocial settings. Folk tale, legend, and myth are true; circumstantial data are real. The two together fuse energetically to create what Balzac terms drama. Well-dressed Mohicans stalk Paris streets, combining the force of the primal with the activities of public life; mythic beauties, clothed as fashionable girls with eyes of gold, stroll Paris parks, joining the transcendent scope of amatory romance to the topical fascination of society's mating games.

Yet the drama Balzac stages is complicated and enriched by his awareness of the ambiguities that result when final truths are costumed in everyday garments. At times he seems unwilling to subject the largesse of romance to the minutiae of the novel. Though he reworks the basic method of Scott's historical fiction—the grounding of absolutism in the plausible field of earthbound common life—Balzac's attitude toward the process is more deeply divided than that of the Waverley novelist. While Scott's allegiance is sometimes claimed by the absolute, his moral perspective usually follows the example of Cervantes in tempering the ideal to the real. The borderland becomes a setting for the deflating contrast between highland extremity and the moral heroism of those who are learning to forego the elixir of epic gestures for the more nourishing manners of civil life. Such translation frequently strikes Balzac as potential trivialization. The relocation of the glories and perils of supreme deeds within the conventions of social order risks setting in motion something like a chemical reaction that will alter and compromise the nature of the former. Both within individual works and in his career-long rush from one type of fiction to another, from philosophic or pastoral romance to novelized epic to novel of manners, Balzac tries to satisfy at once and by turns elemental truths and sociohistorical realities. The banker Nucingen enters at one moment as a rather silly cuckold, a figure of fun and fractured French; at another he is glorified through the tactics of mythopoeic finance into a Napoleon of speculation hurling his armies of stockholders into an epic fray. If all is true, both are true accounts. But even Balzac's enthusiastic dramaturgy cannot quite avoid a tainting and confusing conflation of the two. The novelistic alchemy that creates price war out of real war gives off a certain atmosphere of diminishment. Being in his way both a militant hero-worshiper and a Christian moralist, Balzac often seems to be deploring the socialization he desires.

Such duality, of course, is shared by Scott, Stendhal, and many other novelists of the period. But Balzac goes further than any other in making the tension between the mythic and the Marxian, melodrama and manners, the essential ground of character. The protagonists of his worldly—as opposed to pastoral or philosophic—novels tend to vacillate between the dictates of moral idealism and the practical rewards of social action. Their drama unfolds within the narrative emphases of what Vautrin calls "secret history." Near the end of *Les Illusions perdus*, that satanic arch-empiricist chides the suicidal Lucien de Rubempré for his ignorance of this crucial subject.

> "You don't seem very strong in History. There are two Histories: official History, those lies one is taught . . . then secret History, which contains the true causes of events, a shameful story. . . . Have you studied the means whereby the Médicis, simple merchants, came to be Grand Dukes in Tuscany? . . . Well, young man, they became Grand Dukes in the same way Richelieu became Minister. If you had sought in history for the human causes of events instead of learning lists by heart, you would have drawn from them precepts for your own career."[3]

As a principle of character creation, secret history explains Balzac's focus on the inner circumstances—psychology would be a misleading term—that lead men to become social types, the private motivation that (in a favorite phrase) makes of each "one of those who." The narrative key signature is a version of the gospel according to Goethe's Mephistopheles: in the beginning was the act, the deed, not the word. "Principles don't exist, only events,"[4] as Vautrin tells Rastignac. Or, in the words of Norman Mailer, as much a disciple of Balzac as Lucien becomes of Vautrin: "It is the actions of men and not their sentiments which make his-

[3] *Les Illusions perdus*, in *La Comédie humaine*, ed. Marcel Bouteron (Paris: Bibliothèque de la Pléiade, 1950–55), IV, 1020–21. Translation mine.

[4] I have revised—often sacrificing fluency for an attempt at literal accuracy—Henry Reed's fine translation: *Pere Goriot* (New York: Signet Classics, 1962). Pages from this version are cited following those from Volume II of the Pléiade edition: thus, 940 [Pléiade]; 113 [Reed translation].

tory."[5] For Balzac, a character's private life is a uniquely shaped, and thus obscure or hidden, epitome of the general issues of sociohistory; and such history is the sum and interaction of private lives. Only insofar as the individual is and makes history is he a properly dramatic subject. And individuals can be subspecies within the natural drama of history only insofar as they internalize its goals and processes.

Le Père Goriot is an exemplary outgrowth of this general view. In a celebrated passage, the narrator explains that his protagonist, Eugène de Rastignac, "had seen the three great expressions of society [history in action]: Obedience, Struggle, and Revolt; the Family, Society life [*le Monde*], and Vautrin. He dared not take sides. Obedience was dull, Revolt impossible, and Struggle uncertain" (1057; 243). Obedience, the morally ideal life that Balzac usually portrays in pastoral terms, equates actions and sentiments, and hence lacks the dramatic tension of secret history.

> If there are exceptions to the Draconian laws of the Parisian code, they are to be found in solitude, in men who are never led astray by social doctrines, who live near some clear, fleeting, but ever-running brook; who, faithful to their green shades, are happy to listen to the language of the infinite written all about them and which they discover in themselves as they wait patiently for their heavenly wings while commiserating the earthbound. But Eugène, like most young men who have had a foretaste of splendor, wanted to dash fully armed into the lists of the worldly; having espoused its fever, he perhaps felt in himself the force to dominate it, though without knowing either the means or the end

[5] Norman Mailer, *Advertisements for Myself* (New York: G. P. Putnam's Sons, 1959), p. 477.

of his ambition. . . . As yet he had not shaken off completely the fresh and sweet ideas that surround like foliage a country childhood. He had continually hesitated to cross the Paris Rubicon. (1031–32; 216–17)

Balzac's narrative voice speaks from the Paris side. While clearly more experienced and probing than Rastignac's, it nonetheless agrees that society offers dramatic struggle: a conflict that obscures the ideal, the purity of which is left behind in the sentimental stasis of a better but less engaging realm.

The drama rests in Rastignac's rite of passage from provincial inexperience to tainting experience, from a kind of archetypal innocence to a mixed state wherein ideals are subject to social pragmatism. As Eugène walks back to his shabby boardinghouse after one of his first encounters with the glitter of high society, he speculates:

"If Madame de Nucingen takes me up, I'll teach her how to manage her husband. The husband is in the gold market, he could help me to get a fortune at one stroke." It was not put as crudely as this; he was not yet worldly enough to sum up a situation, understand it, and calculate its possibilities. These ideas floated on the horizon like feathery clouds; and though they hadn't as yet the spirit of Vautrin's, still, if they had been tested in the crucible of conscience, they wouldn't have yielded anything very pure. By a series of such compromises men reach that moral laxity to which our age subscribes. More rarely than ever before do we come upon those upright men of fine will who never bend before evil and to whom the slightest deviation from the straight path seems a crime—such magnificent images of probity as have inspired two masterpieces: Molière's *Alceste* and more recently Walter Scott's Jenny [*sic*] Dean and her father. Perhaps a work of opposite intention, painting the devious ways by which an ambitious man of the world games with his conscience as he tries to skirt round evil, so as to achieve his goal while preserving appearances, would be no less fine, no less dramatic. (954–55; 129–30)

Rastignac develops out of the tense intermingling of pure moral standards with society's impure options. By itself, the young man's demoralizing immersion in the facts of life would satisfy only reader curiosity about social mechanics; told from the vantage of rigid probity, the story would have the flatness of moralistic fable. Balzac, however, gives equal reality to worldly ambition and to the truths of conscience.

Rastignac is energy without form or direction, a tabula rasa on which Goriot's spiritual truth and Vautrin's immoral pragmatism will be imprinted. By the end, the protagonist becomes both a hero of compromise and a compromised hero. He must achieve some kind of parity among selfhood, a worldly identity, and soul. To do this, the extremes of obedience and revolt must be bent to intermediate purposes. The man we see at the conclusion is a socially and morally ambiguous creation, his education points to nothing so clear as a middle way, nothing so deterministic as a pivot of embattled forces. For Balzac's idea of society, compounding realistic curiosity and moral condemnation, is radically uncertain; and Rastignac's character becomes the character of this uncertainty.

The terms of Eugène's initiation and education, of the moral deflation of his potentialities into character, are implicit in the portraits of his two opposing models. Both Goriot and Vautrin are larger than the sociohistory in which they appear. At the same time, both are rendered partially grotesque by their real-life context. In essence, Goriot embodies Family and Obedience, but his exemplary devotion, placed within a corrupting social frame, seems not quixotic but vaguely pathological. When the old man finances a bachelor's flat for Rastignac's affair with his daughter, Delphine's pleasure fills him with ecstasy. He clasps her in an embrace "so savage, so frantic," that she cries out:

> "Oh! you're hurting me!"
> "Hurting you!" he said turning pale. He looked at her with a more than human expression of grief. To paint as it should be painted the face of this Christ among Fathers, we should have to search among the images created by the princes of the palette to depict the passion suffered on the world's behalf by the Savior of mankind. Goriot gently kissed the girdle his fingers had pressed too tightly. . . .
> Eugène, overwhelmed by the man's inexhaustible devotion, looked at him with the naive admiration that in the young constitutes faith. (1026; 208)

Goriot is the absolute manifestation of one of the postures taken by sentiment in popular fiction: the proof of heart and feeling through suffering. Yet the tone and form of his passion deflate his divine model. Instead of the inevitable, serious parody involved in any earthly imitation of a supreme essence, we have a trivializing transposition into alien terms. The occasion and the grief are grotesquely incommensurate. Instead of exalting the fond father, the allusions to Christ (and elsewhere to Lear) tend to ridicule him. Balzac, of course, obviously partakes in the youthful ingenuousness of Rastignac's faith, clearly views the old man as an archetype. Yet this estimate is more than balanced by the validity granted the social perspective that sees Goriot as bathetic or absurd. The father's adoration is compromised both by its objects, the crass daughters, and by its medium, cash. At times the Christ among fathers appears a lapdogish, even a salacious, figure. As a character rather than an archetype the warring gyrations of his deathbed harangue portray him as a crazed and baffled spirit trying to reconcile earthly facts with ideal expectations.

> "Ah! how stupid fathers are! I loved them [the daughters] so much that I kept going back to them like a gambler to the gaming table. My daughters, that was *my* vice; they were my mistresses. . . . I want to see them. Send the police, the troops to look for them! Justice is on my side, everything's on my side: nature, the civil code. I protest. The country will perish if fathers are trodden underfoot. That's obvious. Society, the great world, turns on fatherhood; everything collapses if children don't love their fathers." (1069–70; 259; Balzac's italics)

The Avant-Propos as well as numerous asides stress Balzac's belief in the familial ideals Goriot garbles. But what makes the father's maddened inconsequences so dramatically impressive is not the spectacle of martyred truth, not the echoes of the romantic theme of absolutism trapped within the finite, but rather the inner view of pathetically mismatched contexts. Ideals are not malleable; transported across the Rubicon of social psychology, they foster a state nearer to psychopathology than to sanctity. Balzac anticipates the kind of loosely Manichaean perspective sometimes discovered in Kafka. When in *The Trial* Joseph K. finds the examining magistrate's law books to be cheap pornography, the scene can be read as an illustration of the principle that what in the spiritual realm might be a work devoted to the

Virgin would become erotic trash if brought into the material world. Goriot's ideal paternity, carried into a fallen society, is transmogrified into a gambler's letch for the jackpot of love.

Witnessing the change, Rastignac experiences an almost Gothic violation of his "fresh and sweet" country notions. As in *Oliver Twist* a few years later, society is marked as a Gothic institution.[6] But whereas Dickens presents Oliver as essentially invulnerable, as morally and psychically exempt from the horrors around him, Balzac presents the cumulative shocks to Rastignac's innocence as an education in the Gothic nature of social things: an education necessary to the development of realistic character. Earthly selfhood is the result of a brave gamble, though in spiritual life gambling is wrong. Delphine acts both as the agent of and the prize offered by the game. When she insists that Eugène share the money she wins at the tables, he resists "like a virgin." "But the baroness having told him, 'I'll take you for my enemy if you aren't my accomplice,' he took the money" (970; 147). Desiring, even loving, Delphine, he must play the game. Yet all the while he is "appalled." Typically, when Delphine attends the society ball rather than her dying father, Rastignac's conscience names her an "elegant parricide" (1056; 242).

The gap between truth and social reality is the burden of Madame de Beauséant's and Vautrin's dark sayings.

---

[6] See John Bayley, "*Oliver Twist*: 'Things as they really are,'" *Dickens and the Twentieth Century*, ed. John Gross and Gabriel Pearson (London: Routledge & Kegan Paul, 1966), pp. 49–64, and also my discussion in "Character and Knowledge in Dickens: The Enigma of Jaggers" in *Dickens Studies Annual*, Vol. III, ed. Robert B. Partlow, Jr. (Carbondale, Ill.: Southern Illinois Univ. Press, 1974), pp. 100–121.

Eugène "saw the social world as an ocean of mud; whoever ventured in would be in it up to the neck. 'They commit only shabby crimes,' he said to himself. 'Vautrin is greater' " (1056; 243). There is no institutional equivalent to revolt; only the name, Vautrin. The archcriminal stands against all aspects of the social contract. As in his arrangements for the death of Victorine's brother, he is a demonic stage manager. More usually he is a demonic commentator, a raw voice: "stick to your principles as little as to your words. When they're asked for, sell them. . . . Principles don't exist, only circumstances. The superior man weds himself to events and circumstances in order to control them. If there were fixed principles and laws, people wouldn't keep changing them as they change shirts" (940; 113). Vautrin's accuracy in painting the muddy realities of the Parisian code suggests a fallen omniscience.[7] Given a world that debases Goriot's gold into filthy lucre, moreover, Vautrin's revolt indicates a model for authenticity. Rastignac is tempted.

But Balzac deflates "Cheat Death" and his absolute revolt no less than Goriot and his absolute obedience. The former trivializes Satan no less than the latter defames Christ. Despite his uncompromising words, Vautrin conforms to Madame de Beauséant's social prescription: "if you have any true feeling, hide it like a treasure" (912; 82). Vautrin's identity with revolt is his treasure; to live in society he must hide it. He must live disguised, blurring his exemplary force, squandering his truth. Undisguised, he could not be included among Madame Vauquer's boarders, who represent "in miniature the elements of the whole social order" (860; 21). As part of this order, Vautrin is reduced to a petty demon,

[7] I attempt to outline more fully the concept of "fallen omniscience" in the article on Jaggers cited above.

"the man of forty with dyed whiskers ... one of those whom the vulgar call a 'bright spark' " (858; 19). If one of those, then not unique. In his sardonic mock courtship of the dowdy landlady, in his sentimental, homosexually toned inveigling of his "dear child" Rastignac, and perhaps most clearly in his falling victim to the trap baited by the dull Poiret and the faded Mademoiselle Michonneau, Vautrin shrinks to the mean measure of the society whose meanness he so often makes the butt of sallies "worthy of Juvenal" (859; 20).

Even in the scene of his arrest, his finest moment, Vautrin's archetypal evil must give way to social common sense.

> All hope of flight was cut off ... [The Inspector] gave him so brusque a rap on the head that his wig leapt off, revealing Collin's head in all its horror. Along with the brick-red short hair that gave him the terrifying quality of force mixed with cunning, his head and face and torso as well were clearly lit up as if by the fires of hell. Each of the onlookers understood Vautrin in his entirety: his past, his present, his future, his ruthless doctrines, his religion of selfish pleasure, the regality conferred on him by the cynicism of his thoughts and deeds, the force of a nature capable of anything. ... He sprang back with a movement of such ferocious energy, he roared so, that he tore cries of terror from all the boarders. ... Collin understood his danger when he saw the glint of the cocked guns, and suddenly gave proof of the highest human power. Horrible and majestic sight! ... The drop of cold water that froze his rage was an insight swift as lightning. (1013; 195)

Pure immorality might qualify Vautrin as Rastignac's mentor in an immoral world. But the transition from regal Satan-ism to cunning criminality, no matter how majestic from the viewpoint of normal willpower, underscores the pragmatic omnipotence of marshaled society. Absolute sincerity of being grandly gives way to a simple gesture of self-preservation that even a bureaucratic cog like Poiret can understand. Vautrin's high rhetoric of condemnation lapses into the grossness of criminal cant, and as this happens Rastignac becomes aware that the diabolic brio has always included a shabby social note.

> The prison, with its manners and language, its stark transitions from the facetious to the horrible, its appalling grandeur, its vulgar familiarity, its baseness, was suddenly made plain . . . in this man who was no longer a man but the type of a whole degenerate nation, a savage, logical race, brutal and slippery. In a single moment Collin became a hellish poem in which were painted all human feelings, save one: repentance. His expression was that of a fallen archangel bent on eternal war. Rastignac lowered his eyes, acknowledging his criminal kinship as an expiation of his own wicked thoughts. (1014–15; 196)

Vautrin is carried off, still exhibiting the double meaning of an absolute pulsation of primal energy and the worldly diffusion of such energy into baseness.

Rebounding from the dual impossibility of utter revolt and social disfranchisement, Rastignac turns to Delphine and her father. Through his love he wants to satisfy both ambition and goodness. But Delphine's blandishments also turn the poetry of pure feeling into the crass prose of fact; she inextricably confuses love and gold. "Eugène had questioned himself very seriously that day, and Vautrin's arrest, in showing him the depths of the abyss into which he had nearly rolled, had so strongly reinforced his noble feelings and his delicacy that he could not yield to this caressing refutation of his generous ideas. A profound sadness bore him off" (1024; 206). Yet to reject Delphine is to reject ambition, to return to the unworldly, static life on the other side of the Rubicon. As earlier, in taking his share of Delphine's winnings, now too Rastignac is led to compromise his principles.

A saddened accommodation with what exists becomes the hallmark of Rastignac's emerging character, of his personal share in the confusing tension between the mundane and the moral that typifies social reality. Goriot and Vautrin, uncontained by the ambiguities shrouding the young man, appear as rootless emigrés from earlier sentimental and Gothic fiction. Their primary colors serve nonetheless as contrasts to the chiaroscuro of Rastignac's existence. For him to follow either would be to remain forever a provincial in regard to the issues Balzac presents as real life; for him to revolt against the dense texture of such life would be to deny all vestige of the humanity Balzac presents as possible in this world. After Goriot's funeral, in the concluding passage, Rastignac agrees to struggle for selfhood upon the unclear terrain Balzac has mapped out.

> Rastignac, left alone, took a few steps towards the topmost part of the cemetery and saw Paris spread crookedly along the banks of the Seine where lights were beginning to sparkle. His gaze centered almost avidly on the space between the Place Vendôme and the dome of Les Invalides. There lived the beau monde into which he had wished to penetrate. He cast on this humming hive a glance which seemed already to be sucking its honey, and uttered these high-fllown words:

"Now I'm ready for you!" [*A nous deux main-tenant!*]

And, as the first act in the challenge he was launching at society, Rastignac went to dine with Madame de Nucingen. (1085; 275)

Earlier, announcing his own course to the decent young Doctor Bianchon, Eugène had in a muted fashion taken over the role of instructor in realities: "go, stick to the modest fate your desires harbor. Me, I'm in hell, and I must stay there. Whatever evil you're told about society, believe it! No Juvenal could paint the horror beneath the gold and jewels" (1062–63; 250).

Not only is Rastignac's hell less absolute, less literal, than Vautrin's, but he himself is clearly no evil figure. Why, then, must he agree to act on hell's terms? Balzac's answer is implicit both in the use of Delphine's married name and in the dueling challenge Eugène flings down at Parisian society. In society, the ideal is always married to the real; the approach to love's pure gold is through adultery with the banker's wife. In general, throughout Balzac's world, duels and gambling retain their romantic function: they transpose epic scope into the socially probable acts of individuals, serve as moments of heightened being that the heroic adventurer can store up against the historical loss of his occupation. Energy, for Balzac, as for many of his inheritors, is both a potentially criminal, antisocial force and an essential component of meaningful identity. In *La Comédie humaine* the only field open to expressions of energy is that offered by a sociohistory that blunts, diffuses, and often debases. Goriot and Vautrin both compromise the archetypal good and evil they incarnate, but because they are defined more by these pure cate-

25

gories than by social cross-purposes, they stand forth as epitomes, not historical characters. Their force being an outgrowth of their essence, they are not permitted the kinds of tensions and complications of motive that permit an individual such as Rastignac to taste the rich realities of the world Balzac dramatizes. They cannot conform to Georg Lukács's fine description: "The Balzac characters, complete within themselves, live and act within a concrete, complexly stratified social reality and it is always the totality of the social process that is linked with the totality of the character. . . . these individual destinies are always a radiation of the socially typical, of the socially universal, which can be separated from the individual only by an analysis *a posteriori*."[8]

Rastignac's situation reverses that of his two models. Their purity of meaning precludes any fundamental modification, any incorporation into social typicality. He lacks fixed essence, is only a potentiality. For him the complex contradictions of social processes provide a modus operandi through which he can define his self. Dinner with Delphine, Madame de Nucingen, and all it represents give shape to the previously amorphous energy and values of the nondescript provincial on the make. The character Rastignac develops both responds to and contends with a world in which the voices of his exemplars have become intermingling and uncertain echoes. The young man's education makes him a specific instance of the abstract, polemic category Gide terms the Balzacian ideal. But the tangled emotions, aspirations, and circumstances that go to make up Rastignac's character do not create "purity and continuity of line"; the pattern they produce is anything but consistent. The model Eugène imitates in his concluding duelist's challenge is as in-

[8] Lukács, *Studies*, p. 55.

conclusive as the nature of the society he is calling out to fight; indeed, it depends on the ambiguity of that nature for its form and practical meaning. His character exemplifies "secret history": the struggle between individual and social motives in the creation of meaning and interpretation. Balzac fulfills the promise of privileged insight he makes at the beginning: "Eugène de Rastignac . . . was one of those young men molded by the misfortune of having to work; from their earliest years they know the hopes their families set on them and prepare a fine destiny by calculating from the start the range of their studies, adapting them in advance to the future development of society so as to be the first to exploit it" (854; 14). Worldly reality and individual temperament interact to stage the drama of character. Balzac's idea of character takes form from the field of hidden pressures, the public corruptions and private pathologies, the deviations from value and conjunctions of need that constitute his vision of society. And in this sense the Balzacian ideal of the binding unity of character edges toward a substitution of social process for what Locke termed reflection—the inner, God-given process that holds together sensations and defines the identity of self and soul.

2

HARDY'S MODERNS:

The Ache of Uncertain Character

Hardy's fiction slips away from the terrain of social structure and challenge that Balzac saw as the matrix of Rastignac's character. The great scenes—Sergeant Troy at sword play with Bathsheba in the verdant cleft, Diggory Venn dicing with Wildeve by the light of glowworms—compound in their convincing texture contradictory elements, mixing human, natural, and legendary action. Objecting to the type of satire he found in Hardy's first novel, the publisher's reader who rejected it complained that where Thackeray meant fun, Hardy intended mischief. The reader may perhaps have been reacting to what, instructed by Robert Gittings's account of Hardy's early years,[1] we may now take as simply a naive, working-class image of high society. Yet even after the architect's clerk became socially presentable, something that might—were it not so painful—be called mischief remained. The characters of Hardy's major fiction move confusingly in and out of the definitions by which the previous generation of novelists ordered being and meaning. Both in themselves and in the narratives they inhabit, they resist assimilation with established categories, seem often at odds with mid-Victorian patterns of paraphrasable existence. The earlier characters developed through actions designed to mature their temper, to refine their private nature into the

[1] Robert Gittings, *Young Thomas Hardy* (Boston: Little Brown, 1975).

28

shape of cultural accomplishment, but in Hardy not only do the terms of private being become distressingly uncertain, the shape of any public goals is too blurred as well to allow purposeful growth.

Impulses, intuitions of meaning, fragments of moral order, and the facts of present life all prompt in different directions. Man's aspirations are often the toy of a strange fate whose coincidences make coherent life impossible. The compromises, ambiguities, and perplexing choices that for Balzac were components of efficient action in a fallen world now baffle all experience, mark the hereafter as well as the here and now. In the scene that changes the course of Tess Durbeyfield's life, her horse is killed by a chance encounter with the postman's cart. Just before the accident, the girl, having equated earth with a "blighted star," falls into reverie. "The mute procession past her shoulders of trees and hedges became attached to fantastic scenes outside reality, and the occasional heave of the wind became the sigh of some immense sad soul, conterminous with the universe in space, and with history in time."[2] The bloody mischance, the loss of the family's only income-producing possession, materializes from the beyond. In such passages the real becomes a flimsy raft afloat on a turbulence Hardy cannot document. The lapsing of action out of definable human—let alone social—order creates a kind of amnesia in the conventional scheme of things. And for a writer with so particular a sense of place, so nice a grasp of social and historical process, a writer whose

[2] *Tess of the d'Urbervilles* (London: Macmillan, 1974), p. 60. The text used for all of Hardy's novels is that of The New Wessex Edition, General Editor, P.N. Furbank. Only first references to each book are indicated in the notes; subsequent quotations in the chapter are followed by page references in parentheses.

depiction of circumstantial texture can be so sure, the blank region between human foreground and a background "conterminous" with universal forces becomes as baffling as omnipresent whiteness to one who would paint humanity in its true colors.

The satiric juxtaposition of human shortsightedness with the clarity of religious or cultural purpose frequent in earlier fiction becomes in Hardy a bleak irony that contrasts man's endeavors with cosmic indifference. What Hardy writes in the preface to *Two on a Tower*, a fairly lighthearted tragicomedy about a village astronomer's amatory relations with the local lady of the manor, applies with far more pondered seriousness to the greater Wessex novels: all are "the outcome of a wish to set the emotional history of two infinitesimal lives against the stupendous background of the stellar universe, and to impart to readers the sentiment that of these contrasting magnitudes the smaller might be the greater to them as men."[3] The pitting of human smallness against this stupendous background endows even the most trivial activities with grand significance. At the same time, however, it tends to dismiss the novelistic decorum that translates final things—issues of life and death, of good and evil—into the mediate language of social history. Indeed, Hardy believes that the long years in which humanity has tried to socialize its absolute concerns have served to weaken its ability to deal with naked truth. This is the message of Egdon Heath in *The Return of the Native*. Man's truth resembles the heath's: "a place perfectly accordant with man's nature—neither ghastly, hateful, nor ugly: neither commonplace, unmeaning, nor tame; but, like man, slighted and enduring; and withal singularly colossal and mysterious in its

[3] *Two on a Tower* (London: Macmillan, 1975), p. 29.

swarthy monotony. As with some persons who have long lived apart, solitude seemed to look out of its countenance. It had a lonely face, suggesting tragical possibilities."[4] Social existence, by not preparing man to confront his situation, merely reinforces the vulnerability humanity shares with those man-nurtured groves that in spring suffer "more damage than during the highest winds of winter, when the boughs are specially disencumbered to do battle with the storm. The wet young beeches were undergoing amputations, bruises, cripplings, and harsh lacerations . . . which would leave scars visible till the day of their burning." By contrast, "on the open heath, how ineffectively gnashed the storm! Those gusts which tore the trees merely waved the furze and heather in a light caress. Egdon was made for such times as these" (231–32).

Man, of course, is apart from, usually at odds with, the brute adaptation enforced by natural or universal law. Nature acts with something like a Dostoevskian inconsistency or perversity that is appalling to those who, like most of Hardy's characters, conceive themselves according to some version of the Balzacian ideal. Even Michael Henchard in *The Mayor of Casterbridge*, whose attempt to act in despite of social views we shall consider at length, is so frustrated that he wishes "to wash his hands of life"; "his perception of its contrarious inconsistencies—of Nature's jaunty readiness to support unorthodox social principles"[5] rendering futile the bold ambitions of self-determination. If, in Dickens, society becomes a Gothic institution, in Hardy nature becomes a Gothic scheme. For Hardy, the universe combines

[4] *The Return of the Native* (London: Macmillan, 1974), p. 35.
[5] *The Mayor of Casterbridge* (London: Macmillan, 1975), p. 339.

the depredating bent of Gothic villains with the comedy of Homeric gods, which is usually the tragedy of mortals.

Hardy's pessimism stands as a chorus explaining and bemoaning the conditions of man's drama in an overbearing universe. The pathos extends beyond the at best dubious battle between individuals and the external forces indifferent to them. In many instances, and they are the most telling, the conflict arises within the characters themselves. Impulses and desires gather momentum with an impetus that often casts those who suffer them out of space and time. P. N. Furbank's comment that Hardy "even came to think of human emotion itself as a cruel flaw and mistake in creation"[6] accurately describes the situation in many of the later novels. Yet, at the same time, emotion is the sphere in which Hardy's hope for the future, his idea of a revised ethic that is implicit in the novels and explicit in some of the letters and essays, must take root. The inchoate sense that present bafflement and victimization will at last give way to some livable balance between human endeavor and its darkling limitations rarely lightens the grim tales of immediate misery, but precisely because emotion and nature are allied, there sometimes seems the possibility of a sentimental education grounded in nature's laws.

Neither Hardy's sense of plight nor the terms of his muted hope are unpredictable developments of late-Victorian doubt. His plots tend to center on the traditional interest provided by the confusions, fallacies, and accomplishments of marriage. He accepts the axiom of middle-class fiction that man is a marrying creature; however secularized, the institution still embodies Jane Austen's "truth universally acknowledged." But the meaning of this truth has become

[6] P.N. Furbank, Introduction to *Tess*, p. 12.

radically uncertain; and the institution comes to provide a point of intersection for the warring facts, influences, and values that make up Hardy's "modern" subject. Is marriage of nature or of nurture? If only of the latter, the entire social structure resting on the institution is wholly arbitrary. In marriage, individual desire and cultural purpose should merge, but can they? Since emotion is a tangent of the stupendous energies of the stellar universe, can it be contained within any merely man-made framework? Such complications worry the traditional theme even in the earliest and most benign of Hardy's "Novels of Character and Environment," *Under the Greenwood Tree*. The short pastoral juxtaposes historical change—the dispersal of the old village "quire" upon the introduction of a modern church organ—against an enduring seasonal ritual of courtship and marriage. If community is threatened by the breakup of the quire, it is reaffirmed in the union of Dick and Fancy, who "stand as fair a chance of having a bit of sunsheen as any married pair in the land."[7] Marriage, considered as an achievement of craftsmanship rather than as a social rite, rephrases the rewards of a rural work ethic in the setting of private life. Loyalty and clarity of dedication to honest craft underlie Dick's declaration that "we have no secrets . . . no secrets at all." Yet as the novel ends, Fancy, exhibiting the proclivities of her name, hears the birds singing "Come hither, come hither, come hither!": " 'O, 'tis the nightingale,' murmured she, and thought of a secret she would never tell" (208). Her secret is no dark thing. Earlier, despite her understanding with Dick, she had been briefly infatuated with the townwise Vicar Maybold and had impulsively agreed to marry

[7] *Under the Greenwood Tree* (London: Macmillan, 1974), p. 206.

him. She quickly regretted her vagary and changed her mind. Though unstressed, the episode provides one of the few complications in Hardy's slender plot. Fancy's concealment is not in itself of great moment, but it loosely anticipates the happy-go-lucky matrimonial pragmatism that leads Tess's mother to advise the keeping of a much more serious secret. Insofar as Fancy's character is formed by an opacity akin to that demanded by social life, it is for Hardy mildly duplicitous; insofar as Tess's nature is transparent and truthful, it will be fatal. Even in the early work such matters as the appeal of the socially superior vicar, the tension between private need and public role, and the assumption of feminine impulsiveness forebode disturbing themes. In part, the little mystery simply points to Hardy's relation to the novels of the sixties and to Wilkie Collins, whose influence is clear in *Desperate Remedies*, published the year before. Moreover, rural sanity and resiliency hold natural folly in check. Yet marriage does not insure quite the comic, happy resolution that pastoral romance usually promises.

The uneasiness surrounding Fancy's character is intrinsic to Hardy's sense of human experience. When Dick's mother complains that the tales told by a local storyteller are "quite coarse to a person o' decent taste,"

> "Well, now," replied Reuban, with decisive earnestness, "that sort o' coarse touch that's so upsetting to Ann's feelings is to my mind a recommendation; for it do always prove a story to be true. And for the same reason, I like a story with a bad moral. My sonnies, all true stories have a coarse touch or a bad moral, depend upon't. If the story-tellers could ha' got decency and good morals from true stories, who'd have troubled to invent parables?" (80)

Reuban, of course, is refashioning a tenet of the novelistic realism Hardy inherits. Yet in Hardy's practice this yoking of true stories and bad morals comes to challenge the Victorian equation between realistic and moral truth: to undermine the reformist, optative belief that the bespattered facts of seemingly indecent coarseness can be reconciled with cultural purposes. In Hardy, the truth-telling impulse behind the concluding reference to Fancy's secret is at odds with the values and certainties traditionally conveyed by her marriage.

The protagonists of the major novels live out the ensuing perplexity. Particularly in *Tess* and *Jude the Obscure*, the ambiguities centered on marriage infect the treatment of childhood, that "season of youth" so dear to the Victorian novel of moral development. The faith that an individual, a David Copperfield or a Dorothea Brooke, can employ the facts of sociohistory as a tool in the creation of culturally valuable character, the very faith in the possibility of some form of organic maturity, disappears from these novels. Characters lose the growing space built into social mediation; they become essences rather than potentialities. The unswerving trajectories of pure being that Hardy records seem equidistant from the developmental optimism of George Eliot and the commitment to "becoming" central to D. H. Lawrence's fiction. When Tess christens her child "Sorrow," she has in mind a fixed condition, not the name of an individual capable of growth. She herself is imprisoned in a fixed duality: paralyzed between Angel Clare, the distorted projection of her innate morality, and Alec d'Urberville, the reduction to sensual mindlessness of her physical being, her peony lips.

The moral dilemma embodied in Tess and Sorrow is

repeated in *Jude*, Hardy's most programmatically pessimistic novel. The impossibility of real names, and of the complex, open-ended individuality for which they stand, is reiterated in Father Time, Jude's and Arabella's child. Father Time kills his siblings and then himself. "It was in his nature to do it," Jude explains. "The doctor says there are such boys springing up amongst us—boys of a sort unknown in the last generation—the outcome of new views of life. They seem to see all its terrors before they are old enough to have staying power to resist them. He says it is the beginning of the coming universal wish not to live."[8] The explanation is reminiscent of Werther's suicide and Chateaubriand's *vague des passions*, two central expressions of the counter-Enlightenment conception of balked character. But whereas Chateaubriand stressed the turbulent disorientation of exceptional feeling ("the imagination is rich, abundant, marvelous; existence poor, dried-up, disenchanted"[9]), Hardy sees the condition as part of the life of ordinary, practical mankind. Tess and Jude exhibit no romantic yearning for ideal fulfillments or imaginatively privileged transcendences. The fate that overtakes them and their children is only an intensification of the common lot.

Such intensification is the basis of Hardy's most compelling characterizations. His pessimism shapes his idea of character, but does not obliterate his conviction of plausible multidimensionality, the rich artistic allegiance to the possibility of human completeness that he shares with midcentury realism. Were the loosely Schopenhauerian ideology that increasingly darkens his perspective to dominate his field of

[8] *Jude the Obscure* (London: Macmillan, 1974), p. 356.
[9] François-René de Chateaubriand, *Génie du christianisme* (Paris: Garnier-Flammarion, 1966), p. 309. Translation mine.

vision, his creations and their world would resemble the dooming of Thomson's *The City of Dreadful Night*. This does not happen. Unlike counter-Enlightenment fictions in which absolute fatalities engulf the humanity of those subject to them, Hardy's novels portray the vagaries of an often deadly fate from within the indelible uniqueness of distressed individuals.

Except in *Jude*, Hardy tends to play down the rigid predeterminations of class. The frequently painful restrictions imposed by class blend with cosmic law to close down the range of possibility. But at the same time, the limitation of scope to common desires and ideas serves the purposes of intensification. Outside and beneath the pigeonholing definitions of class exist a freedom and a variousness that social strata inhibit; the pressure of the social fixities and their conventions, which are always at least half-seen, creates the density of being that so often appears in Hardy's borderland world. Many of the protagonists are as rich in characterological potential, as open to life, as Balzac's Eugène de Rastignac. But in Balzac social structure delineates both an inner and an outer form, ultimately a character, for this potential. In Hardy, character emerges out of the tense intersection of individual raw material with the complexly ramified forces that constitute the data of pessimism. When Rastignac has internalized the processes and conflicts of social reality, when his amorphous gifts have been tarnished yet focused by compromise with real social fixity, he is rewarded: his willingness to fight for wholeness on the terms of a fallen world gains the only character possible in such a world—an achievement confirmed later in *La Comédie* when he becomes a peer of France. After the relatively early *Far from the Madding Crowd*, no such reward awaits intensity of being in Hardy.

Those who attempt to temper their energies to the terms of universal Will, to align its dictates with their individualities, are usually rendered tame and uncertain, perplexed into a nervous inefficiency that Hardy terms Laodicean. The others, more striking figures who refuse to bend, usually rage brilliantly against the bleak backdrop of what appears to be an inevitable victimization, and then burn out. These latter figures live out a desperate decorum that for Hardy, and often for his readers, recalls Greek tragedy.

What Hardy describes is something like the experience of a minor member of the chorus or of a walk-on player who must suddenly act the entire tragedy by himself. When a simple citizen of Thebes must live Oedipus's high drama, the commonplace matters of life lose their conventional meaning and take on a hallucinating and unfathomable intensity. The technique Hardy refines to his purpose combines the suddenness of Gothic confrontation with the usurpation of dailiness by mystery that Wilkie Collins perfected. Repeatedly, the Wessex characters experience profoundly ramified versions of the shock that forces its way into the life of Collins's Walter Hartright when he first encounters the "woman in white": "I, and this woman, whose name, whose character, whose story, whose object in life, whose very presence by my side . . . were fathomless mysteries to me. It was like a dream. Was I Walter Hartright? Was this the well-known, uneventful road, where holiday people strolled on Sundays?"[10] Removed from the mechanical suspensefulness of Collins's type of novel, rationalized and made psychologically resonant by Hardy's intensely empathic seriousness, this type of situation suggests the taut confusion that results

[10] Wilkie Collins, *The Woman in White* (Boston: Houghton Mifflin, Riverside Editions, 1969), p. 15.

when Tess's normal sensuousness carries her unprepared into a cosmic plot. In the kind of universe revealed through Father Time's killings and explicable only through something like the doctor's far-ranging pessimism, even common vulgarity can take on a heightened role: a gesture like Arabella's throwing the pig's pizzle at Jude can imply in its stunning coarseness a type of heroic assertion.

The universe deems human action laughable; human beings in their differing ways, and in their smallest as well as in their greatest acts, achieve character by resisting the judgment. The universe would work its Will by belittling and abstracting. Hardy's realism of time and place, and his realism of character portrayal, challenge categorical abstraction by insistent particularity. Reversing the usual Victorian derivation of the typical, the valuably normative, out of the raw material of individuality, Hardy views any abstraction from private uniqueness as an invitation to the alienating fate that the cosmos is always ready to impose on men. Characters in earlier fiction were usually viewed as incomplete essences that could achieve fulfillment only through cultural, rather than personal and particular, action. Hardy shares the commitment to larger sympathies but fears that any effort to move beyond the individual may play into the hand of destiny's typifying bent. The roundedness that once stood for an integration of private particularity with marital, familial, or communal categories of aspiration now tends to become a desperate assertion of the facts of self against the cosmic forces that would abstract and flatten. This is the background against which we are to understand Angel Clare's belated education. "Cynical things he had uttered to himself about [Tess]; but no man can be always a cynic and live; and he withdrew them. The mistake of expressing them had arisen

39

from his allowing himself to be influenced by general principles to the disregard of the particular instance" (389–90).
Granting differences in terms, the passage is similar to Dickens's or George Eliot's demand for moral sympathy. But the
stakes are no longer those of a cultural imperative. The necessity for particularity, the need to ground existence in the
special details of individual ideas and emotions, is now almost
a precondition of survival. Hence Father Time: "Children
begin with detail, and learn up to the general; they begin
with the contiguous, and gradually comprehend the universal. The boy seemed to have begun with the generals of life,
and never to have concerned himself with the particulars"
(296).

Hardy intends a dramatic counterpoint between the
darkness of abstract law and the glow of particular being.
Yet Father Time's too ready immersion in the former is frequently approximated in Hardy's own tendency to veer
from individual instances into generality. Though Tess's fellow dairymaids, each of them in love with Angel, are minor
figures, still the description of their sad nights suggests the
confusing alternation of narrative focus that recurs in the
treatment of many of the major characters.

> The air of the sleeping-chamber seemed to palpitate
> with the hopeless passion of the girls. They writhed
> feverishly under the oppressiveness of an emotion thrust
> on them by cruel Nature's law. . . . The incident of the
> day had fanned the flame that was burning the inside
> of their hearts out, and the torture was almost more
> than they could endure. The differences which distin-
> guished them as individuals were abstracted by this pas-
> sion, and each was but portion of one organism called
> sex. (187)

The powerfully compassionate view of universal victimization blurs the specific humanity of the victims: representation verges on extreme illustration, pathos on melodrama. The middle ground of plausible individual response is elided. The dairymaids' subsequent stories veer off into the kind of extremity that leads Kleist's Michael Kohlhaas to react to the impounding of his horses by challenging all the powers that be. One girl attempts suicide, another takes to drink. Izzy, acting hysterically against the grain of the native decency Hardy has been at pains to stress, agrees to elope with the now married Angel, though he quickly decides against the move.

Carried into the major portraits, this disequilibrium between the vastness of depersonalizing forces and the vulnerable values of individuals might logically result in a general amorality: in extended versions of Izzy's quest for a modicum of joy in a grim universe. Mankind, being the sport of "cruel Nature," might do well to heed the dictates of its selfish needs and desires. If general law is indifferent to the demanding and usually unrewarding restrictions of decency, perhaps it might make sense to follow the egoistic pleasure-taking of Alec D'Urberville, Sergeant Troy, and others. Hardy does not condemn such behavior out of hand, but it does not interest him deeply. The egoists ally themselves with the way of the cosmos; they slip free from what Hardy considers both the cross of human dilemma and the future ground of human triumph: that innate morality that would do battle with the mechanical logic of external laws. If the universe turns the stories of moral culture into arbitrary parables, the latter still tell of man's colossal desire to endure on his own best terms. Acknowledging the need for sweeping social reorientation, Hardy clearly clings to more or less progressive Victorian premises. He believes neither in any unprecedented cultural covenant nor in the radical conclusions that D. H. Lawrence and other twentieth-century readers would impose on his stories. However hopeless it often appears, the task of his characters and the burden of his characterization involve the reconciliation of indecent actualities and innate decencies. Though not traditionally good, most of his central figures are morally better than a strictly pessimistic ideology might expect. No character discovers the pulse of a universal heart of darkness horribly beating in his own breast. Though Hardy no longer represents moral culture as in any way a logical framework for life, he persists in presenting it as a vital component of his characters' value. Without her moral instinct Tess would be beneath the dignity of Hardy's tragedy; without his Christminster dream Jude would be little more than crude Arabella's fit mate.

Like their author, the protagonists inherit the aspirations of Victorian moral realism; like him, they are compelled to acknowledge that this inheritance must be re-formed to present conditions. Clym Yeobright, Hardy's returning native, cannot accept his mother's desire for his social advancement. His sense that moral action and ambition do not go hand in hand is hardly original. But even the hope of becoming an obscure yet culturally committed teacher to the workers on the heath is threatened by his share in his generation's uncertainties. "His scheme was far enough removed from one wherein the education of youth should be made a mere channel of social ascent. He had no desires of that sort. He had reached the stage in a young man's life when the grimness of the general human situation first becomes clear; and the realization of this causes ambition to halt awhile. In France it is not uncustomary to commit suicide at this stage;

in England we do much better, or much worse, as the case may be" (211). Clym is the first of Hardy's explicit examinations of the self-distorting temperament of modern man. Like his successors Angel and Jude, he is both a partisan of moral culture and a victim of "the chronic melancholy which is taking hold of the civilized races with the decline of belief in a beneficent Power."[11] In such characters, what Hardy terms melancholy saps the vitality and elasticity that they would need to put their high values into action.

Like several of the other modern men, Clym discovers the force he lacks in a woman, Eustacia Vye, and would marry it. Physical desire becomes inextricably bound with a craving for her obvious energy. Unhappily, however—as Fancy's secret predicted—feminine nature confuses, sometimes contradicts, the moral aims not only of would-be husbands but of the women themselves. Hardy's strong women live out a mysterious power not unlike that of Egdon Heath. Eustacia seems a passionate tangent of Egdon's sublimity; she too appeals "to a subtler and scarcer instinct, to a more recently learnt emotion, than that which responds to the sort of beauty called charming and fair" (34). In Hardy's dramatis personae, dark ladies are to be the new heroines and wan, baffled men the new heroes. Yet what Clym adores as fine vitality is for Eustacia an intense confusion. She dislikes the heath; he loves it. Her passionate inconsistencies include both a desire to live a life of urban vanity and a yearning to be a good woman. Her native energy, divided against itself, surges only to tragedy. Nonetheless, Eustacia, Bathsheba, Tess, and the other heroines who share their traits lie close to the heart of Hardy's idea of character in the throes of contemporary dilemma. Eustacia's combination of dynamism,

[11] Hardy is speaking of Angel Clare in *Tess*, p. 156.

rampant instinct, and beleaguered decency particularizes the general extremity that has overtaken life. A blighted star fallen among men in human guise, Eustacia is a fitting embodiment of unmediated existence. In her company, Hardy's drastic turns of story can seem plausible. In *The Return of the Native*, Wildeve's melodramatic flounderings, Clym's near-blindness and cruel fate, and the many occasions of bald coincidence are assimilated into a realism of commonplace sublimity by Eustacia's convincing presence.

As the treatment of Sue Bridehead in *Jude* attests, Hardy is no feminist. His point rephrases the traditional assumption that women are closer to the pulse of nature than men. Adjectives describing nature and its ways describe women as well. Fancy's secret is much like the antic coincidences the universe employs to thwart rational conclusions and goals. Yet few of the women are malign or consciously cruel. They simply need to fulfill the often errant proclivities of their being. Moreover, because they are both natural and human, their resilience sketches the new integration Hardy seeks: a model for character whose contract will be, not with society, but with cosmic circumstance. Until Hardy divides femininity into two opposing camps—pitting Arabella against Sue in his last novel—the instability of his forceful women bears a hopeful promise as well as a present threat. Though hedged and at times almost subverted, the essential joy with which *Far from the Madding Crowd*, the first of the major novels, concludes remains as an undercurrent throughout the fiction. Echoing in his name—Gabriel Oak—both higher revelation and heart of oak moral solidity, the manly hero joins pastoral virtue to the kind of idealized work ethic George Eliot embodies in Caleb Garth. However, Gabriel's strengths have been overtaken by an early version of the debilitating melancholy seen in Clym and Angel. The good man lacks the energy of purpose that would sinew his virtues. In his love for Bathsheba, he finds firm direction, though at the sacrifice of the tradition and the self-reliant ambitions with which he begins life. Bathsheba's force appears the crucial element lacking in the cultural aspirations Gabriel inherits. Revising the presocial, vibrant, and often morally anomalous traits of Scott's dark ladies and their avatars, she becomes a model for mankind's innate ability to endure present blight. After Sergeant Troy's death, she unflinchingly caresses the bloody corpse. "Deeds of endurance which seem ordinary in philosophy are rare in conduct, and Bathsheba was astonishing all around her now, for her philosophy was her conduct, and she seldom thought practicable what she did not practise. She was of the stuff of which great men's mothers are made. She was indispensible to high generation, hated at tea parties, feared in shops, and loved at crises."[12] Versions of the eternal feminine, Hardy's heroic women can at times soar free from trivializing social life and from the doubts that beset their modern men. Bathsheba emerges as a type of Achilles to Gabriel's Hector; her native absolutism complements his more civil bent.

Such reversals of traditional sex roles anticipate the revolutionary reappraisal undertaken in much of Lawrence's fiction. But for Hardy the phenomenon is more a symptom of current confusion than a promise of truer relations. In the past, internalized social codes assisted by superior masculine rationality molded the strong emotionalism frequently identified with women's nature to the good purposes of culture. Now, however, Hardy finds the codes inappropriate or

[12] *Far from the Madding Crowd* (London: Macmillan, 1974), pp. 402–3.

worse and views his modern men as incapable of exerting rational or moral authority. At crises, women's enduring strength springs forth. But existence is not a permanent crisis; it is composed of long stretches of difficult dailiness. Bathsheba's astonishing qualities are not much help in the daily management of her estate. She needs Gabriel as her overseer; were it not for his assistance, she would squander her inheritance. Indeed, she cannot manage her own nature, and comes close to squandering the very gifts that make her indispensible to "high generation." In Bathsheba, Fancy's mild infatuation with the vicar is transmuted into an ardor for the flashy, self-absorbed virility of Sergeant Troy. Smitten with the sergeant, she demonstrates "the element of folly distinctly mingling with the many varying particulars which made up" her character; "though she had too much understanding to be entirely governed by her womanliness, [she] had too much womanliness to use her understanding to the best advantage." Her love is "entire as a child's" (219); untutored and presocial, her unmediated reactions both manifest truths that society evades and reveal that unpreparedness for complex life that the doctor finds in Father Time. Bathsheba's conduct often recalls the behavior of Gabriel's novice sheep dog, which early in the novel bankrupts its master by doing its job too blindly and running the flock off a cliff—thereby providing an "instance of the untoward fate which so often attends . . . [those] who follow out a train of reasoning to its logical conclusion, and attempt perfectly consistent conduct in a world made up so largely of compromise" (74). Following, not reason, but her nature, Bathsheba rushes into marriage with Troy and is rescued to fulfill her grand potential only by his death.

For Hardy, social compromise distorts both human and

universal truth; but since man's position is vulnerable both to chaos from within and to cruel indifference from without, some kind of intermediate state is necessary: enduring character must be grounded in some existential compromise. What Hardy has in mind is a set of checks and balances, a somber art of the humanly possible wrought out of a tangle of moral idealism, physical passion, and the vast forces that play upon and with men's lives. Women such as Bathsheba, Eustacia, and Tess anticipate Freud's incorporation of Schopenhauer's cosmic Will into the structure of the human id. Hardy's heroines are human raw material manifesting the implacable nature of the universe in a form at least potentially amenable to the processes and goals of civilization. The challenge posed by these strong women repeats that which earlier writers saw in the vital force of their hero/villains; such energy must be domesticated—as Clarissa puts it in regard to Lovelace, must be "humanized." The note of challenge confronted and transformed into human resilience sounds through the happy ending of Bathsheba's and Gabriel's story. The couple will marry at last; their "substantial affection," a bond nurtured "in the interstices of a mass of hard prosaic reality," results in a "good fellowship—*camaraderie*— . . . superadded to love between the sexes." Where "happy circumstance permits its development, the compounded feeling proves itself to be the only love which is strong as death" (419).

Yet the happy circumstance recorded in *Far from the Madding Crowd* is closer to the youthful pastoral optimism of *Under the Greenwood Tree* than to the coincidences and miseries that preside over the late fiction. Two large areas of ambiguity that merely loom on the horizon of Fancy's and Bathsheba's marriages will become increasingly ominous.

Hardy's intermittently judgmental attitude towards Bathsheba's love for Troy raises questions about his moral perspective that go unanswered. If by her nature Bathsheba is
more apt to prove a danger than a partner to true love, she
cannot be held personally accountable. But Hardy frequently treats the inborn defects of her virtues as subjects
for blame. She is not just passionate, but culpably emotional,
making "no attempt to control feeling by subtle and careful
inquiry into consequences" (219–20). In a duality shared by
Zola, Hardy shows, on the one hand, that conventional moral
categories do not apply to modern circumstances—are, in
fact, moribund; on the other hand, he presents such categories as conclusively necessary. When she is not a heroine
as of old, Bathsheba is a carrier of modern disorder. John
Bayley's description of Tess as "a woman of the new novel
who is as it were compelled to live in the world of the old
novel"[13] points to the ambiguity that surrounds Bathsheba's
heirs.

A second, even more disturbing, set of characterological
and thematic perplexities grows out of Hardy's emphasis on
the reversal of male and female gifts. The dynamism of the
women reflects slightingly on the paralyzing uncertainties
that mark the modern men. Here too, the realities of the new
novel impel in one direction; the moral conventions that
Hardy shares with the old novel, in another. He believes that
men should be the chief actors in humanity's moral drama.
The fallowness of masculine powers is a sign of contemporary decadence. Women can endure, can be heroic mothers
and epic partners, but the force of sustained rationality

[13] John Bayley, Introduction to *Far from the Madding Crowd*,
p. 25.

needed to manifest what hope there is must, in Hardy's vision, come from men. To conceive such men, however, involves allowing them the power of a Bathsheba or a Eustacia. If a woman is prone to wreak disorder, how much more so a man who joins her élan vital to the traditional superiority of male strength?

Several of Hardy's most provocative, and most ambiguous, characterizations attempt to reverse the shift in sex roles. In each case the portrait involves a profound instability of attitude on Hardy's part: a blurring of the lines between male heroic power and Gothic temperament that recalls romantic narrative. Boldwood, the gentleman farmer to whom Bathsheba frivolously sent a valentine, foreshadows melodramatically the dangers posed by Michael Henchard, Hardy's most extensive treatment of the new woman's qualities within a man's nature. Prior to Bathsheba's careless sparking of his passions, Boldwood had been a saturnine solitary; his was "the perfect balance of enormous antagonistic forces —positives and negatives in fine adjustment." Afterwards, "his equilibrium disturbed, he was in extremity at once. If an emotion possessed him at all, it ruled him. . . ." Unleashed, Boldwood becomes a rather Byronic *homme fatal*, a "hotbed of tropic intensity" (153). The fatality to which his colossal emotions lead is too weighty for the still more or less pastoral plot, and Hardy shoves him somewhat hastily out of the way. But the Twilight suggestiveness and confusion produced by the conjunction of women's presocial resources and man's force, the terrifying misalliance between the somber majesty of Egdon and the requirements of moral culture, return twelve years later as the keynote of *The Mayor of Casterbridge.*

Michael Henchard

The alternatively fierce and sad protagonist of *The Life and Death of The Mayor of Casterbridge: A Story of a Man of Character* is something of a throwback. With its insistent animal imagery and its suggestions of a presocial shame culture, Michael Henchard's story recalls Henry King's encounter with prehistory in *A Pair of Blue Eyes*. Dangling perilously over a cliff, King sees before him a fossil of "one of the early crustaceans."

> Time closed up like a fan before him. He saw himself at one extremity of the years, face to face with the beginning and all the intermediate centuries simultaneously. Fierce men, clothed in the hides of beasts, and carrying, for defense and attack, huge clubs and pointed spears, rose from the rock, like the phantoms before the doomed Macbeth. . . . Behind them stood an earlier band. No man was there. Huge elephantine forms, the mastodon, the hippopotamus . . . —all, for the moment, in juxtaposition. . . . Folded behind were dragon forms and clouds of flying reptiles . . . and so on, till the lifetime scenes of the fossil confronting him were a present and modern condition of things.[14]

Henchard often stalks and glooms like a relic of past hugeness revivified amid the alien surroundings of nineteenth-century culture. He descends unexplained, as if from the realm of Tess's fantasy, "conterminous with the universe in space, and history in time."

Hardy's novel has struck many readers as atypical. As Desmond Hawkins puts it: "The primary narrative theme

[14] *A Pair of Blue Eyes* (London: Macmillan, 1975), pp. 240–41.

in all his novels—except *The Mayor of Casterbridge*, so often
the odd man out—is the conventional romantic one of young
lovers striving to reach the goal of happy union."[15] Hardy's
opening—Henchard's besotted sale of his wife Susan, the
ramifications of which will be pursued with a unity of action
in itself atypical—stands starkly apart. The plot offers no example of the wanly perplexed modern man, no descendant
of the forceful female. Though there are amatory occasions,
neither the tone nor the goals of romantic striving are much
in evidence. Hardy's usual emphasis on human desiring
caught in the toils of cosmic forces gives way to a consideration of unmitigated selfhood caged both in social relativism
and in inscrutable fate.

Transposed into the dominant key of male assertion,
Bathsheba's or Eustacia's headstrong traits now directly challenge both the social contract and capricious universal law.
Breaking the former, Henchard will be exceptionally vulnerable to the latter. His need to stand alone requires a
mighty, if not heroic, refusal of all intermediate postures.
Henchard sells Susan because he cannot submit to the limits
her simpleminded dependency imposes on his ambitious
strength. The shock value of the act depends upon the value
Hardy and his readers place on marriage. It is as if George
Eliot's Lydgate had cast off Rosamond. What would be in-
conceivable in *Middlemarch* is plausible in Hardy, but the
sale nonetheless offends the idea of union around which so
many of Hardy's themes cluster. Moreover, it violates Henchard's own soberly self-generated sense of justice. Upon
awaking the next day, he knows that he has erred and desires to atone. He undertakes "to put up with the shame as

[15] Desmond Hawkins, *Hardy: Novelist and Poet* (New York:
Barnes & Noble, 1976), p. 167.

best he could. It was of his own making, and he ought to bear it. But first he resolved to register an oath, a greater oath than he had ever sworn before: and to do it properly he required a fit place and imagery; for there was something fetichistic in this man's beliefs" (49). Henchard's sense of fault is presocial; his "ought" is an imperative of a primal code. Neither here nor elsewhere is there evidence of those internalized social terms that mark the Balzacian ideal. The self-imposed oath not to drink is "greater" than the social sacrament of wedlock. In standard Victorian usage, character combines individual qualities with public role and moral definition; Hardy's "man of character" would establish himself out of wholly personal impulses and aims.

Recalling heroes of old, Henchard appears a fit inhabitant of a universe that would compel its inhabitants to revive the stark extremities of precivilized life. His "one talent" is that "of energy." "Mentally and physically unfit for grubbing subtleties from soiled paper; he had in a modern sense received the education of Achilles" (106). Had Bathsheba been indeed a "great man's mother," her son might well have resembled the mayor. Like her, he is "constructed upon too large a scale to discern . . . minutiae" (207). "Though under a long reign of self-control he had become Mayor and churchwarden and what not, there was still the same unruly volcanic stuff beneath the rind of Michael Henchard as when he had sold his wife at Weydon Fair" (141). Finding himself burdened by a social lot that yokes his sovereignty, he tries to rear free. Yet the sold wife, Susan, though she is the lowest common denominator of the theme of human interdependence, keeps alive Hardy's acknowledgment that raw energy must be sheltered by communal purpose. Man is a victim in the scheme of things, and Henchard cannot simply buy himself out of slavery to a partner who—with her "hard, half-apathetic expression of one who deems anything possible at the hands of Time and Chance except, perhaps, fair play" (36)—epitomizes victimization and dependence.

Henchard's force has the ruthless drive of unmediated egoism, but the ambition this force must serve leads him into often baffling realms beyond what he knows and can control. Embodying cruel nature's coarse truths, Henchard's sense of life is crude. We are forewarned that the mayor's "personal goodness, if he had any, would be of a very fitful cast —an occasional almost oppressive generosity rather than a mild and constant kindness" (64). From any moral point of view, in domestic or civil matters, Henchard's impulses are indecently at sea; he behaves by rote, imitating a pattern the meaning of which lies outside his ken. When, after the apparent death of the sailor who had bought and "married" her, Susan comes to Casterbridge with Elizabeth-Jane, her now grown-up daughter, the mayor immediately resolves to right his past wrong by remarriage. He has "schooled himself in a course of strict mechanical rightness towards this woman of prior claim" (111).

> He pressed on the preparations for his union, or rather reunion, with this pale creature in a dogged, unflinching spirit which did credit to his conscientiousness. Nobody would have conceived from his outward demeanour that there was no amatory fire or pulse of romance acting as a stimulant . . . nothing but three large resolves—one, to make amends to his neglected Susan; another, to provide a comfortable home for Elizabeth-Jane under his paternal eye; and a third, to castigate himself with the thorns which these restitutory acts brought in their train. (112)

Schooling, conscientiousness, and resolution are high values in Victorian novels of moral development and character. Used to describe Henchard, they become items in a curriculum he knows to be important but cannot learn. "With all domestic *finesse*," as indeed with all cultural modes that might train his ego's bent, "he was hopelessly at variance. Loving a man or hating him, his diplomacy was as wrong-headed as a buffalo's" (142).

Henchard's many-faceted contradictions seem intended to create ambiguity rather than understanding. A celebrated passage contrasts the mayor to the benignly efficient, rational Scotsman Farfrae. "Character is fate, said Novalis, and Farfrae's character was just the reverse of Henchard's, who might not inaptly be described as Faust has been described—as a vehement gloomy being who had quitted the ways of vulgar men, without light to guide him on a better way" (143). Both the reference to Carlyle's recasting of Faust and the allusions to such works as Shelley's *The Revolt of Islam* cast Henchard as a romantic overreacher, an *homme fatal* raging against limits and trying to bend them to his will. At the same time, since Henchard is of the rural laboring class, his implicit challenge to social restrictions and conventions continues the realistic refashioning of Promethean struggle notable in the stories of a Julien Sorel or a Becky Sharp. Yet though a certain class animus and distrust are insinuated throughout Hardy's fiction, the mayor's story seems only vaguely related to the general concern. Unlike Jude, Henchard is not portrayed through the optic of class. He resembles the forceful women in being of a race apart; his energy is his nature. And his energy is too self-involved to focus for long on the issues of condemnation and revolt that preoccupy Balzac's Vautrin. Regarding the grander role Hardy's allusions suggest, Henchard's solipsism, joined to his animal-like powers, makes it hard to view him as any sort of romantic Promethean. If the aura of Byronism surrounds his private vehemence, the effect is of incongruity, of striking coincidence wrought by the chance of history, rather than of premeditated revolt.

The society that Hardy often portrays as inert certainly needs the energy Henchard manifests. Yet not just society but all the civil values in which Hardy believes exist in contradiction to the mayor's kind of force. What keeps them apart is implicit in the idea of a "better way." Henchard's may well be the appropriate character for what Hardy, discussing architecture in *A Laodicean*, dubs a "neo-Pagan" age.[16] The term is descriptive but also pejorative. Somehow the mayor has been born an alien to the better purposes that should harness his volcanism to the advantage of the commonweal. Moreover, as a projection of unruly nature, he is invulnerable to education; unlike such neopagans as Dickens's street sweeper Jo in *Bleak House*, he is no subject for moral colonization. Indeed, the fact that Henchard stands so wholly apart from the higher meaning of his civil titles— "Mayor and churchwarden and what not"—makes his very existence a threat to such meaning. His utter egosim becomes a danger to the moral web of duties and responsibilities that makes culture better than paganism.

To the extent, however, that the realities determining Hardy's world are neopagan, any moral estimate must be modified. Somewhere in Henchard's combination of rural gifts and native energy there must be a corrective to the present hollowness, evasiveness, and decadence. But just this possibility appears to be one source of Hardy's elusive at-

[16] *A Laodicean* (London: Macmillan, 1975), p. 39.

titude. Behind Henchard lies Hardy's complex response to the often indecent practical strengths of the laboring class out of which the mayor has grown. At times we see a figure of colossal promise capable of exercising the crisis virtues of Bathsheba; at other times Henchard seems much like the uncouth rustic Christopher Coney, who digs up Susan's corpse to steal the pennies weighting her eyes. Hardy's characterization reflects the ambivalence evident in his stylistic alternation between vibrant description and the heavy-handed diction of high culture. Yet the tension by no means simply projects Hardy's own duality. The warring elements in Henchard dramatize some of the most tormenting issues of late-century concern: the value of primitivism to a declining West; the value still attached to a culture that in major respects no longer commands allegiance; the extent to which individual self-creation can accord with the moral ideal of man as a social being.

The character Hardy creates responds with ungainly extremity to these and other uncertainties. Henchard is aware both of the circumstances that confine his strengths and of his inability to understand the sophisticated system of values from which these circumstances derive. He knows his gifts but senses at times that they are at odds with a set of unclear needs: an intangible dimension of existence that might relieve the solitude his force seems to carry with it. After Susan's death, he is drawn to Elizabeth-Jane, whom he believes to be his own flesh and blood. The girl, however, believes that Newson, the sailor who bought her mother, is her father.

Henchard always looked like one bent on resisting pain when Elizabeth-Jane spoke of Richard Newson as "father." ... "Was Newson a kind father?"

"Yes, sir; very."

Henchard's face settled into an expression of stolid loneliness which gradually modulated into something softer. "Suppose I had been your real father? . . ."

"I can't think it," she said quickly. "I can think of no other as my father, except my father."

Henchard's wife was dissevered from him by death; his friend and helper Farfrae by estrangement; Elizabeth-Jane by ignorance. . . . His mind began vibrating between the wish to reveal himself to her and the policy of leaving well alone. (150)

The mayor's stern sovereignty warily stalks the perimeters of interdependence. His private shame culture both fears and desires communal civilization. His tentative softer feelings are balked when he discovers that Elizabeth-Jane is Newson's daughter after all—his own child having died a few months after the "sale." As if to revenge his previous weakness, he treats the girl with bitter cruelty. Yet his longing remains. He turns to Lucetta, with whom he had been intimate during the time he had believed Susan to be dead. Lucetta had tended him when he was ill, and their relationship had compromised her in the eyes of her Jersey neighbors. Now an heiress, she has settled in Casterbridge hoping that, with Susan out of the way, he will marry her. Following his impulse to wipe the slate of past injustices, the mayor is willing. "His bitter disappointment at finding Elizabeth-Jane to be none of his, and himself a childless man, had left an emotional void in Henchard that he unconsciously craved to fill." "It was by no means with the oppression that would once have accompanied the thought that he regarded the moral necessity" of a union with Lucetta (175). Yet he is in no hurry to court and wed. The promptings of loneliness lead to no subtlety, no amenity in his approach. Grudging his very need, Henchard acts like a caveman trying to drag a mate into his den. His majesty derives from a primitive self-sufficiency. By the same token, he lacks any sense of a middle way, of a better principle that would abate aggrandizing self-hood before the threshold of others' lives. Predictably, he loses Lucetta to Farfrae's insinuating suit.

The pathos of Hardy's portrait is that Henchard is not a grand animal, lion or buffalo, not a romantic overreacher challenging mortal limits. He joins huge will to the material goals of his time and place. His energy is uncommon, but his devotion to cash as the purchase price of sovereignty is vulgar. His world, however, offers him no better purpose—though Hardy at times implies that he would not know the better if it were at hand. But material success offers no real escape from the moral shortsightedness of primitivism. A potentially valuable character unsupported by any true sustaining values, Henchard is preternaturally vulnerable to the victimizing fate Hardy sees as threatening all human endeavor. Late in the novel Henchard nearly kills Farfrae in a fit of enraged frustration. Afterwards, alone in the loft from which he might have thrown the Scotsman, he subsides into exhaustion: "So thoroughly subdued was he that he remained on the sacks in a crouching attitude, unusual for a man, and for such a man. Its womanliness sat tragically on the figure of so stern a piece of virility" (297). Just as the mayor's virile fierceness extends the unruliness of some women's strength, so his inability either to act out nature's blind force or to accept any stabilizing social compromise portrays him as an extreme instance of the existential bewilderment that Hardy associates with women. Naked virility is helpless; virile femininity is mistaken; the softer roles assigned men and women are unavailing in a harsh universe. Against this bleak background, Henchard's particular situation presents a harrowing spectacle.

Nonetheless, Henchard's naked egosim violates, and by violating victimizes, and by victimizing demonstrates the necessity for, some mediating order—for some structure of mutual, social existence. Near the end, Henchard becomes reconciled to, finally reliant on, Elizabeth-Jane, only to discover that—Farfrae's first wife, Lucetta, having died—the girl has become secretly engaged to the Scotsman. This time Henchard reacts, not with rage, but with a conviction of hopeless futility. He believes the couple will dismiss him as

> an irksome obstacle whom they would be heartily glad to get out of the way. Embittered as he was against society, this moody view of himself took deeper and deeper hold of Henchard, till the daily necessity of facing mankind, and of them particularly Elizabeth-Jane, became well-nigh more than he could endure. His health declined; he became morbidly sensitive. He wished he could escape those who did not want him, and hide his head for ever.
> . . . .
> He proceeded to draw a picture of . . . himself living like a fangless lion about the back rooms of a house in which his stepdaughter was mistress. . . . It was terrible to his pride to think of descending so low; and yet, for the girl's sake he might put up with anything; even from Farfrae; even snubbings and masterful tongue-scourgings. The privilege of being in the house she occupied would almost outweigh the personal humiliation. (330)

A "shorn Samson," "a dark ruin, obscured by 'the shade from his own soul upthrown' " (346), Henchard totters on the bitter threshold of dependence. Yet his presocial code works to raise his ruin above the merely social pathos. Hardy has earned the application of Shelley's *Islam* to his protagonist's fall. The former mayor bears his breast to scourging and humiliation because he believes he has deserved them. Love and pride merge in his decision to reject the "privilege" of community. Exhausted but untamed strength combines with an almost heroic conviction of unworthiness to preside over Henchard's last days. He prowls the country as a day laborer, finally burrowing into the lonely heath. Farfrae and Elizabeth-Jane seek him out too late. He has left only a brief penciled will: "That Elizabeth-Jane Farfrae be not told of my death, or made to grieve on account of me. . . . & that no murners walk behind me at my funeral. . . . & that no man remember me. To this I put my name. Michael Henchard" (353).

The power is clear. Hardy has created a character transcending conventional understanding and evaluation. The mayor partakes of a grandeur his times dismiss. But Hardy's practical morality, if not his ideal vision, belongs to these times, and Henchard does violence to the conditions of mankind's only present safeguard against chaos. The heroic note, unaccompanied, falls flat; indeed, it produces a cacophony that destroys any hope of general harmony. As we have seen, Henchard's character comes disturbingly close to the distinctly neopagan types who form an uncouth stratum in Casterbridge and its environs: the furmity woman, Jopp, and the disreputable dwellers in Mixen Lane. True achievement in Hardy is intertwined with the moral life. Henchard is a moral hazard, a social near-criminal. He sells bad bread to the townspeople without compunction. When Elizabeth-Jane's actual father reappears, Henchard tells the sailor that the young woman is dead: "stimulated by the unexpected coming of Newson to a greedy exclusiveness in relation to her; so that the sudden prospect of her loss had caused him to speak mad lies like a child, in pure mockery of consequences" (315). Unlike Bathsheba's childlike intensity of passion for Sergeant Troy, Henchard's tantrum of possessiveness is wholly typical of his essential nature. And Hardy's insistence on the point is equally typical. When Henchard explains to Elizabeth-Jane that he and not Newson is her father—a "fact" he has as yet no reason to doubt—Hardy describes him as showing "a respect for the young girl's sex and years worthy of a better man" (151).

The pattern of Henchard's rise and fall hints at the time-honored plot of social decline and moral ascent, of egotism tempered into goodness. But such stories are, for Hardy, cultural parables, not true accounts. Shortly before the end, once more a simple laborer, Henchard finds himself at the fairground where he had sold his wife.

> He experienced not only the bitterness of a man who finds, in looking back upon an ambitious course, that what he has sacrificed in sentiment was worth as much as what he has gained in substance; but the super-added bitterness of seeing his very recantation nullified. He had been sorry for all this long ago; but his attempts to replace ambition by love had been as fully foiled as his ambition itself. His wronged wife had foiled them by a fraud [her silence about the death of his own daughter] so grandly simple as to be almost a virtue. It was an odd sequence that out of all this tampering with social law came that flower of Nature, Elizabeth. Part

of his wish to wash his hands of life arose from his perception of its contrarious inconsistencies—of Nature's jaunty readiness to support unorthodox social principles. (339)

The ponderous progress of Henchard's character from egoistic extremity to a degree of fellow feeling—from shame to sorrow, ambition to sentiment—is frustrated by the nature of things. His willingness to abdicate his sovereignty means nothing. The uncaring universe has shriveled his goals and energies to no visible purpose.

> And thus Henchard found himself again on the precise standing which he had occupied a quarter of a century before. Externally there was nothing to hinder his making another start . . . [and] achieving higher things than his soul in its half-formed state had been able to accomplish. But the ingenious machinery contrived by the Gods for reducing human possibilities of amelioration to a minimum—which arranges that wisdom to do shall come *pari passu* with the departure of zest for doing—stood in the way of all that. He had no wish to make an arena a second time of a world that had become a mere painted scene to him. (340)

Against the backdrop of Hardy's pessimism, Henchard's wearily earned awareness—his rudimentary turning toward social and sentimental existence—is obscured. Moral development or education devolves into the cry of human victimization: "I, an outcast, an encumberer of the ground, wanted by nobody, and despised by all, live on against my will!" (340).

The energy that once served ambition makes one last gesture toward accommodation, a final effort to wrench free of the pain character has earned and the universe abetted.

Henchard decides to bring a wedding present to Elizabeth-Jane. A "caged goldfinch met his eye. The cage was a plain and small one, the shop humble, and on inquiry he concluded he could afford the modest sum asked. A sheet of newspaper was tied round the little creature's wire prison, and with the wrapped up cage in his hand Henchard sought a lodging for the night" (342). His unexpected arrival at the wedding party the next day causes his stepdaughter to stammer in surprise: "Oh—it is—Mr. Henchard!"

> "What; Elizabeth?" he cried. . . . "What do you say?—*Mr.* Henchard? Don't, don't scourge me like that!"
> . . . .
>
> Henchard's lips half parted to begin an explanation. But he shut them up like a vice, and uttered not a sound. How should he, there and then, set before her with any effect the palliatives of his great faults—that he had himself been deceived in her identity at first . . . [that his lie to Newson] had been the last desperate throw of a gamester who loved her affection better than his own honour? Among the many hindrances to such a pleading not the least was this, that he did not sufficiently value himself to lessen his sufferings by strenuous appeal or elaborate argument. (346)

From sovereign beast to fangless lion to caged bird. Henchard hurriedly retreats, leaving his gift behind in the garden bushes, where a week later the housemaid discovers a cage with a dead bird.

The melodramatic literalness of the symbol is apt. For unlike socialized figures whose faith helps them translate a communal cage into a true shelter, Henchard cannot create the metaphors culture employs to alleviate the starkness and solitude of the human condition. Even when he is willing to enter Farfrae's and Elizabeth-Jane's household, Henchard sees nothing before him but a prison that, his honor and self-esteem lost, is merely better than death. Such literal-mindedness exposes truth without any way to survive truth. But Henchard's true story is an unnecessarily extreme position on a spectrum that leads from untenable fact to evasive parable. At the opposite pole are Farfrae and Lucetta. The latter, in her vain, unquestioning, wholly social nature, embodies Hardy's satiric dismissal of the kind of characterization encouraged by the Balzacian ideal. Farfrae, however, seems to offer an acceptable modus operandi, a middle ground of socialization.

The Scotsman appears sufficiently malleable and at the same time sufficiently strong to withstand nature's buffeting. "The curious mixture of romance and thrift in the young man's composition" (297) blends sentiment and the realities of trade in a "remarkably pleasant" way (69). When Elizabeth-Jane first encounters him, on her first night in Casterbridge, she is much impressed. Farfrae entertains the townspeople with poignant songs and then instructs them with statements that

> showed him to be no less thoughtful than his fascinating melodies revealed him to be cordial and impassioned. She admired the serious light in which he looked at serious things. He had seen no jest in ambiguities and roguery, as the Casterbridge toss-pots had done. . . . He seemed to feel exactly as she felt about life and its surroundings—that they were a tragical rather than a comical thing; that though one could be gay on occasion, moments of gaiety were interludes, and no part of the

actual drama. It was extraordinary how similar their views were. (85–86)

Elizabeth-Jane is a sensible girl. Her views are often close to Hardy's, and her admiration must be taken seriously. So too, however, must her mild disappointment when she comes to know Farfrae.

> "You are anxious to get back to Scotland, I suppose, Mr. Farfrae?" she inquired.
>
> "O no, Miss Newson. Why would I be?"
>
> "I only supposed you might be from the song you sang . . . about Scotland and home, I mean—which you seemed to feel so deep down in your heart; so that we all felt for you."
>
> ". . . But Miss Newson"—and Donald's voice musically undulated between two semitones, as it always did when he became earnest—"it's well you feel a song for a few minutes, and your eyes they get quite tearful; but you finish it, and for all you felt you don't mind it or think of it again for a long while. O no, I don't want to go back! Yet I'll sing the song to you wi' pleasure whenever you like. I could sing it now, and not mind at all?" (123)

Farfrae's reasonable attitude is that of an amenable, relaxed *homme moyen*. Yet there is something missing.

A few pages earlier, during Henchard's first long talk with his new manager, the mayor—as always confessional about his own concerns—tells of the complications surrounding his involvement with Lucetta years before: "in my illness I sank into one of those gloomy fits I sometimes suffer from, on account o' the loneliness of my domestic life, when the world seems to have the blackness of hell, and, like Job,

I could curse the day that gave me birth" (108). Farfrae's rejoinder—"Ah, no, I never feel like it"—seems somehow incommensurate, a bland denial of a complete perspective on life. The Scotsman deals in emotions; he never suffers from them. While likable and virtuous enough, his character hardly competes with the drama of Henchard's. Farfrae's qualities, moreover, are always slightly tarnished by an admixture of the cunning Hardy associates with the Scottish nature. When Elizabeth-Jane's stepfather disappears after the wedding, Farfrae wants to call off the search because "to go much further afield would reduce them to the necessity of camping out for the night; 'and that will make a hole in a sovereign' " (351).

The reservations implicit in Hardy's portrait do not contradict Farfrae's pleasantly serious traits and general attractiveness. Like the attitude of one of the characters in *The Hand of Ethelberta*, his temperament proves "its value frequently; for it [is] . . . impersonally human."[17] Indeed, were his natural accommodation with life less successful, were he to live at a sharper emotional pitch, Farfrae would not be able to shelter the much-tried Elizabeth-Jane. Yet if we follow the realistic novelists of the previous generation in equating valuable character with the possibility of growth and development, we must find Farfrae deficient: a given, essentially unchanging worldly man. His qualities are even less susceptible to molding than Henchard's, who at last verges on development. The two men stand as extremes between which Elizabeth-Jane, the moral though not the dramatic centerpiece of Hardy's conception, is flung as she gradually defines the conditions of her selfhood.

The young woman appears to be Hardy's model for

[17] *The Hand of Ethelberta* (London: Macmillan, 1975), p. 86.

plausible acculturation to the hard lessons of the Twilight. The process involves cruel loss, a sacrifice of Henchard's potency and Farfrae's charm. For Elizabeth-Jane, social existence becomes, not an abstract repository of moral and humane virtue, but a necessary defensive strategy. She would counter "Nature's unorthodox social principles" with a militant orthodoxy. "Any suspicion of impropriety was to Elizabeth-Jane like a red rag to a bull. Her craving for correctness of procedure was, indeed, almost vicious. Owing to her early troubles with regard to her mother a semblance of irregularity had terrors for her which those whose names are safeguarded from suspicion know nothing of" (239–40). The animal image, the violent ambition to escape her origins, and the extremity of reaction all associate Susan's daughter with the mayor. But Elizabeth-Jane's character is very differently organized. "If there was one good thing more than another which characterized this single-hearted girl it was a willingness to sacrifice her personal comfort and dignity to the common weal" (75). Her morality—which seems closely parallel to the omniscient judgments scattered throughout the narrative—is the stern result of the tempering of conventional appraisals by untoward experience. At the end, Elizabeth-Jane stands forth as an exemplum of truth passed through the fires of contemporary disorder.

> From this time forward Elizabeth-Jane found herself in a latitude of calm weather, kindly and gateful in itself, and doubly so after the Capharnaum in which some of her preceding years had been spent. As the lively and sparkling emotions of her early married life cohered into an equable serenity, the finer movements of her nature found scope in discovering to the narrow-lived ones around her the secret . . . of making limited oppor-

tunities endurable; which she deemed to consist in the cunning enlargement, by a species of microscopic treatment, of those minute forms of satisfaction that offer themselves to everybody not in positive pain. . . .

. . . Her position . . . afforded much to be thankful for. That she was not demonstratively thankful was no fault of hers. Her experience had been of a kind to teach her, rightly or wrongly, that the doubtful honour of a brief transit through a sorry world hardly called for effusiveness, even when the path was suddenly irradiated at some half-way point by daybeams as rich as hers. But her strong sense that neither she nor any human being deserved less than was given, did not blind her to the fact that there were others receiving less who had deserved much more. And . . . she did not cease to wonder at the persistence of the unforeseen, when the one to whom such unbroken tranquillity had been accorded in the adult stage was she whose youth had seemed to teach that happiness was but the occasional episode in a general drama of pain. (353–54)

These last lines of Hardy's novel recall "Monk" Lewis's parting with those who survive his plotting of Gothic horror: their "remaining years . . . were as happy as can be those allotted to Mortals, born to be the prey of grief, and sport of disappointment."[18] Conclusive ending is reserved for the demonized monk; those who can live on are less compelling subjects. Hardy, of course, stems from a tradition in which the Ambrosios have been rationalized and the focus turned upon the realistic chiaroscuro in which common life takes place. Yet even in this tradition the sad trailing off represents a marked reestimation of what is plausibly possible. The

[18] Matthew Gregory Lewis, *The Monk* (London: Oxford Univ. Press, 1973), p. 420.

ending radically revises George Eliot's type of beleaguered yet still hopeful idea of an inevitable compromise between human desires and the destinies reality permits. Hardy phases Elizabeth-Jane out of active struggle and into the weary decency of unpredictable survival. Fatigue rather than goodness or happiness is the dominant note. One must lie low before life's storms, must maintain moral balance in a vertiginous position. The education of the "flower of Nature" instructs in the possibilities of a vulnerable indoor plant.

The greater the human value, the more telling the experience of life's depredations. Ideally, Henchard's stern dynamism and his stepdaughter's moral beauty should work together. But as the two are not blood kin, so their qualities are not kindred. Excluded from the human enclave Elizabeth-Jane has always yearned for and finally helps create, Henchard becomes a threat; his needs abet the tyranny of things. Finally his frustration turns in upon itself and is engulfed by indifferent nature. Neither rampant energy nor mannerly convention can cope with the Twilit facts of our blighted star. A new type of character is required. And however paradoxical it may at first seem, the nature of a pessimistically conceived cosmos becomes a taskmaster instructing humanity in the character of survival. The forces pressing in from beyond the human pale—the atrocious alternatives Conrad will evoke in Kurtz's summarizing last words, "The horror! The horror!"—must teach, not just appall.

As Hardy's clear affection and his insistent use of the vocabulary of education indicate, Elizabeth-Jane is the prize pupil of the new curriculum. Vision and growth are not lost in her, but their scope is reduced. She retains the strength to act; she quits "her safe and secluded maiden courses for the speculative path of matrimony" (156). But Hardy's muted celebration of her marriage to Farfrae, as well as his un-excited estimate of the Scotsman's qualities, rewards the young woman with what is at best a cramped, defensive, and miniaturized happiness. Her possibilities have lost the reso-nance of that "narrowed lot" that George Eliot permits most of her central figures. Elizabeth-Jane is for her author the best of women, combining moral strength with something of Bathsheba's gifts, yet she is scarred permanently by the storms unleashed upon her springtime.

Elizabeth-Jane's compound of stubborn selfhood and moral dignity conveys Hardy's diminished yet still vital terms for hope. By encircling us, tragedy helps shape an order more truthful than that once provided by society. The traditional conflict between egoistic energy and the in-ternalized cultural values that constitute the English version of the Balzacian ideal of character has given way to a strug-gle between the darkness of things and the native morality most men share. To emerge against the grain of cosmic law, man's character must be "withal singularly colossal." In some unclear way, moral character is stronger than the probabili-ties opposing it. As the narrator says of some residents on Casterbridge's squalid Mixen Lane: "amid so much that was bad[,] needy respectability also found a home. Under some of the roofs abode pure and virtuous souls whose presence there was due to the iron hand of necessity, and to that alone" (279). The perdurance of decency, however distressed, and that of resilience, however tried, states Hardy's revision of the strand in the Victorian sense of transition that believes hard times to enforce testing, not tragedy.

The embers of this faith set Hardy apart from his early modern successors who often equate the achievement of identity with that of art itself and for whom the metaphoric

value of character replaces the goals of moral culture. Clinging to his immediate predecessors' idea of character and immersing it in the newly alien circumstances he calls modern,
Hardy frequently seems to verge on the themes of determinism and victimization common to much late-century literature. Yet here too he is atypical. He believes that moral
nurture has in the course of time and testing developed into
a definitive component of human nature, that a tendency
toward goodness is not a superimposition but a truth. Elizabeth-Jane is meant to bear this out. Her survival carries into
action Henchard's blurred craving for something "better."

Indeed, Elizabeth-Jane's development provides one of
the few major instances of Hardy's subdued meliorism.
Usually, grimly advertised fatality and modern vulnerability
form so bleak a warning that the strain of hope is obscured.
Yet there is in Hardy a central area of intention for which
the title of the penultimate chapter of *Far from the Madding
Crowd*, which tells of the triumph of Gabriel Oak's long-
suffering love, might serve as an epigraph: "Beauty in Loneliness—After All." Hints that existence need not be as maul-
ingly grim as the foreground of his monitory dramas might
suggest are not uncommon, though their message is often so
muted as to be moot. In *The Return of the Native* it is not
just an extension of Hardy's earlier concession to the sanguine spirit of a serial-reading public that can account for
his retaining Thomasin's marriage to the reformed reddle-
man Diggory Venn as the conclusion to the novel. At the
end of *Tess*, Angel Clare and Tess's now-grown sister remain
for a long while "absolutely motionless" after the hanging
that closes the gods' cruel sport, but then they find strength
to arise, join hands, and move on, perhaps toward the mutual
solace Tess had desired for them. Only in *Jude* does there

seem no room for growth, for the possibility that mankind can make its "limited opportunities endurable."

Yet the trimming of Elizabeth-Jane to the measure of modern limitation, her emergence as the protagonist of present truth, are not enacted with novelistic assurance. We are unprepared to learn that the young woman is a "flower of Nature"; the praise has not been earned by Hardy's portrait. Elizabeth-Jane stands illustrationally for the ideal of tempered character, but she does not receive the dense representation that makes Henchard memorable. Her endurance seems more an example of the "persistence of the unforeseen" than of an education undertaken before our eyes. By contrast, Henchard and the strong women are the triumphs of Hardy's characterization: forceful, complex versions of the "restless aspiring" energy manifest in a Pip or a Dorothea Brooke.[19] But for Hardy such power is that of a fractured wholeness. The mayor's strength cannot join what has been sundered; his will, in fact, precludes his role in any story of future realignment. He combines the effect of elegy with the vivid presence of ballad. Loss and tragic melodrama are the environment of Hardy's novelistically successful characters. Frustration and stalemate are their substance.

[19] The quoted words are from Pip's self-estimate in Chapter 14 of *Great Expectations*.

3

ZOLA

Characters in the Fields of Force

> *"Vous êtes tout de même d'une jolie force, vous."*
> *("All the same, you're a fine force, you are.")*
>
> —Clorinde to *Son Excellence Eugène Rougon*

The melodramatically unmanageable individualities and cosmic distress of Hardy's swarthy Twilight are "quite coarse to a person o' decent taste." Zola's account of the historical, genetic, and legendary blight that withers character defies such categories as coarseness and decency. In staking out the territory that is called naturalism, Zola largely dismisses the private and innate dimension of the Balzacian idea of character, while emphasizing the external, situational factors that determine thoughts, feelings, and behavior. The actors and the narratives that contain them are purged of the unique, unrepeatable configurations of inwardness and are left naked before the play of primal and social influences. Like Hardy, Zola narrates the collapse of traditional structures of value and insists on the human toll any rebuilding must exact. But whereas Hardy premises the cruel indifference of universal law and tries to conceive a humanity that can live with the fact, Zola depicts a humanity whose sexual, social, and intellectual abominations express the nature of an epidemic malaise. To the major extent that character is formed by external models and pressures, character is disease.

One reason for the proliferation of those mobs whose action Zola charts so masterfully is the erosion of any private selfhood that might resist the pressure of transitory definition. This aspect of Zola's fiction—the spasmodic induction of individuality into the ranks of a general or archetypal identity—has had a widespread influence on modern narrative. Zola's example stands behind *unanimisme*, the sociohistorical synopses of expressionistic naturalism (as in Dos Passos and Alfred Döblin), and through a series of distortions behind socialist realism. Particularly in his pronouncements about the experimental novel, Zola appears to sanction such extensions. But the twenty novels making up *Les Rougon-Macquart* are grounded in dualities and contradictions strikingly similar to those that shape Hardy's and Chekhov's fiction. The documentary message of the novels concludes with judgmental satisfaction, "character is dead"; the positivistic vision insists, "long live character." The novels fail to dramatize a convincing transition. Zola accepts the ideal of organic human wholeness so often staged by earlier novelists: the model is clearly evident in Gervaise in *L'Assommoir*, and is refracted in the presentation of the decent miners in *Germinal* as well as in the glimpses of the many integral lower-class lives that populate the chronicle. Yet the strongest emphasis is on the displacement and dispersal of such wholeness by contemporary corruption. And the expression of loss and decay, though intended to mirror only a destructive phase, obscures the promise of rebirth.

Zola envisions a progressive alchemy of Schopenhauerian Will into an energetic multidimensionality that will restore the valuable humanity potential in France's good earth. Man's stricken capabilities can be revitalized only when caught up in the elemental, cleansing impetus associated with "force." Unlike Hardy's carefully textured reincorporation of the phases and rites of nature into the fabric of late-century experience, Zola's evocation of the abiding determinisms of force is quasi-mystical: a materialistic version of Dante's "love that moves the sun and the other stars." Nature and mankind dance to the plangent rhythms of this essential élan vital; Zola's art responds to them with its fullest fervor. Shorn of force, life is fallow or worse—its futile contortions a subject for satire; its sentimental virtues bloodless. Innocence and goodness exist, but like the village girl Miette in *La Fortune des Rougon*, the first novel of the series, they are ineffectual. When Miette enters, she is nice, but bland. Then force impinges on her life as she and her beloved watch a procession of insurgent republicans.

> A singular drunkenness rose from this crowd heady with noise, courage, and faith. These beings half seen in moonlight, these adolescents, these ripe men, these old men brandishing unaccustomed weapons, clothed in the most varied costumes, from workers' smocks to bourgeois frockcoats; this endless file of heads that the hour and occasion made unforgettable masks of energy and fanatic zeal at length took on in the young girl's eyes the vertiginous impetuousness of a torrent. At times it seemed to her that they no longer marched, but were borne forward upon *la Marseillaise* itself, upon that hoarse and sonorous chant. She couldn't make out the words; she heard only a continual rumbling, going from bass notes to shrill, piercing as nails randomly driven into her flesh. This howl of revolt, this call to battle and to death, with its tremors of rage, its burning desire for liberty, its amazing mixture of murderous and sublime forces, striking her heart so unremittingly, more deeply with each brutal rhythm, filled her with

the voluptuous agonies of a virgin martyr standing and smiling under the lash. . . .

Certainly, Miette was a child. She had blanched at the approach of the troop, . . . but she was a courageous child, an ardent nature that enthusiasm readily exalted. . . . She became a boy; willingly would she have taken up a weapon and followed the insurgents. As the rifles and scythes filed before her, her white teeth showed longer and sharper from between her red lips, like the fangs of a young wolf eager to bite.[1]

Specific psychology and the data of social circumstance fall away; the thirteen-year-old is recreated as a typical figure in *Les Rougon-Macquart*. Beginning with probable reactions, Zola veers off into what we shall come to recognize as a general psychopathology of force. And just as Miette is carried from realism into a mode anticipating expressionism, so Zola's description passes from bourgeois realism to a hectic catalog of extremes that recalls popular Gothic fiction. Mass emotion, violence, pain, ecstasy, sexual excess all enter into the definition of force; and force transforms the simple girl into an enraged animal.

Zola admires the high patriotism of the republicans and hymns the energy their march unleashes as purposeful, essentially moral. Yet despite his allegiance, there are even in this first novel signs of thematic difficulties to come. Gripped by force, Miette escapes the private and social disorder, the he-

---

[1] I have translated all quotations from Zola from the five-volume Bibliothèque de la Pléiade edition of *Les Rougon-Macquart* published under the direction of Armand Lanoux, with commentary, notes, and variants established by Henri Mitterand (Paris: Éditions Fasquelles et Gallimard, 1960–67). The passage in the text is from Volume I, pp. 31–32. Subsequent quotations are cited to volume and page number in the text.

reditary *nervosité* and endemic malaise of her era, but she does so at the cost of the complex selfhood earlier novelists were so often concerned to portray and Zola himself desires to see reborn. To be sure, Zola intends a kind of abeyance. The tempering of Miette's simple goodness in the acid of truth predicts the necessary immersion in primal nature that is a precondition of what is called in *L'Argent* "the right reason of health" (V, 375). As Zola insists throughout *Le Docteur Pascal*, the final novel of the series and its thematic gloss, present decay is an inexplicable accident; France must be regenerated into "a cultural medium for healing in which, both physically and morally, the individual can be remade and saved" (V, 1209). The circumstances of the accident are detailed formidably; the presence and workings of potentially purgative force are evoked with powerful art. But the effects of Zola's potent prescription upon character are often distressing. Frequently, the self is purged along with the sickness. Once the medicine is withdrawn, life appears to be de-energized. Again, Zola's treatment of Miette anticipates a major difficulty in the later novels. Coming after her exultant identification with the insurgents, the description of her budding love seems weakly conventional.

> This month of joyful tenderness rescued Miette from her mute despair. She felt her affections reawaken: the happy childish carelessness so long repressed by the hateful solitude in which she had been living. The certainty that someone loved her, that she was no longer alone in the world, allowed her to bear the proddings of Justin [her mean cousin] and the town urchins. There was now a song in her heart that kept her from hearing the hooting. . . . Her dawning love was like a refreshing daybreak calming her feverish distress. At

> the same time, she learned the cunning of a girl in love. She told herself that she must keep up her mute attitude of revolt if Justin's suspicions were not to be aroused. But despite her efforts, her eyes remained gentle even when the boy pained her; she could no longer adopt her black, harsh look. (I, 184)

Sympathy is clear, but the images and diction are lax, generalized, uninvolved. Conventional emotions do not inspire the intense art awakened by the collision of human nature and primal force. If force submerges Miette's particularity, stereotyped description washes out her budding individuality.

Throughout the Rougon-Macquart novels, the presentation of probable, ordinary life remains distant, even uninterested. But against this blurred background the primary colors of rampant extremity appear with an ever more shocking pyrotechnic effect. A person singled out to be a carrier of force, whatever its specific expression, transfigures circumstances much as Nana does in her role as Venus in a music-hall burlesque of Olympus and its amorous deities.

> When Nana raised her arms, the golden hairs in her armpits could be seen in the glare of the footlight. There was no applause. Nobody laughed any longer. The men's faces were serious, their nostrils narrowed, their mouths prickly and parched. A wind seemed to have passed over the audience, a soft wind laden with hidden menace. All of a sudden, in the good-natured child the woman stood revealed, a disturbing woman with all the impulsive madness of her sex, unveiling the uncharted world of desire. Nana was still smiling, but with the sharp-edged smile of a man-eater. (II, 1118)

Each of the last sentences takes a common word—*wind*, *woman*, *smile*—and subjects it to potent redefinitions. Nana's aphrodisiac effect on the audience does the same.

> A wave of lust was flowing from her as from a bitch in heat; it had spread further and further until it filled the whole theater. Now her slightest movements fanned desire, and with a twitch of her little finger she could stir men's flesh. Backs arched and quivered as if unseen violin bows had been drawn across their muscles. . . . The audience was suffocating, the very hair growing heavy on sweating heads. In the three hours they had been there, their breath had filled the air with a hot human smell. . . . The entire house swayed, seized by a fit of giddiness in its fatigue and excitement, possessed by those drowsy midnight urges that fumble between the sheets. And Nana, before this rapt audience, these fifteen hundred human beings jammed together and overwhelmed by the nervous exhaustion that comes towards the end of a performance, remained victorious in her marble flesh with that sex of hers powerful enough to destroy the whole gathering without losing a jot of its own force. (II, 1119–20)

Force, Nana, the audience, and Zola's vivid command of the dynamics of stress collaborate in transforming the commonplace occasion. Melodrama urges vulgarity and anonymity towards myth.

Here and in many similar scenes Zola marshals the intensity of a two-fold inversion: force usurps character; contemporary decay—*malaise* is Zola's repeated term—turns the regenerative rhythm of force into a danse macabre. Nana and the fifteen-hundred human beings resemble nerves manipulated in a primal foreplay. Their individuality is carried off by a spate of simile, hyperbole, and synesthesia; separate egos are merged by the pressure of active verbs and participles. But at the same time, the nature of these egos, their hereditary share in a general corruption, perverts the energy flooding through them. In itself, force has no moral definition. Yet it can and must be made to serve the revitalization of the fundamentally traditional human, cultural, and patriotic virtues in which Zola believes. The decadence of present character and society traduces this potential. Nana corrupts "a whole religion, a whole world of poetry" (II, 1112). The fertile mystery whose pulses Zola records is befouled, vitiated by the murderous rut society has become.

Particularly in the novels devoted to the Parisian bourgeoisie, Zola's depiction of social life passes far beyond any castigation of a vanity fair. *Pot-Bouille* with its simmering stew of sterile lusts and egomaniacal ambitions provides a typical view: the hypocritical lives of the middle-class dwellers in a pretentious new apartment building are played out against comments and sights from the servant's court, a "sewer" draining off the vileness behind the whitewashed facade. Near the end, the local priest and doctor try to sum up what they have witnessed. The former comments that God has forsaken these lives. "Don't drag God into it," the doctor objects. "They're sick or badly nurtured, that's all."

> He launched out at the women, some corrupted or stultified by their dolls' upbringing, others whose sentiments and passions were perverted by hereditary bad nerves: all of them surrendering themselves filthily, foolishly, with no more desire than pleasure. He wasn't any gentler with the men: strapping fellows who, under the hypocritical cover of their fine bearing, ended

by ruining their constitutions. And through all this Jacobin transport sounded the death knell of a class, the decomposition and breakdown of the bourgeoisie whose rotting props were cracking. (III, 363)

Zola clearly seconds "the just observations of an experienced practitioner who knows in depth the hidden affairs of his district." Yet the passage suggests contradictory impulses. The reformist perspective that might advance a cure for illness or bad nurture is bound by different standards than those implicit in the revolutionism of "Jacobin transport." An underlying animus vies with scientific estimate. Zola parts company with the doctor when the latter is carried away by revolutionist wrath: radical surgery is not needed; the rotten props will and should collapse by themselves. However, Zola's moral absolutism cannot leave the bourgeoisie alone to their fate. The servant's comment with which the novel concludes strikes a note of equivocal bitterness: "C'est cochon et compagnie"—"It's Swine and Sons."

The cast of *Pot-Bouille* is a collection of characterless types acting out filthy desires. The few decent figures vary the moral paralysis of the put-upon father, M. Josserand. Zola's central concern is not with individuals who might be saved but with the nature of a setting that must be analyzed before it can be remade. Yet not only does the larger focus expand the tension between experimental investigation and infuriated judgment, it also points to a further complication. As in the description of Nana's performance, rage at the misappropriations of force readily gives way to imaginative participation in the pulsations of disorder; diagnosis is compromised by artistic empathy with the melodramatic flaring up of the disease. The long sections during which the fevers of decay simply smolder portray a commonplace stupidity and wrongdoing so dully repetitious that the moments of egregious foulness—whether in the servants' lives or the masters'—come as a relief. Zola's moral indignation is undoubted, but it is confusingly associated with what appears to be an enraged frustration at the crass limits habitual sinning sets upon both the regenerative impetus of force and the aspirations of forceful art. Zola's animus against bourgeois bad faith at times resembles what a Van Gogh might feel were he compelled to work only in pastels.

Extreme malaise calls forth the best of Zola's art. When decay topples into collapse, we glimpse through the chaos those truths that normal life has evaded. If Miette's story in the first novel predicts Zola's difficulty in accommodating pure energy to decent dailiness, the quasi-incestuous affair between the bored, blasé wife Renée and her stepson in *La Curée*, the second novel of the series, reveals the artistic advantages of a collusion between force and decadent character. Treated by her husband, the speculator Saccard, only as a conspicuously lovely possession, Renée yearns for intensities to quicken her "dead heart." At the beginning, she can still find a certain tranquillity in nature, in "the murmuring shadows of the park whose voices counseled peaceful happiness." But her temperament, which sometimes seems a distorted projection of her author's sensationalism, has lost the capacity for sustaining simple joys. "The ardent impulses of a sensual woman, the caprices of a sated woman awoke within her" (I, 357–58). She is gripped by desire for her husband's son Maxime, a "neuter being, blond and pretty, his manliness dimmed from childhood." "This pretty little man, . . . this failed girl . . . with tiny laughs and bored smiles, became in Renée's hands one of those decadent debauchees who at certain times in a rotten nation exhaust the flesh and unhinge the brain" (I, 485, 486). As in Hardy, the inversion of traditional sex roles is a symptom of general disorder. Though sometimes the erosion of conventional definitions allows truth to emerge, usually women's preemptive passions and men's unmanly passivity are condemned by Zola's vehemently conventional chauvinism about such matters. But indignation here fuels art. Extreme perversion results in an utter abdication of character before the facts of force. "Maxime and Renée, their senses corrupted, felt themselves carried away into the potent nuptials of the earth. The sun burned their backs . . . hot droplets fell on them from the tall palms. The sap that rose in the trunks of the trees coursed through them as well, endowing them with a mad desire for immediate increase, for gigantic reproduction" (I, 487). Just as Nana embodies and defames the powers of Venus, so the two voluptuaries enact and parody elemental potency. Desiring only to reduce force to private titillation, Renée lacks the character that might order the process she has set in motion. She is absorbed. She becomes "the burning daughter of the hothouse. Her kisses flamed and faded like the red flowers of the giant mallow that last but a few hours and are reborn unceasingly, like the bruised, insatiable lips of a colossal Messalina" (I, 489).

Renée both demonstrates present derangement and is cast into a telling repetition of archetypal harlotry. She is the spawn of Lilith, not Venus. Zola's belief in a mystic fecundity that Renée violates connects him with an important aspect of the late-century reestimation of nature.[2] Yet at the same time, his commitment to a revised form of Balzacian

---

[2] John Alcorn examines the English tradition born of this movement in *The Nature Novel from Hardy to Lawrence* (New York: Columbia Univ. Press, 1977).

social premises, to the cultural mission of character, militates against the organic grounding of character in untrammeled nature that Gide will intermittently advocate and D. H. Lawrence will pervasively exalt. Renée's sexuality is evoked with an artistic thrust that carries beyond culture, with a descriptive participation that complicates any simple condemnation of bourgeois filth. According to the underlying message of Zola's fiction, the forces coursing through Renée must both quicken art and serve the revitalization of French culture. But the former intention succeeds at the expense of the latter. Renée's corruption and the social misappropriation that the hothouse performs upon primal energy are clear; but nowhere in the novels is the positive, let alone redemptive, value of the primal rites upon which the bored wife intrudes made dramatically available to characters who might put it to good use. Force is of nature, and our examination of *La Faute de l'abbé Mouret* will illustrate Zola's contradictory exaltation of the energy of nature and fright at its indifference to human purposes. As all the novels show, unprecedented strength of character is demanded if force is to be tamed to the decencies of civilization.

Many of the characters Zola proposes for this role are women. And given his male bias, the choice suggests a perpetuation of dilemma rather than a source of remedy. Unlike Hardy's strong women, Zola's heroines rarely revolt against traditionally dependent roles. Their special quality intensifies obedience and endurance. They must sacrifice all to charm their men out of the neurasthenic self-involvement that prevents them from collaborating in the fecundity Zola esteems as women's highest gift. Variations on Miette's moment of transformation abound. Most of these women join the pastoral lass in experiencing "the voluptuous agonies of a virgin martyr standing and smiling under the lash." Pauline in *La Joie de vivre*, the most extreme example, struggles heroically to maintain her good nature amid a Job-like catalog of woes. "Happiness, she believed, depended on neither men nor things but on the reasonable way one accommodated oneself to them" (III, 1002). Zola's account of the various connotations of "Douleur" transforms accommodation into martyrdom. Pauline must cling to joyous dutifulness in a devastated environment alien to the hopes and works of men. An orphan brought from Paris to a seaside fishing village, she witnesses the piecemeal destruction of every house. The crass, ignorant fisherfolk stand by and jeer at Lazare, her husband, as he tries to build a breakwater that might save them. Pauline's own home is safely on a hill above, but her home life is even more dolorous than that of the villagers. Her aunt, Lazare's mother, lapses from grudging decency to miserly meanness, and then, having robbed and tormented her niece, dies suddenly and graphically from dropsy. The uncle, an ineffectual, self-centered man, pleasant enough on the infrequent occasions when he is free of pain, is tortured by exhaustively described bouts with chronic gout. The family's aged dog bleeds to death, its kidneys having degenerated. Enduring all this, and more, Pauline becomes an exemplar of the force of health. On the next to last page, homage is paid her "renunciation, love of others, and the goodness" she spreads "over miserable [*mauvaise*] mankind" (III, 1129). Nonetheless the novel concludes with the mysterious suicide of the servant who has been the family's mainstay.

Zola intends his title as exhortation and praise, not irony. But Pauline's joyful commitment to life seems as ironically out of place as a sanguine sermon in a plague-stricken state.

The message she embodies precludes any portrait of complex consciousness. She remains an enclave of mental health, ever opposed to what Zola presents as her husband's emasculating pessimism. If she is her author's hope for the future, Lazare, despite intervals of enthusiasm and flurries of joy, is the very type of late-century exhaustion.

> Dominating all, drowning all, his ennui became immense: the ennui of an unbalanced man so sickened by the ever-present idea of looming death, by the pretext of life's nothingness, that any action, the mere dragging oneself through existence, seemed loathsome. Why exert yourself? Science was of no use, could neither prevent nor determine anything. His was the skeptical ennui of his generation; unlike the romantic ennui of the Werthers and Renés bemoaning a lost faith, his was that of the new protagonists of doubt, of the angry young researchers who, unable to discover life all at once at the bottom of their retorts, dubbed the world impossible.
>
> In Lazare ... the unspoken terror of ceasing to be went hand in hand with a braggart insistence on nothingness. His very terror, the imbalance of his hypochondriac nature, drove in upon him the theories of pessimism, a fierce hatred for existence. He believed life a fraud from the moment he could not believe it immortal. He reveled again in the ideas of the "old one," as he called Schopenhauer, whose most vehement passages he recited from memory. He spoke of killing the will to live in order to halt the barbaric imbecile march of life. ... To suppress fear, he would suppress life. (III, 1057–58)

Zola's displeasure with the husband is as intrusive as his flattery of the wife. In both cases, omniscient pontification works against imaginative projection. Lazare's racial weakness is as mysterious a fiat as Pauline's strength. Since he must illustrate the disfranchisement of character, however, his hollowness serves Zola's theme: he acts as a dissonant aeolian harp to sound the nature of malaise. But Pauline's reduction to sentimental abstraction damages Zola's case. Nothing in the account of her parents, in *Le Ventre de Paris*, prepares us for her heroic nature. They are, to be sure, joyful purveyors and consumers of the fat of the land, but their bourgeois complacency hardly seems a likely breeding ground for a psychology of renunciation.

Leaving aside the first and last novels, *La Joie de vivre* is the most programmatic of the series. Pauline's active resignation is to balance Lazare's defects. But just because the model Pauline must provide is so crucial, Zola overprotects it. Even in such private matters as her first terrified and then joyous initiation into womanhood, Zola's desire to illustrate and instruct preempts the individual reactions necessary to his demonstration. The major difficulty, however, arises directly from his insistence upon the traditional limits of a woman's place in life. Believing even the social behavior dictated by this role to be natural, and believing that only through their naturalness can women teach us how to utilize germinal force, Zola insists that his exempla be women as of old. The point is clearest in *La Débâcle*. Zola concludes his social history of a family under the Empire by recapitulating Lazare's weakness and Pauline's strength in the "profound difference" between Maurice and his twin sister Henriette.

> He was as high-strung as a woman, shattered by the sickness of the epoch, going through the historical and social crisis of his race, capable from one moment to the next of passing from the most noble enthusiasms to the

deepest discouragements, while she, so weak-looking, a self-effacing Cinderella with the resigned appearance of a little housewife, had the firm brow and brave eyes of the blessed stock of which martyrs are made. (V, 558–59)

Like Pauline, Henriette can endure. Such heroic helpmeets can transform victimization into exemplary martyrdom. But, being women, they cannot exert the force needed for renewal. And Zola's loose equivalents to Hardy's strong women, his Nanas and Renées, are unfeminine, unnatural, and unworthy.

Society offers no usable ground for redemptive action. To counter the sickness that society merely worsens, both men and women must somehow acculturate the forceful *gai saber* explicit in scenes such as the harvest feast in *La Terre*.

At eleven they all sat down to bread and cheese. It wasn't that they were hungry, for they'd been cramming themselves with grapes since dawn: their gullets sticky with sugar, bellies bloated and round as barrels. The grapes churned inside them, as good as a purge. Already every few minutes some girl had to slip behind the hedge. Naturally, everyone laughed, the men getting up and shouting "oh—oh!" to help them on their way. In short, a fine gaiety, something healthful, refreshing. (IV, 664)

In *Le Ventre de Paris*, the artist Claude Lantier divides his countrymen into two categories: the Fat and the Thin. The latter distort or ignore the bounties of nature; their lean and hungry intellectualism or monomania of vision desiccates their lives. Zola prefers and usually applauds the Fat, those who project the values of the harvest scene. In *Le Ventre*, Madame François carries something of her beloved countryside with her as she brings her produce into the Paris markets. She gives "the effect of a healthy, robust plant, as well developed as the vegetables grown in the compost of her kitchen garden" (I, 804).

Similar types occur often in the novels, but their roles are minor, and their presence, while pleasant, lacks force. The refreshment of healthy gaiety rarely inspires major character. Not only do the realities of Zola's sick epoch make health implausible, but when fecund fatness, as a dimension either of setting or of character, is accorded full scope, the results are usually appalling. Madame François's kitchen garden has charm; its produce transported into and multiplied in Les Halles, the vast Paris markets that form the setting for *Le Ventre*, swells into the bloated congress of foodstuffs that nauseates the protagonist Florent. The subliminal suggestion of animals being fattened for slaughter that slightly taints the harvest episode becomes explicit in Zola's epic catalogs of food and refuse. Florent, a utopian who has taken a job as market inspector after his return from political exile, sees fertility burgeon disgustingly into a

> sated, digesting beast sprawling over Paris, wallowing in fat, ponderously propping up the Empire. The markets encircled him with huge throats, monstrous haunches, sleek gullets that were like endless arguments against his martyr's thinness, his yellow, discontented face. Here was the belly of shopkeeping, of a decent enough mediocrity puffing itself out, happy, glistening in the sunshine, finding that all was for the best, that never had peaceable folk grown fat so handsomely. (I, 732–33)

The shift from shared revulsion at bourgeois glut to the milder tone of the last sentence points to Zola's divided attitude. He agrees that mindless appetite debases France but then undercuts Florent's outrage by insisting on his sickly, bloodless nature. The burghers' corpulent complacency and the rampant fecundity that inspires some of the best passages in the novel are ambiguously linked. Florent's thinness and his abstract revolutionism threaten both the rich extremity to which Zola's art is drawn and the patriotism that he views as a product of manly nerves and immersion in vital coarseness.

The duality evident in the treatment of Les Halles and Florent recurs whenever absolute force impinges on character. The utopian rebel is judged because he retreats from forceful life. Yet such life does not permit acceptable character. Those caught up in it usually court not judgment so much as horror. Though the extravagances of *La Terre* and *La Bête humaine* reflect the crises of Zola's biography in the eighties,[3] their crude excess is fundamental to all the fiction. In the repeated variations on the idea of the *bête humaine*, it is never certain which should be the adjective and which the noun. Zola's attraction to often bestial immoderation strains against his goal of human and humane achievement. When, in *La Terre*, the wastrel brother Jésus-Christ makes use of his special talent and frightens off the bailiff by farting in imitation of a shotgun, the effect is of comic coarseness "as good as a purge." But when, in *La Bête humaine*, Misard defeats his wife's cunning suspicions about his scheme to get hold of her money by murderously putting rat poison in her enemas, we perceive an obsessional crudeness. Zola's imagination so responds to what Conrad's Marlow terms the "fascination of the abomination" that the hope of man's ultimate

[3] See in particular Chapters 9 and 12 in F. W. J. Hemmings, *Émile Zola*, 2d ed. (London: Oxford Univ. Press, 1970).

triumph over the raw plots of his animal nature comes to appear an improbable idealism. Like Hardy, Zola conceives of decency and a degree of moral order as innate, but these qualities prove no match for an equally engrained bestiality. Jacques Lantier, the locomotive engineer who is the primary study in Zola's gallery of *bêtes humaines*, knows himself to be cursed by an inextricably associated sexual and murderous lust. He strives to avoid the promptings of his sick heredity, but cannot. He kills the woman he loves; suddenly he hears

> a bestial snorting, a wild boar's grunting, a lion's roaring. Then he relaxed: it was his own breathing. At last, at last! He was satisfied; he had killed. Yes, he had done it. A frantic joy, a vast delight rose in him with the consummation of his eternal desire. He felt a proud surprise, an expansion of his masculine sovereignty. The woman, he had killed her, possessed her as he had yearned for so long to possess her, utterly, to annihilation. She no longer existed, would never exist for anyone. (IV, 1298)

Zola's proto-expressionism lavishes upon one man the force marshaled in the miners' rampage in *Germinal* or the gruesome field-hospital scenes in *La Débâcle*. And the spectacle of male sovereignty so foully expressed destroys not only the individual involved but also the positivistic message that manliness may be re-formed to hope. It is extremely hard to view the action as just a destructive phase in humanity's progress.

Jacques, of course, is an egregious instance—perhaps the most so in Zola's fiction, though there are close competitors. But the beast in Jacques stalks everywhere. Contemporary society veneers animality with stupidity and hypocrisy—dressing *bête* within *bêtise*. Nana joins "the golden beast, oblivous as a force, whose very odor corrupted the world" (II, 1271) to the "woman of fashion, a partner in male stupidity and filth, a marquise of the fancy sidewalks. . . . a celebrity of the chic world, thrust into the daylight of its financial follies and besmirching excesses . . ." (II, 1346). Her animality flows naturally into a mindless debauching of culture. As once she travestied Venus on stage, later she ruts on a vast silver bed chased with scenes from mythology. In her gaudy house, "two porcelain statues, a woman in her chemise hunting for fleas and another stark naked walking on her hands with legs in the air, . . . were enough to foul the salon with a taint of elemental stupidity [*bêtise originelle*]" (II, 1348). An agent both of force and of its corruption, Nana becomes a composting chemical to hasten the rot that must precede fertility; she carries the fever of a revolution both more effective and more organic than that foreseen by Zola's usually abstract and confused utopians.

> An accumulated inheritance of poverty and drink . . . in her case had taken the form of a derangement of the sexual instinct. . . . a plant nurtured on a dungheap, she was avenging the paupers and outcasts who had produced her. With her, the rot that was left to ferment among the lower classes was rising to the surface and moldering the aristocracy. She had become a force of nature, a ferment of destruction, unwittingly corrupting and disordering Paris between her snow-white thighs. (II, 1269)

As an experimental study of what happens when a fixed temperament is placed in certain circumstances, Nana is not meant to reveal density of character. She demonstrates the socialization of animality; her psychology and sentiments become data, parallel to the punctiliously recorded details of milieu. But the scientistic method that describes the animal loses sight of the human; indeed, it victimizes the protagonist's humanity as surely as the sociopolitical and hereditary processes the novel indicts. Experimentally recorded, the courtesan's life would read as but another flatly reportorial response to the fashion for accounts of lower-class prostitutes begun by Edmond de Goncourt in *La Fille Élisa*. In fact, praising *Marthe*, Huysmans's venture into this vein, his English biographer Robert Baldick contrasts the achievement of "febrile charm" both to Goncourt's "portentous solemnity" and to Zola's "monotonous crudity" in *Nana*.[4] Certainly a good deal of Zola's treatment is monotonous: the social mechanics of decadence are often repetitious; the vagaries of social *bêtise* are expounded at ponderous length. But the many scenes in which sexual crudity resonates with force, and the many details, such as the porcelain statues, that press social satire to elemental grotesquerie, represent Zola at his best. The difficulty with *Nana*, as with many of the other Rougon-Macquart novels, derives not from an overaccumulation of gross details but from the tension between individual character and the intermittently applied tenets of the experimental method. The latter tends to disallow the former. Zola's affiliation with the characters he creates compromises his positivistic mystique. Like Jacques, Renée, and a host of others, Nana often resembles a machine, a doll programmed to act in predetermined ways. Yet just as the protagonist of E. T. A. Hoffmann's "The Sandman" falls in love with an automaton and treats her as complexly human, so Zola keeps verging on an empathic identification with his mechanical subjects.

[4] Robert Baldick, *The Life of J.-K. Huysmans* (London: Oxford Univ. Press, 1955), p. 33.

Were it not for the laboratory method, Nana would be hard to distinguish from Balzac's harlots. And at times the experimental intention lapses: we are close to a revision of the characterologically vibrant realm of *La Cousine Bette*. The quite traditional narrative structure of rise and fall that Zola employs appears to carry with it fragments of traditional portraiture. A thwarted young lover kills himself.

> Nana sat stupified, still with her gloves on and her hat on her head. The mansion relapsed into heavy silence ... and she remained motionless, not knowing what to think, her head buzzing with this event. A quarter of an hour later, Count Muffat found her still in the same place. But then she relieved herself with a flood of words, telling him her misery, repeating the same details twenty times over, picking up the blood-stained scissors to demonstrate Zizi's gesture when he stabbed himself. Above all, she was intent on proving her innocence. (II, 1446)

The passage suggests a mode as far from the expressionistic intensity of the music-hall scene as from the deterministic explanation of Nana's sexual derangement. Though hardly probing, the mixture of detail and psychology is an outgrowth of Balzacian realism. Nana's bafflement, her shocked inability to understand, and even her guilty assertions of innocence all suggest the individual character of her moral underdevelopment. And when this novelistic shading of degenerate instrumentality into human chiaroscuro is accompanied by Zola's convincing adaptation of lower-class diction into narrated consciousness, another individualizing technique reinforces the creation of character. Reacting to an unwanted pregnancy, Nana feels "a perpetual sense of surprise, as if her sexual parts had been deranged; so they still made babies, even when you didn't want them to and used them for other business? Nature exasperated her . . ." (II, 1412). The note of moral condemnation, which will develop in the novels of the nineties into an obsessive loathing for all who tamper with organic generation, is clear; so too are the terms of experimental explanation. Yet the tone approaches charm: a person's voice, not that of a type or class.

The emergence of this individual note is neither consistent nor long-lived, though moments in the daughter's narrative hark back to the much richer portrait of the mother, Gervaise in *L'Assommoir*. Moreover, the memories of realism's roundedness must be considered setbacks to Zola's intention. Responding sympathetically to Nana as a person, we tend to forget the fascinations and abominations of force, the rot that must compost renewal. Nana must be treated as a faulty machine—cast off, not viewed with a fond eye to repair. Both *Nana* and *La Bête humaine* conclude on the threshold of *La Débâcle*, of the Franco-Prussian War in which the deranging diseases of Louis Napoleon's Empire burn out, opening the way to health. At the end of Jacque's story, after he and his assistant fall beneath the wheels in a murderous fight, their troop train speeds on unguided, its mechanical fervor becoming a key signature for Zola's chronicle. "What matter the victims that the machine crushed in its course? Was it not bound for the future, heedless of spilt blood? Without a driver, through the shadows, like a blind and deaf beast unleashed amid death, it roared . . ." (IV, 1331). The beast in man and the beast that man has created converge. They must be assimilated and brought under control. Both must be engineered to truth, patriotic meaning, and authenticity of function. In this process those such as Nana and Jacques are not only dispensable, they must be dispensed with.

Character as previously known must be discarded. Zola's hope is for a French race living out a version of the state the cavalryman Prosper experiences during a charge in *La Débâcle*: "he was riding in a dream, feeling as light and disembodied as a man in his sleep, with an extraordinary vacuum in his brain that left him without a single idea—in fact, a machine functioning with irresistible impetus" (V, 660). Mindlessness becomes a virtue when it clears the way, not for wanton desire, but for the influx of a grandly communal instinct such as patriotism. Retrospectively, we are to understand that the many episodes in which force preempted private life have been distortions of this necessary development. The impetus that frees Prosper from himself can, if raised to conscious choice, liberate all humanity from its sick thralldom. But this can only happen if virile prowess is added to the abnegation of egotism practiced by women like Pauline.

The man who is to begin the task is Jean Macquart, a former soldier. Having in *La Terre* married into a land-ravenous family that casts him out after his wife's death, he reenlists at the commencement of the Franco-Prussian War. Jean's qualities are those of France's enduring strength. Even when badly wounded, he struggles on "out of a keen need to live, to use his tools or plough again, to rebuild his home, as he put it. He was of the ancient earth, stubborn and wise, of the land of reason, work, and thrift" (V, 716). Possessing all these virtues, however, Jean is simple, almost illiterate, untouched by the achievements of French civilization. Through comradeship with the wellborn, neurasthenic Maurice, onto whose weak shoulders the inheritance of high culture has fallen, Jean must fulfill the cultural imperatives of renovation as well as the needs of the ancient earth. When Maurice, a callow, terrified, and exhausted soldier who does not know why he ever enlisted, is about to fall by the way and be left behind, Jean lifts him up.

> Maurice let himself go in Jean's arms, let himself be carried like an infant. No woman's arms had ever held him with such heart-warmth. Amid total collapse, amid this extreme misery, face to face with death, it was a sweet comfort to feel a being who loved and cared for him. And perhaps the thought that this heart, now all his, was that of a simple man, a peasant who had remained close to the land, a man whom he had at first disdained, added a grand savor to his gratitude. Was not this the brotherhood of the world's earliest days, the friendship that came before culture and class? . . . Jean, without analyzing his feelings, experienced joy in protecting the refinement and intelligence that he himself had not yet achieved. Since the frightful drama of his wife's death he had believed himself without a heart, had sworn never again to look on women, those creatures who cause so much pain. . . . Thus, for both men, friendship became a sort of broadening. (V, 521)

Brotherhood precludes fecundity. Jean's admiration for Maurice's qualities passes over into love for his friend's sister, the blessed, brave Henriette. But the time is not yet ripe for happiness. Jean and Maurice, after a long separation, come together again on opposite sides of the Commune's barricades. Not recognizing Maurice, Jean fatally wounds him. Epic friendship fails; the dream of a union with Henriette becomes impossible. After heroic but futile efforts to save Maurice's life, Jean leaves the wasted city. "The ravaged field was fallow; the burning house fallen to earth; Jean, the humblest and most miserable of men, set off, walking towards the future, towards the great, the ungainly need to remake all France" (V, 912).

The concluding lines resound with Zola's hope; the complex plot, with its scenes of suspenseful adventure, war, wounds, and agonizing civil strife often shows Zola at his most effective. But as a character, Jean, like Pauline, remains unconvincing. The repeated assertion of his virtues intervenes between the action and the man who must realize its force. The virtues are not only too abstract, they are too conventional to survive, let alone to heal, the disastrous miseries Zola paints. Moreover, the plot, which intensifies but does not fundamentally alter conventional motivation, development, and complication, frustrates the impetus of innovative vision. Adapting John Bayley's comment on *Tess*, we can say that even were Jean successfully projected, he would still be a character of the new novel confined within the boundaries of the old.

Zola contends in *Le Roman expérimental* and elsewhere that radical revision of narrative should correspond to and support the renewal of character. Yet the techniques that might respond to the challenge are not in evidence. The two most widely admired novels, *L'Assommoir* and *Germinal*, both moving studies in victimization, demonstrate Zola's command of character in defeat. But they do not counterpoint this defeat of the old with any compelling structure capable of realizing the future that the premise of the Rougon-Macquart vision holds out. Zola's dream entails the sacrifice of the kind of character cherished by the preceding generation of novelists. Because figures such as Jean are to be fulfilled, not in themselves, but through a healthy reorientation of the mob psychology Zola describes so well, the densities and strengths shifted away from character must be restored elsewhere: revitalized narrative must seed reconceived humanity. The earth rhythm that concludes *Germinal* and resonates in other passages throughout the series points to this goal. Yet only once, in his radical rescoring of the pastoral tradition, his perfervid narrative of a Second Empire Adam and Eve, does Zola confront at full length and with sustained artistic energy the demand implicit in his vision.

La Faute de l'abbé Mouret

In Zola the longing for some other existence took a different form. In him there was no desire to migrate to vanished civilizations; . . . his sturdy, powerful temperament, enamoured of the luxuriance of life, of full-blooded vigour, of moral stamina, alienated him from the artificial graces . . . of the eighteenth century. . . . On the day when he too had been afflicted with this longing, this craving which in fact is poetry itself, to fly far away from the contemporary society he was studying, he had fled to an idyllic region where the sap boiled in the sunshine; he had dreamt of fantastic heavenly copulations, of long earthly ecstasies, of fertilizing showers of pollen falling into the palpitating genitals of flowers; he had arrived at a gigantic pantheism, and with the Garden of Eden in which he placed his Adam and Eve he had created, perhaps unconsciously, a prodigious Hindu poem, singing the glories of the flesh, extolling, in a style whose patches of crude colour had something of the weird brillance of Indian paintings, living animate matter, which by its own frenzied procreation revealed to man and woman the forbidden fruit of love, its suffocating spasms, its instinctive caresses, its natural postures.[5]

That Huysmans's master artificer Des Esseintes should prefer the often torrid style of *La Faute* to the prosaic narrative of *L'Assommoir* is not surprising. That Zola should have written a novel inviting such tropic praise *is*. Both Des Esseintes's aesthetic enclave and Zola's Paradou, however, fulfill the late-century craving for regions exempt from conventional codes and definitions. Both novels challenge what their authors consider the deadening modes of strictly documentary realism. Both seek alternatives to an existence tortured by Schopenhauer's Will, and both end by acknowledging the bitter truth of the Twilight translation of *l'idéal* into *l'impossible*.[6]

Zola's ideals, of course, differ basically from those Huysmans expresses in *À Rebours*. Des Esseintes isolates the second of the three sections: the heady compounding of Adam and Eve with Daphnis and Chloe in what might well appear to be a set of artificial tableaux vivants. But even in this section, *La Faute de l'abbé Mouret* employs the extravagant postures of its rhetoric to hymn natural force; neither Zola nor his spokesman—Serge Mouret's uncle, Doctor Pascal—condones artifice. What Des Esseintes takes as an attack on social institutions is intended as a condemnation of all behavior that warps organic development. Huysmans's protagonist delights in Zola's attempt to dispense with the shaping mediations of sociohistory. But again the intention has

[5] J.-K. Huysmans, *Against Nature*, trans. Robert Baldick (Baltimore: Penguin Books, 1959), p. 184.
[6] See A. G. Lehmann, *The Symbolist Aesthetic in France, 1885–1895* (Oxford: Basil Blackwell, 1968).

little to do with Huysmans's desire to create a privileged aesthetic precinct. Zola's extensive documentation—taken from horticulture and Catholic ritual—provides material essentially unfixed in time and place that is then fashioned into a sweeping, antiphonic allegory: noumena confronting phenomena; mind, body; cultural imperatives, physical impulses. Throughout, the novel is contrapuntal rather than incremental. The sections do not conclude, but are juxtaposed: Serge's maddened Mariolotry; his rebirth in the overgrown pleasure park and his love for the new Eve, Albine; his return to his church and the Old Testament militancy that supplants his love for the Virgin. The timelessness of the action is in part a component of Serge's fall, of the heredity that dooms him to the absolute. And the binding motif of Doctor Pascal's ideal of reengineered health involves a return to history.

Serge's dilapidated church rises above the village of Artauds, a bleak setting that announces Zola's elemental frame. The descendants of the first Artaud family form, "behind this desolate belt of hills, a separate nation, a people born again from the soil, a race of three hundred beginning time over again."[7] Like the grasping, rutting peasants in *La Terre*, the villagers are without higher values, alien to the fertile temperament Zola often associates with the good earth. In Artauds, the earth is fever-struck: "an enflamed horizon, the twisted lines of this passionate dry country swooning in the sun, sprawled like an ardent but sterile woman" (1240). The febrile land has burned out all faith. As Serge's assistant, the crude Friar Archangias—himself a peasant—complains, the villagers "act just like their animals. They don't go to

---

[7] Volume I, p. 1232. Subsequent references to *La Faute de l'abbé Mouret* omit the volume number.

Mass; they make fun of the commandments of God and the Church. They love their bits of earth so much they'd fornicate with them" (1237).

As later in *La Joie de vivre*, the brutal character of the setting extends into the abbé's home, though, unlike Pauline, he craves a private purity abstracted from surrounding persons and events. Excepting the temperamental but usually good-hearted servant Teuse, Serge's companions illustrate competing ideas, are not intended as representational beings. Désirée, his sister, is a healthy, happy innocent completely immersed in her collection of livestock. "No doubt it was her mental poverty that drew her to the animals. She was at ease only with them; . . . in default of reasoning power, she had a kind of instinct that put her on their level . . ." (1262). The Cybele of her barnyard, a reeking precinct of fecundity and dung that sickens Serge much as the Paris markets disgusted Florent, Désirée is impervious to the intellectual, metaphysical, or spiritual yearnings Zola finds typical of the Thin. Mindless animal richness, however, is clearly preferable to the vulgar, puritanic materialism that serves Friar Archangias for religion. The friar's tirades begin with attacks on women and sexuality and go on to deny all mystery. Serge shrinks from and yet envies this simpleminded faith. Archangias's "crudity made him the true man of God, without earthly ties, completely given over to the will of God, humble, uncouth, his mouth filled with ordure to use against sin." Serge "despaired because he couldn't go even further toward stripping himself of his body, because he was not ugly, vile, stinking with a saint's vermin. When the friar revolted him with his crude comments, his overeager brutality, he accused himself immediately of delicacy and inborn pride, as if these were true faults. Should he not be dead to all worldly weakness?" (1239–40).

Offended in different ways by his sister and his assistant, afflicted by what Doctor Pascal terms hereditary *nervosité*, Serge appears to be another in Zola's catalog of victims. Yet while the deterministic emphasis is clear, too much attention to it blurs Zola's central design. Just as Nana will confusingly carry and pervert primal sexuality, so Serge is both a vehicle of a vast mystique of spiritual force and a maimed human being. What confuses the experimental demonstration is that the maiming appears a precondition to the expression of such force. Artistically, the prosaic facts demanded by human regeneration conflict with, are sometimes eclipsed by, the perfervid prose poetry that seeks to render Serge's yearning for the infinite. The kind of complex ambivalence that will beset Conrad's treatment of the darkness beyond civilization's pale enters into Zola's attempt to convey the fascination of pure ideality. The compulsions of the *bête humaine* and the convolutions of *bêtise* are countered by a mystery that matches their factuality. "For years [Serge] had not known the sun. He still did not know it; his eyes were shut, fixed on his soul, having only contempt for fallen nature. ... he had dreamed of a hermit's desert, of some mountain lair where nothing lived, no being, no plant, no water could disturb his contemplation of God. It was a surge of pure love, a horror of physical sensation. There, dying to himself, his back to the light, he could have waited for existence to end, could have lost himself in the sovereign whiteness of souls" (1232).

Like the pathogenic murderer Jacques Lantier, Serge is one of those extreme types cast up by a sick age. His horror of sensation is produced by a deranging nurture. But Zola is equally concerned with the surge of pure love. Not only does his attitude recall Balzac's essential allegiance to his maddened idealist Louis Lambert; his style, in its effort to transcend the commonplace and to enter the sovereign purity of a sheerly suggestive art, parallels the abbé's craving to abandon the tainting limits of material reality.

> Often, through calm nights, when Venus gleamed all blond and dreamy in the soft air, he forgot his self, let fall from his lips like a delicate singing the *Ave maris stella*, that tender hymn that flowed from him as, beside blue shores, a delicious sea lit by a smiling star large as a sun is barely stirred by caressing winds. Once again he recited the *Salve Regina*, the *Regina coeli*, the *O gloriosa Domina*—all the prayers, all the canticles. He read the Office of the Virgin, the holy books in her honor, the little Psalter of Saint Bonaventura, his tenderness so devout that tears kept him from turning the pages. He fasted, mortifying himself so he could offer her his bruised flesh. From the age of ten, he wore her livery, the holy scapular, the double image of Mary sewn in cloth, the warmth of which he felt with trembling happiness against his back, his chest, his naked skin. Later, he had taken the chain to show himself love's slave. But his greatest act remained always the angelic Salutation, the *Ave Maria*, his heart's perfect prayer. "Hail Mary" —and he saw her approach, full of grace, blessed among women; he cast down his heart for her gentle feet to tread on. He repeated, he multiplied this greeting in a hundred ways, straining his wits to make it more telling. He said twelve *Aves* in memory of the twelve stars encircling Mary's brow; he said fourteen for her fourteen delights; he said seven dozen to honor the years she had

passed on earth. He rolled the beads of his lesser rosary for hours. Then, at length, on certain days of mystical meetings, he undertook the infinite whisperings of the greater rosary. (1290)

Religious pathology and the data of Mariolotry open out into a kind of incantation. Here and elsewhere in Book I Zola attempts the ineffable; tries to capture the rhythm and texture of that supernatural dimension to which Huysmans and the Symbolists so often direct their art. Otherworldliness inspires an aesthetic idealism clearly influenced by Baudelaire and by the Flaubert of *La Tentation de saint Antoine*. Zola seems to press beyond the conventions of realistic characterization and the determinants of the positivistic utopia at the heart of his own faith.

Yet in less exalted form the impetus of Serge's quest is as fundamental to the Rougon-Macquart vision as the bedrock of empiricism. In his summation to the series, *Le Docteur Pascal*, Zola clearly shows that rational materialism, no matter how heroic, is insufficient to the needs of a new life. The figure of hope is Clothilde—the doctor's niece, lover, and exemplary pupil—who has learned to balance passion for material truth with a commitment to the unknown. The latter adds the human to the animal, provides the higher aim and cultural justification for the ballast of physical fact. Serge is all too human in this sense, incompletely animal. Regeneration requires physicality. But the teeming forces of the physical swell incontinently into the orgiastic glut Zola catalogs so impressively. The abbé's grand refusal would deny such messiness. "I want to believe that this virginity lives on from age to age in endless ignorance of the flesh. Oh! to live, to grow, far from the shame of the senses! Oh! to multiply, to procreate without the abominable need for sex, through the simple communion of a celestial kiss!" (1313). Serge is hysterical, on the verge of near-fatal brain fever. He is as extreme a case as Jacques. To obliterate the vile mixture of death and lust that the murderer exemplifies, the abbé would uproot the entire physical world.

> "Yes, I deny life; I say that the death of the species is better than the continual abomination that propagates it. The fall [*la faute*] spoils everything. It is a universal strench fouling love, poisoning the marriage chamber, the cradles of the newborn, mounting even to the flowers swooning in the sun, to the trees letting their buds burst forth. Earth bathes in this impurity whose least drop seeds shameful vegetation. But for me to be perfect, O Queen of angels, O Queen of virgins, hear my cry, grant my prayer! . . . Oh! death, death, venerable Virgin, give me utter death. I shall love you in the death of my body, in the death of all that lives, of all that multiplies." (1314–15)

There is no middle ground, or at least none that elicits Zola's fullest art. At the same time, some middle way must be found. Serge's refusal overleaps with paradoxically virile thrust the cherished but unconvincing abnegation practiced by Zola's good women. His obsession with the crudeness of carnal generation not merely carries to an extreme the fear of life of a Lazare or a Maurice, it becomes a transcendental form of the gluttony of the Fat. Moreover, though Zola's style and narrative art participate in the aspirations of the abbé's yearning, there is an uneasy air of misdirection. Book I denies the documentary realism dominant in most of the other novels; it seems to flirt with a plotlessness far from the traditional, even melodramatic, storytelling through which

Zola usually presents his cases. To be sure, the depth psychology of mania is a plot, but the expressive participation in florid tenderness as well as in reverberant disgust suggests a commitment beyond psychological representation. Repeatedly, the effects Zola seeks point to an attempt to create an art as "pure" as the state Serge craves. But just as the abbé's goal perverts Zola's, so the techniques employed to convey the symphony of disembodied purity seem responses to a temptation at odds with the novelist's earthbound responsibilities.

The analogy between theme and art becomes clearer in Book II. The first section ends abruptly with Serge's nervous breakdown. To save his nephew's life, Doctor Pascal carries him off to Paradou, a deserted estate nearby. In a sense, Serge's prayer has been granted, for the amnesia following his collapse resembles a perfect blankness. Though Paradou, once a pleasure park for the games of eighteenth-century worldliness, is a riot of shameful vegetation, Serge has forgotten his loathing. Here, nursed by Albine, the niece of Doctor Pascal's acquaintance who serves as caretaker, Serge must begin again. Theme and art are to collaborate in a demonstration of recuperation. Paradou's original, artificial design has been buried under a century's rampant growth; the couple's inherited, conventional nature is to be overturned; Zola's art is to return to the pristine sources of narrative—a blend of the pastoral, lyric, and mythic—to express the genesis of a new action. Reversing the usual direction of pathetic fallacy and anthropomorphism, Serge and Albine become the vehicles for the elemental message.

> The next day, the fair weather was spoiled: it rained. Gripped again by fever, Serge passed a day of suffering, his eyes fixed desperately on the curtains

through which passed only a cavernous, suspect, ash-grey light. He could no longer make out the sun; he searched for the shadow that had frightened him [the day before], the high branch that, washed out now in the downpour's pallid blue, seemed to have carried the entire forest off with it. Towards evening, disturbed by a brief delirium, he wept, sobbing to Albine that the sun was dead, that he heard the whole sky, the entire countryside weeping at the sun's death. She had to console him like a child, promise him the sun, assure him that it would come back, that she would give it to him. But he also suffered for the plants. Their seeds must be in pain underground, waiting for the light; they had nightmares, dreamed that they were climbing along a tunnel blocked by cave-ins, fighting furiously to get to the sun. And he began to cry more softly, saying that winter was a sickness of the earth, that he would die along with the earth if spring did not come to cure them both. (1321)

Reborn, Serge is again a nervous child. But his anxiety is not that of any civilized reflex; it personifies part of a seasonal ritual—and anticipates a fatality implicit in man's identity with nature. Gradually, however, the beckonings of spring and Albine's coaxings give him strength to leave his bed-chamber in the old lodge. He ventures outdoors with the girl who seems to incarnate health. With massive rhetorical power, Paradou becomes the couple's teacher, classroom, and curriculum, wholly supplanting the culture and acculturation central to novels of social development. When, with as yet untutored ardor, Serge declares his innocent love for Albine, the park hugely orchestrates the simple melody of their chaste embrace.

They remained clasped in one another's arms. . . . Around them the rose bushes bloomed. It was an insane, amorous flowering, filled with red laughter, pink laughter, white laughter. The living flowers opened like naked things, like blouses revealing the treasures of breasts. There were yellow roses shedding gilded skin like that of native girls, straw roses, lemon roses, roses the color of the sun, all the subtle shades of necks bronzed by blazing skies. Then the flesh tones softened: tea roses possessed a delectable moist skin, displayed hidden modesties, parts of the body that are not shown, of a silken smoothness lightly blue with the tracery of veins. Then the laughing rose-life beamed: the white rose, barely tinted by a deep red spot, the snow of a virgin's foot testing the water of a spring; the pale pink rose, more discreet than the warm white of a half-glimpsed knee, than the gleam with which a young arm brightens a wide sleeve; the bold red rose, blood under satin, naked shoulders, naked hips, all woman's nakedness, caressed by light; the brilliant pink rose, flowers like budding nipples, like half-parted lips breathing the perfume of warm breath. And the climbing roses, great bushes raining white flowers, bedecked all the others, all this flesh, with their lacework clusters, the innocence of their delicate muslin; while here and there wine-rich roses, almost black, were bleeding, puncturing this bridal purity with passion's wounds. Nuptials of scented wood leading May's virginity to July and August's fertility; a first naive kiss gathered like a bouquet on a marriage morning. Even in the grass, moss roses in their spreading robes of green linen awaited love. Along the length of the sun-spotted path flowers prowled, faces stretched forward, calling to the gentle winds. Beneath the unfurled tent of the clearing, all the smiles bloomed.

No blossom resembled another. Each rose had its own way of loving. Some, very timid, hearts blushing, would only open their buds halfway; while others, stays unlaced, quivering, opened full, seemed disheveled, their bodies fatally crazed. There were little ones, gay, alert, going in file, a cockade in their caps; huge ones, swollen with sensuality, with curves like sleek sultanas; brash ones, harlotlike, tempting slovens, showing off petals whitened with cosmetic wiles; virtuous ones, with correct low-necked bourgeois gowns; aristocratic ones, inventing new modes of undress with the supple elegance of originality that their rank permitted them. Roses with cup-shaped blossoms offered their perfumes as from a precious crystal; roses inverted like urns let theirs spill forth drop by drop; roses round as cabbages exhaled the regular breath of sleeping flowers; roses as yet still in bud clasped their petals tightly, giving out only their virginity's vague sigh.

"I love you, I love you," Serge repeated softly.

And Albine was a great rose, one of the pale pink roses opened that morning. (1340–41)

Human and social anatomy burgeons horticulturally in an overwhelming stylistic transposition. The variations sweep up Serge's hesitant tune, preempt Albine's personal response, and plunge young love into so bravura a suggestiveness as to transform the rose garden into a cradle of erotica. Zola begins with the pastoral motif of the innocent rightness of natural experience—a theme repeated in many passages of epic horticulture in Book II. Serge and Albine are urged to consummation by the flowers and trees. Yet the excitement of Zola's exuberant prose, of the social and sexual patterns acted out by the roses, leaves in its wake several crucial thematic ambiguities. The traditional pastoral distinction between Arcadia and society is confused when pre-lapsarian Paradou throbs with the metaphors, costumes, and modes of social description.[8] There is a curious affiliation between the rites of Edenic spring and the priapic cupids that disturb and perplex the innocent couple when they examine the decorations in the lodge. The park seems more like Renée's hothouse than Madame François's healthy garden. At the same time, the judgmental atmosphere surrounding Renée and other contemporary figures caught in the throes of force is largely absent. The passage invites a feeling of release. In an early sketch for the novel, Serge and Albine are identified as a modern Adam and Eve, but their garden is cast, not as Eden, but as the tempter, Satan. Since the organizing thematic question of the novel—whether *la faute* is man's or nature's—appears to be answered and man exculpated, there is no need for shame or blame. But what then can be the position of character? Where do Serge and Albine fit in? Paradou prompts them to physical completion—a good thing—but the energy of the park seems as indifferent to them as persons as the Schopenhauerean Will that Zola blames his neurasthenic men for accepting. Both the biblical and the pastoral elements at times indicate a desire to return to those earliest days before class and culture that Maurice discovers in Jean's comradeship. But comradeship in the primal setting Zola evokes seems born of threat and a need for refuge. Paradou hardly provides any model for unselfconscious natural community.

> The vegetation was enormous, haughty, powerfully untamed, brimming with chance displays of monstrous

[8] My comments on the pastoral tradition are based largely on Renato Poggioli, *The Oaten Flute: Essays on Pastoral Poetry and the Pastoral Ideal* (Cambridge, Mass.: Harvard Univ. Press, 1975).

blossoming unknown to the gardener's spade or water-
ing can. Left to herself, free to increase without shame
in the depths of a solitude protected by the existing
shelters, nature each spring cast off more restraints. . . .
She seemed in a rage to overturn all that man had made;
she rebelled, unleashed a stampede of flowers over the
path, . . . tied the necks of the marble statues she had
toppled with a sinuous rope of climbing plants. . . . her
rampage extended until it claimed the least cultivated
spots, which she molded to her own image, planting in
them like a rebel flag some common roadside seed that
she turned into a gigantic growth. . . . the garden was
now nothing but a turmoil, a truant battering the walls,
a suspect place where drunken nature hiccoughed ver-
bena and carnation. (1345–46)

Certainly such a setting destroys conventional nurture, ap-
proximates Rimbaud's *dérèglement des sens*. But its purgative
force is the other side of a dynamism alien to human purpose
or control. The excesses of Zola's deranged Second Empire
suddenly appear to derive, not from racial and social determinisms, but from an anarchy at the very core of creation.

And indeed, behind Serge and Albine's uneasy confusion at the garden's sexual prompting, there is often a fearful
intuition that to give way will somehow prove their undoing.
The pastoral perplexities of untried love blend into a more
modern, generalized, and ominous anxiety. "The park caused
a mute disquiet that they could not explain. In the bend of
some path a danger was lying in wait; it would grab them
by the neck, throw them to the ground and harm them. They
never opened their mouths to speak of these things, but in
timid glances they confessed this anguish that separated them
like enemies" (1384). The contamination of sexuality with

violent aggression, notable throughout Zola, passes over into a boding atmosphere of organic evil. The couple try remaining in the lodge, but the decorations now appear somehow noxiously unclean, unhealthy. They feel forced back into the park.

> No longer was there the happy languor of aromatic plants, the musk of thyme, the incense of lavender. They were trodding over vile-smelling herbs: wormwood, with its acrid alcoholic fumes; rue, with the smell of rank flesh; scorching valerian, streaming with aphrodisiac sweat. Mandrake, deadly hemlock, stinking hellebore, belladonna dizzied them, overcame them with a torpor that left them staggering in each other's arms, utterly vulnerable. (1387)

The lascivious cupids are no worse than nature in this guise; the fetid atmosphere of the bourgeois novels, no more foul. Nor can loathsome nature be taken as a correlative of the couple's festering passion. Serge and Albine have been portrayed as vehicles of the park's force, not vice versa. Whereas the roses enthusiastically express the nature of some sensual aesthetic deity, the herbs exude the curse of a Gothic Rappaccini. The relation between the two, and, more broadly, between so ambiguous a milieu and the lovers, raises questions about the coherence of Zola's intentions.

Nowhere is this indefiniteness more confusing than at the climax of the Paradou section. The coursing forces urge the recalcitrant Serge and Albine toward the mysterious center of the garden, toward the shade of a grove over which towers the new tree of knowledge: "good, sturdy, powerful, fecund, it was the dean of the garden, the father of the forest, the pride of the plants. . . . Its sap had such force that it

streamed from the bark, bathing the tree in prolific vapor ..."
(1404). Here, spurred by "the very virility of the earth,"
innocence is to become experience.

> It was the garden that had willed their fall [*faute*].
> For weeks it had lent itself to the slow apprenticeship of
> their tenderness. Then, on the last day, it had led them
> to this verdant alcove. Now it was the tempter whose
> every voice taught love. From the flowerbeds came
> odors of swooning flowers, a long whispering that told
> of the nuptials of the roses, the thick delights of the vio-
> lets; never had the solicitation of the heliotropes a more
> sensual ardor. From the orchard came the windblown
> scent of ripe fruit, a thick smell of fecundity: vanilla
> of apricots, musk of oranges. The meadows spoke in
> deeper tones ... the great moan of multitudes in heat,
> the nakedness of running waters along which willows
> dreamed aloud of desire. . . . And in this mating of the
> whole park the most primitive embraces resounded from
> afar, from those rocks whose heat-split stones were
> swollen with passion, whose thorny plants loved tragi-
> cally, unslaked by the nearby springs, themselves afire
> with the burning star that had entered their bed.
> "What are they saying?" Serge murmured, be-
> wildered. "What do they want of us that they torture
> us so?"
> Albine, without speaking, clasped him to her.
> (1407–8)

Giving way to "the fatality of generation," the couple joins
in the "huge fornication of the park." "It was a victory for
the animals, plants, everything that had willed the entry of
these two children into the eternity of life. The park applauded thunderously." Relieved of will and shame, "they

experienced an absolute perfection of their being. The joy of creation bathed them, made them equal to the mother forces of the world, made of them the very force of earth. And there was also in their happiness the certainty of a law obeyed, the serenity of a goal logically achieved, step by step" (1410–11).

Serge and Albine become part of the springtide. Yet the joyous certainty and serenity of this consummation cannot be called a logical achievement of the narrative or a point of departure for reconstituted character. The engorged prose drowns Serge's painfully pleading question just as it overrides the tragic dissonance of the rock plants' passion. The style Zola reserves for triumphant force swells into a superlative militant ecstasy unrestrained by the specific circumstances and human structures that elsewhere channel its course. Social and conventional impurities are left behind, but so too are the individual tonalities on which the ideal of reborn character rests. The absorption of human particularity into the "mother forces of the world" would constitute ideal fulfillment only if Zola's vision were that of the Hindu poem Des Esseintes finds in Paradou.

And Zola intends no vision of nirvana. At the moment of transfiguration, all suggestions of looming threat fade; contradictory possibility retreats from view. Just as the massive burgeoning of the earth with which *Germinal* concludes outsounds the anarchistic uproar raised by Souvarine, so here the harmony of completion dissolves the earlier dissonances in Zola's treatment of the garden. But in the moment of climax, Paradou fornicates; Serge and Albine must make love. And the discrepancy between animal and human completion broaches the theme that will dominate the sad aftermath. The perfection that has been experienced is that of matter, not of human character. Such freedom is compatible only with those who resemble Serge's retarded sister, whom Doctor Pascal with rueful fondness calls the *"grande bête."* Participation in nature's rites is a precondition to organic selfhood, but the indifferent force conducting the ceremony must be made to serve consciousness and order. Nature and man are separate: a fact that gives rise to the necessary sophistication —or sentimentality, as Schiller terms it—that underlies the *faute* central to the novel's theme. The view of man's intermediate position between spirit and matter is traditional. Yet Zola's belief in the primacy of natural experience in the dialectic, his idea that material nature rather than spirit contains the mysterious key to the good life, frustrates the aspirations for otherworldly value that are presented as the source of human order and purpose. Most of the novels emphasize the disturbances resulting from man's attempt to impose his faulty nature upon elemental force, but *La Faute* (along with such works as *L'Oeuvre* and *Le Rêve*) examines the reaction of spirit to the hegemony of nature.

Having been initiated in the roots of primal joy, Serge should develop a new and balanced character. He should realize the hopes of Doctor Pascal's experiment: "The shadow of trees, the fresh breath of that child, all that youth would have put you back on your feet. At the same time, the child would lose her wildness, you would humanize her; the two of us would have turned her into a lady ready for marriage. It was perfect . . . " (1452; Zola's ellipsis). Such balance and developmental compromise, however, are no more part of Serge's character than of his author's. When the young man recovers consciousness after his ecstatic experience and finds that his flesh has acted in despite of his soul, he cowers, tries to hide his nakedness: "we have sinned, we deserve some terrible punishment" (1416). Ignoring Albine's misery-stricken refrain—"Do you love me?"—much as the park had ignored his own fears, he immediately accepts the accusations of Friar Archangias, who bursts onto the scene like a crude combination of an angry god and a marauder violating a pastoral Arcadia. "You have disobeyed God, you have murdered your peace. Temptation will gnaw at you forever with its burning teeth; from now on you won't have your ignorance to combat it with. . . . So this is the tramp who tempted you, is it? Don't you see the serpent's tail twined in her hair? The very sight of her shoulders makes one puke . . . Leave her; don't touch her; she's the gateway to hell . . ." (1417; Zola's ellipses).

Book III begins with Serge back in his pulpit, about to preach a marriage sermon. Gone is his initial delight in the Virgin. He speaks sadly, sternly, of the battle between nature and spirit. Through Doctor Pascal, Zola insists that the abbé's pain is that of an individual hereditary flaw, not of a generalizable instance of human malaise. Serge and Désirée simply carry to an extreme the genetic division of their family. Gazing at the sister's barnyard, the doctor muses: "Yes, simple brutes, that's all we need. With them, things would be fine, gay, strong. Ah! that's the dream! . . . It's good luck for the girl, who's as happy as her cow. It's bad luck for the young man, who's dying in his cassock. A little more blood, a little better nerves, and all would go well with him. He's missing his life . . . A true Rougon and a true Macquart, that's what these children are. The tag end of the pack, the final degeneration" (1454; Zola's ellipses). Clearly, these experimental speculations, while they may do all the justice possible to Désirée, hardly suit the ambiguities of Serge's drama. Zola's mythopoeic imagination and its style have followed trajec-

tories of implication outside the scope of positivistic rationalism and its novelistic techniques. The continuing struggle
that makes up Book III outdistances any strict deterministic
bent and in so doing recalls the Gothic absolutism that challenged rational limits and anticipates the archetypal reach of
much early modern fiction.

Serge's story now takes place against the pathos of Albine's victimized normality. Emerging from her previous
ancillary role, the girl comes to learn the sober lessons that
preside over Elizabeth-Jane's education in *The Mayor of
Casterbridge*. But in Zola's narrative a sane sense of diminished possibilities lends itself only to further diminishment.
Deserted in Paradou, pregnant by a man who has disappeared entirely into his cassock, Albine has been raised from
natural simplicity into what Doctor Pascal would term a
higher state only to be left adrift. She mourns her loss, envies
Désirée: "that wholly fleshly life amid the hot fecundity of
a flock of animals, that purely animal blossoming. . . . She
dreamed of being loved by the tawny rooster and loving in
her turn, naturally, without shame, as trees grow, her veins
open to the coursing sap" (1461). Even given the little we
have come to know of Albine, this conscious embracing of
mindless fertility seems out of character. Zola introduces the
role of victimized womanhood only to press almost immediately beyond it. Soon it seems that the girl, instead of being
"humanized" into a "lady," has been transformed into the
protagonist of the nature myth that is the antiphon of Serge's
spirituality.

> "What's the good of suffering, of death?" she an-
> swered. "O Serge! if you could remember! You told
> me, that day, you were so tired. I knew you were lying
> because the weather was so fresh and we'd only walked

a quarter of an hour. But you wanted to sit, to take me in your arms. There was, you know it well, a cherry tree deep in the orchard beside a stream which you couldn't pass without needing to kiss my hands with little kisses that climbed along my shoulders to my lips. The season of cherries had passed; you ate my lips . . . The faded flowers made us cry. One day you found a warbler dead in the grass, you turned pale, pressed me to your breast as if to keep the earth from taking me."

The priest drew her before the other Stations of the Cross.

"Quiet!" he cried, "look again, listen again. You must bow down in pain and pity. . . . Jesus sinks under the weight of His cross. The path to Calvary is rough. He has fallen to His knees. He doesn't even wipe the sweat from His brow. He gets up, continues on His way. . . . Jesus, again, sinks under the weight of His cross. At each step He staggers. This time He has fallen on His side so violently that He is breathless for a moment. His torn hands have left the cross. His pained feet leave bloody prints behind Him. An abominable weariness overwhelms Him, for He carries on His shoulders the sins of the world . . ." (1470–71; Zola's ellipses)

Two positions speak; character is secondary. Albine is the joy, the fullness, of the physical world. She offers fertile empathy to leaven pain. The deepest misery of her thesis is that it brings into being, seems almost to require, Serge's antithesis: "death is here, it is death I want, death which delivers, which rescues us from corruption . . . Listen! I deny life, I refuse it, I spit on it. Your flowers stink, your sun is blind, your grass leprous to all who lie on it, your garden a charnal house where the corpses of all things decompose. Earth sweats abomination. You lie when you speak of love, of light, of the happy life within your verdant place. You have only shadows. The trees distill a poison that turns men into animals" (1473; Zola's ellipsis). Albine is charming, innocent, lovely; but we have seen the nature she loves transformed into the vile forms Serge abominates. The abbé's maddened transcendentalism gives compelling voice to the logic that Zola rejects in his account of Lazare's pessimism. Sounding above history, contemporary circumstance, and the distortions of private lives, the grand refusal attains a purity of negation unavailable to Pauline's indecisive husband. The abbé refines absolutely the disaffection of Zola's pale rebels, the dreams of his would-be saints. For once, the aria of spirit is allowed to peal above the orchestration of matter.

Albine, though so minimal a characterization, is still too particular an individual to conduct the elemental music Serge refuses to hear. In the abbé's apocalyptic vision, which is the climax of the narrative, her role is taken over by the forces of blindly rioting fertility.

> Then the scattered rocks, the roadside stones, all the valley's pebbles, loosed themselves, rolling, roaring, as if thrust forward by the need for movement. In their turn, the bogs of red earth, the few fields that had been conquered by mattock blows, launched into the flow, thundering like unleashed rivers, washing down in the tide of their blood fertilizing seeds, burgeoning roots, copulating plants. . . . A multitude recruiting new forces at each step, a people in heat whose breath, the tempest of life at furnace heat, drew near, bearing all before it in a hurricane of colossal birth-giving. Starkly, the attack came. From the horizon the entire countryside hurled itself at the church: hills, stones, earth, trees. The

church cracked under the first blow. The walls gaped,
the tiles flew off. But the massive Christ, though shaken,
did not fall.

The pastoral, amorous innocence of springtime Paradou,
even the delights of Albine, seem in retrospect only facades.
Hypertrophied by hallucination, militant and disordered
nature surges to the fore, toppling the church triumphant.
As the statue of Christ falls, the "tree of life began to swell
heavenward." "Abbé Mouret applauded this vision wildly,
like one of the damned. The church was vanquished. God
no longer had a house. For the moment God would no longer
vex him. He could rejoin Albine, since she had triumphed."
Even when Serge awakens: "He no longer understood, he
remained in frightful doubt, caught between the invincible
church restored from its ashes and all-powerful Albine
whose every breath could totter God" (1487–90).

A tragic dilemma: on the one hand Serge's negation of
material life; on the other, an explosion of life force so
violent as to abolish all hope of human order. Grace or
anarchy. The few scenes that follow seem intended to deny
any middle ground. Serge considers heeding the promptings
of his vision, tries to make up his mind to return to Albine
and Paradou. But he is immediately baffled by commonplace
contingencies that are as irrelevant to his sense of life as they
have been absent from Zola's drama.

> Twenty times he tried to fix upon a plan for their elope-
> ment, to arrange their existence as happy lovers. He
> came up with nothing. Now that desire no longer mad-
> dened him, the practical side of the situation stunned
> him. . . . Where would they get horses to carry them
> away? If they went on foot, wouldn't they be stopped
> as vagabonds? Besides, would he be able to find work,

to discover some occupation that would assure his wife bread? He had never learned such things. He was ignorant of life; searching his memory, he found only scraps of prayers, details of services. . . . Even unimportant things embarrassed him. He asked himself whether he would dare give his wife his arm in the street. . . . Vainly would he try to wash away his priesthood, there would always be the sad pallor, the odor of incense. And if one day he had children? . . . He felt a strange repugnance. He would avoid this horror he felt. . . . Then the hope of being impotent was sweet. No doubt all his virility had left him during his long adolescence. That settled it. In the evening he would flee with Albine. (1496–97)

For the first time in the novel Zola approaches the kind of psychological analysis employed by traditional realistic fiction. Serge's predicament is quite movingly understood and conveyed. Symptomatically, however, the abbé—or perhaps Zola himself—forgets that Albine is already pregnant. The issues of quotidian psychology are almost bemusedly incongruous when set against the preceding intensities. There is even a mild note, again for the first time, of satire. Set upon the ground of practicalities, Serge's spirit is as displaced as that of Baudelaire's deck-waddling albatross. There has been no preparation for this opening to the social and emotional context of Balzacian characterization. Extremity creates agents, not human beings.

Serge goes back to Albine in Paradou not because she is all-powerful, not because he is compelled by renewed temptation. Having, he feels, been ejected from his priesthood, he has lost all sense of purpose and meaning. Doctor Pascal has upbraided him for wronging the girl; he desires to do right. But he is half paralyzed by the prospect of a "humanized" life and love. He lapses into frigid distraction as Albine paints their future life.

> "In winter, we won't stay on in the garden like two savages. We'll go where you want, to some big city. We'll love each other just as peacefully among men as among trees. And you'll see that I'm no good-for-nothing who only knows how to hunt birds or walk without getting tired. . . . When I was little, I wore embroidered skirts, open-work stockings, fine scarves, flounces. . . ."
>
> He was no longer listening; he said suddenly, with a soft cry, "Ah! I remember!"
>
> Then, when she questioned him, he did not want to answer. He had just remembered the feel of the seminary chapel on his shoulders, the frozen garment that turned his body to stone. He was recaptured invincibly by his priestly past. The vague memories . . . imposed themselves with sovereign authority. While Albine went on telling him of the happy life they would lead together, he listened to the bells sounding the elevation, saw the monstrances tracing fiery crosses above the great kneeling crowd. (1504–5)

Albine's memories of ladylike childhood and the hopes she draws from them seem trivial in view of Serge's dilemma and Zola's theme. Her dream may be health, but Serge's anguish appears, by contrast, heroism. To the extent that she speaks as a potentially successful product of Doctor Pascal's experiment in the taming of wildness and the regeneration of sick character, the vividness of malaise emerges as more valuable than the blandness of cure.

This penultimate section, brief as it is, tends to undermine the exciting extravagances of Zola's elaborate allegory. The motor force of the novel's power sputters. Quoting the original sketch in which Paradou is cast as Satan, "who tempts Serge and Blanche [Albine] and beds them beneath the tree of evil," F. W. J. Hemmings sees the plot as embodying Zola's "fundamental ambiguity" towards sexual love.[9] Such ambiguity and its relation to the novel are beyond doubt. But it is one ambiguity among many. For finally the novel expresses in its competing plangencies the fact of unending duality. The animal component of sexuality cannot be assimilated to normal life and marriage except at the cost of vitalizing force. Before the fall into consciousness, there can be no protecting order—no meaningful culture; after it, there can be no joyous, healthy immersion in physical truth. Instead of becoming a meeting ground for nature and spirit, consciousness becomes a quicksand. The interaction of Albine's native wildness and Serge's spirituality that takes place under the garden's prodding leads to the threshold of a conventionality that, Zola believes, would squander both their qualities in dulling habit. Compromising the concluding idea that spirit cannot marry nature is the implication that such opposites ought never to blend: that the plausible, integrated character that would result could only dim their potent meaning.

Unhumanized, nature plunges from bud to fruit to "winter's doom"; unnaturalized, spirit soars off onto something like Mallarmé's blank page. Albine kills herself, filling her room with the suffocating scents of decaying autumn blooms. In Serge, "the church was victorious; . . . the world no longer existed. Temptation was extinguished like a fire no longer required to purify his flesh. He entered a more than human peace" (1510). In the last lines, as the abbé conducts Albine's funeral, Désirée rushes in from her barn-

---

[9] Hemmings, *Zola*, pp. 106–7. I have translated the fragment from Zola's preliminary notes.

yard. " 'Serge! Serge!' she yelled, clapping her hands, 'the cow has made a calf!' " (1527).

The retarded girl's shout counters Serge's abstraction with fecund animal health. But the human promise of the theme is now betrayed by "the fatality of generation." Brought to consciousness in the pregnant Albine, the same processes that produce the calf involve nemesis. The dramatic irony Zola intends is clear, but its elements raise unanswered questions. Serge is abnormal, more or less than human. Yet Zola's spokesman Doctor Pascal has proposed him as Albine's fit complement. The scheme cannot but go awry. The idea of authentic character and marital balance contained in the doctor's prescription is a deficient counterweight to the hyperbolic destinies Zola dramatizes. There is a force beyond positivism's best laid plans. Some malice at the heart of things assimilates Paradou to the worldly decadence of the original pleasure park. Like the goals of Serge's spirit, the rites of this nature seem so frequently unnatural that we understand why Huysmans's rebel against material fact should greet the section with such enthusiasm. From a different perspective, the temptation the garden expresses comes to approximate the dynamic diabolism of Balzac's Vautrin, and Zola's perfervid treatment almost matches the earlier writer's appalled fascination. In *La Faute* the vehicles that should point to the mystical metaphor of natural force are somehow bent into the service of man-made distortions. Serge and Albine are cleansed of social, impure particularities only to become pupils of a curriculum that teaches new *liaisons dangereuses*. The garden's precepts hark back to those ancestors of Vautrin who exploited the *système de la nature* to justify villainy.

Yet despite the contradictions that bewilder interpretation, Serge's and Albine's plight is impressively rendered. Balked by uncontrollable force on one side and social malaise on the other, they are victims indeed: pained beings seeking nonexistent fulfillments. Both the abbé's ecstasy and Albine's suicide are in every way opposed to Zola's principles, but both reverberate with a tragic inevitability that challenges these principles. The artificial man and the natural girl finally seem to have their being outside the judgmental framework that complicates Zola's response to the defeat of worldly types. Cast out of history into allegory, their lives parallel Hardy's account of cosmic cruelty. Doctor Pascal's experimental plans, which are Zola's as well, cannot encompass these apparent illustrations of the impossibility of restored health, integration, and character.

L'Assommoir and *Germinal*

Zola's experiment in *La Faute* misfires because of the extremity of its materials. Balance and moderation have little chance. Hence nothing is proved. Doctor Pascal's theories might apply to more stable, more probable subjects. And *La Faute de l'abbé Mouret*, though its absolustistic allegory usually overrides the probable, nevertheless does at times suggest the terms of more conventional action. Indeed, such matters as Serge's inability to manage even the idea of a common married life both invite a degree of normative satire and suggest a rationale for his fate. However extraordinary, he is an example of Twilight insufficiency. Even Albine's less complex poignancy can elicit a similar diagnosis. She is in some way accountable for the weaknesses that destroy her. Her willingness to leave Paradou for a city life as Serge's wife hints that her early bourgeois upbringing has tainted her. Doctor Pascal's chiding reference to her wildness suggests that her later years in the pleasure park have sapped her ability to cope with the stringent facts of contemporary life. Certainly, nothing suggests that she is any better equipped than Serge to manage existence "among men."

Such comments must rest on elusive, often contradictory, evidence. Certainly, Zola's compellingly pathetic picture makes the idea of Albine's participation in her misery at once unlikely and offensive. She is too innocent, too little like even the best of probable women, to be responsible. But accountability is crucial if a character is to represent possibilities open to all. One method of obviating the difficulty is to relocate Albine's qualities within a probable world. Decent, dutiful proletarians like the laundress Gervaise in *L'Assommoir* may combine the social probabilities of realistic characterization with the undistorted truths of innocence. Existing beneath the level of bourgeois contaminations, Gervaise can exemplify the healthy roots of the plant that her daughter's corrupt career blights. The mother joins the joyous plenitude Zola praises in the harvest scene with an essentially Balzacian grounding in social particularity. Happily married, pregnant, she returns home from the markets. Her labor pains are just beginning in earnest.

> The spasm passed; she was able to open the door, relieved, thinking she'd definitely been wrong. She was cooking mutton stew with short ribs that evening. Things went well while she peeled the potatoes. The ribs were in the pan when the sweats and pains returned. She stirred the sauce, lumbering in front of the stove, blinded by big tears. If she was giving birth, that was no reason to leave Coupeau without food, was it? At last the stew was simmering over the banked fire. She

went back into the other room, thinking she had time to set a place at the other end of the table. But she had to put down the wine at once; she didn't have strength enough to get to the bed. She fell and gave birth on a straw mat on the floor. (II, 467)

The flexible narrated consciousness protects the scene both from moral-pointing and from the falsifying vocabulary of bourgeois distortion. The data of daily life among men, the motifs of good appetite, healthy coarseness, and natural germination, merge into a portrait of rounded being rare among Zola's characters.

The episode, of course, belongs to the brief period of Gervaise's well-being. A product of a doomed family and citizen of a demented Empire, she will be carried off in the general collapse. But her sick heredity enters organically into her appeal; it is like her gimpy leg that, hardly noticeable in good times, becomes apparent only when life goes amiss. In the same way, her social and economic deprivations, and the injustices they represent, are sometimes minor, sometimes all-important components of her sense of self. Her joys, virtues, and flaws collaborate and interact with the thematic social documentation to achieve the Balzacian balance between individuality and typicality. There is no need for exclamatory emphasis of the type we find in the parallel story of the girl Lalie, Gervaise's neighbor, who struggles to care for her motherless siblings until her besotted, sadistic father carries his drunken beatings too far and kills her. In comparison to this vilely victimized Little Nell, the laundress appears to be accountable for her own decline and yet innocent. To be sure, the minimal goals she speaks of to Coupeau before their marriage are all pointedly frustrated: her story ends without her having a steady job, a decent place to sleep, a

man who won't beat her. Yet the full-blooded normality she
provides for these hopes offsets the melodrama of their futility. Even her major flaw—her inability to follow her decent
impulses—is far from the excess that thrusts two of her sons
into archetypal violence. Her Provençal temperament, with
its cheerful somnolence of will, readily takes the imprint of
the epoch. Stoic endurance turns to sloth; healthy appetite,
to disordered craving; acquiescent sensuality slips into the
promiscuous carelessness that lets her sleep indifferently with
both her returned first lover and her husband. By the end,
drink and penury have blasted her unexceptional goodness.
A starving sloven, unsuccessful even in her clumsy attempt
at prostitution, she drifts into death.

   We mourn the loss, the waste, because Zola's portrait
is as richly vivid as those in the best realistic novels of the
previous generation. But Gervaise is quite without personal
force. Exempt from the outrageous behavior that marks her
sons' lives, she is also defenseless against the outrages of the
reality Zola presents. The internalization of social malaise
into character—a clear variation on Balzacian technique—
results in the equation of character with victimization. The
appealing, if ambiguous, normality Zola creates has no way
of dealing with the mythic pulsations that define his sense of
cosmic reality. Gervaise's qualities have no share in the absolutism that, for example, attracts the saintly Madame Caro-
line in *L'Argent* to the egomaniacal financeer Saccard.

> [Caroline] remembered some of Saccard's ideas, bits of
> his theory of speculation. . . . without speculation there
> would be no great, no living, fertile enterprises, just as
> there would be no offspring without lust. Such excesses
> of passion, such crudely expended and squandered life,
> were needed if existence were to continue. . . . Money,

the poisoner and destroyer, became the fertilizer for the great works that would join the world's peoples and pacify the earth. (V, 224–25)

Saccard's financial satyriasis is a special version of squandered élan vital; the form is relatively unimportant, but the forceful essence is crucial. The laundress too squanders promise, and even the most squalid episodes in her decline inspire pity; but grand expenditure, tremendous even in its misdirection, is not in her nature.

Lacking this, Gervaise can only be foredoomed. She breathes the taint of her time and place, and can no more resist the sick course of things than she can refuse her drunken husband's demand that she break off work to serve his passing mood. "The deep kiss they exchanged amid the filth of her trade was like a first fall in the slow degradation of their lives" (II, 509). The Empire's dirty laundry exudes a morally contaminating reek quite different from the fertile stench so offensive to Florent and Serge. The synthesis of weakness and goodness risks coming apart; judgment intervenes. If Gervaise's unwitting participation in decay rescues her from the abstractly asserted goodness of the women martyrs, it also unfits her for any part in the future achievement of health.

Zola's characterization largely leaves such matters unstressed. The laundress is flawed; the flaws lead to her fate. But the flawed epoch that presides over the action is rather passed over—though the thematic emphasis on family alcoholism and the ambiguously illustrational role played by Lantier do carry forward Zola's general concerns. The novelistic and moral truths that enter so vitally into Gervaise appear to be differently determined than those that elsewhere produce the massive doses of truth-telling. Yet between

Gervaise's pathos and Zola's hopes lies the difficult bridge that must connect force to responsible action. Decency must be sinewed by force to create a mode of being fully accountable to the moral, cultural, and patriotic values in which Zola believes.

Of the Rougon-Macquart novels, *Germinal* comes closest to achieving this. By attempting to create the communal character of a milieu, Zola strives to retain the human appeal he often captures in his passages of narrated decent consciousness while avoiding the weaknesses and misdirections he associates with individual egos. W. J. Harvey clearly summarizes the technique and some of its effects.

> Surely there is no single character in this novel who remains powerfully in the mind as an individual. . . . What, then, does one remember as the source of the novel's power? First, there are individual *gestures* as distinct from individual characters—Moquette flaunting her bum in derision. Then there are superbly melodramatic scenes. . . . Above all there is the symbolic power of the book—the mine, for example, seen as an animal, finally wounded and collapsing in its death throes; counterpointing this, the miners seen as animals, the human figure almost being submerged into the natural. . . . All these things derive from Zola's control of the mass; nowhere is he finer than in his mob scenes. . . . Here is a community in action; the coarse vigour of the book is appropriately chanelled through a number of characters who hardly ever achieve more than a background status.[10]

Incremental and intersecting, the fragments of dailiness and extremity build into a free-floating atmosphere of character.

[10] W. J. Harvey, *Character and the Novel* (Ithaca, N.Y.: Cornell Univ. Press, 1965), pp. 57–58.

Victimization, accountability, natural force, cosmic determinism, and social injustice overlap. Zola's penchant for
judgment and extravagance is dominant in individual cases—
the representatives of capitalism; Jeanlin, the degenerate;
Chaval, the villain—but is held in check by a general impression of the miners' essential decency. Both the good and the
bad, of course, are wasted by malaise. Many perish. The defeat, however, unlike Gervaise's futile decline, can be shown
as a sacrifice: a bleak season in the progress of hope.

The community, of course, is unable to conceive, let
alone to articulate, its relation to larger developments. To
perform this function Zola introduces Etienne Lantier, a
starving engineer compelled to take whatever work he can
find. Better educated and more self-conscious than the
others, Etienne superimposes a degree of cultural awareness
both upon the socioeconomics of the general plight and upon
the treasures and demonisms of the primal, subterranean life
of the mines. Etienne is a Balzacian figure. Though economic
need has displaced him from the conventional plot of the
ambitious young provincial bound for action in the city, he
is clearly more a man on the make than he is a potential
Jean Macquart. Yet like the untempered Rastignac, he is
sensitive to injustice and eager to charge into the battle-
ground of real things. When the already meager pay is low-
ered, he urges and tries to lead a strike that will put into practice his diffuse socialist theories. The strike soon becomes an
outlet for mob fury; troops are brought in and brutally take
charge. A failure, rejected by his former followers and
friends, he returns to work only to be buried—along with
the girl he loves and the miner he hates—in a mine collapse
engineered by the black anarchist Souvarine. Miraculously

escaping alone, he departs for Paris and a hoped-for career as a labor leader.

Insofar as Etienne's story involves an education in social processes, he provides an example of the misdirection of contemporary energies. His gradual affiliation with the bourgeoisie again recalls Rastignac. But whereas Balzac presents such initiation as ambiguous, a loss of moral innocence and a gain of complex selfhood, Zola's treatment is wholly negative. Society can teach nothing that it will not tarnish Etienne's value to learn. Not so much the content as the very existence of his abstract social theories blinds him to truth. Moreover, leading the strikers, he becomes vain, develops "the soul of one of those bourgeois he detested" (III, 1460). His outrage at the squalor of the miners' lives, a responsible reaction, shades into a distaste for their healthy coarseness.

This false education, however, contains another, a true one that the reader must learn. Etienne is the product of outmoded patterns and goals; he is not natural or coarse or wise enough to comprehend the message of his own experience. When the miners' march becomes a rampage carrying him along, he is appalled at the others and at himself. Yet the reader must harvest the meaning implicit in "this huge, blind, irresistible mass of people, passing like a force of nature, sweeping all before it, overturning rules and theories" (III, 1521). Paradou's energy can be reborn among men. The wrecking of the mines and the hounding to death of the nasty owner of the company store, who is posthumously castrated for his crimes, show force avenging itself upon the agents of misrule. The riot strengthens Etienne's desire for bourgeois safety and his disaffection with his comrades. He fails to perceive the latent truth that will press even nearer the surface during his subsequent adventure. The intense melodrama of the cave-in episode signals, as always in Zola, the presence of essential meaning. Trapped with Etienne are Catherine, whom he would have chosen had not conventional restraint held him back, and Chaval, the brutal, bestial miner who has, in fact, made the girl his own. The trio quite neatly illustrate Jung's libido, anima, and shadow. Subterranean floods press them ever deeper into the mine's entrails, finally forcing them onto a narrow ledge at the dead end of a small tunnel. Chaval taunts his natural enemy, tries to get Catherine away from the man she now acknowledges as her true love. Provoked into hereditary murderousness, Etienne kills him. Catherine, crazed by starvation and fatigue, drifts into an hallucination of pastoral freshness and light. She and Etienne make love as Chaval's corpse, dissolution made actual, floats back to bob at their feet. Eros and Thanatos merge into the single force of earth. After Catherine dies, Etienne falls into semiconsciousness. He half hears the approaching pick strokes of the rescuers—sounds that announce the leitmotif of the brief remainder of the novel. After recovering, he at last takes to the Paris road, bent on a new career. Beneath him in the mines those few who have escaped bullets and fatal poverty are again at work, having had to accept the company's terms. "A brimming sap flowed through the whispering voices, the sound of seeds expanding into a vast embrace. Again, again, more and more distinctly, as though they were rising through the soil, the comrades hammered. In the fiery rays of earth's star, in this young morning, the countryside was heavy with sound. Men were springing up, a black avenging army sprouting slowly through the furrows, swelling for a coming century's harvests, a host whose germination would soon burst open the earth" (III, 1591).

Unlike the lovers' consummation in Paradou, this conclusion is not only deeply felt but logical in its rhetorical orchestration. The allusion to the legend of avenging warriors burgeoning from dragons' teeth provides a rich crescendo for the theme of germinal force; the passage integrates the novel's social motifs and hyperbolic scope. But the strains trumpeted beneath Etienne's departing steps can have little meaning for the tone-deaf youth; he is a budding bourgeois, whom Harvey, with only slight exaggeration, calls a "mere dummy." [11] The reader must divorce Zola's lofty tenor from its worldly vehicle. Moreover, there is a disturbing parallel between this abstract evocation of better times aborning and Etienne's departure from the scene of the miners' defeat. Most of those we have come to know are dead; those who survive may perhaps be more conscious of the uses of group action—Zola does not examine the point—but they are condemned to work at miserable wages and amid the ruins of their lives. Pathos and victimization mark the characterization of the community no less than they did that of the fated Gervaise. Hopeful vision and present fact remain disjointed.

Yet the effort toward communal rather than individual character is a vital development. Zola reaches forward toward the belief, which forms a large strand in the modern tradition, that sovereign egos must be transcended and that this can happen only by means of a grueling rite of passage. The difficulty is that Zola, unlike many of those who later adapt his experiments, is of two minds about the implications of such a revolution. No more than Hardy is he will-

[11] Ibid., p. 57.

ing to part with the expansive virtues and possibilities his tradition associates with individuality. And the force, however expressed, that carries men beyond themselves appears to be incompatible with the moral values that, however reformed, still constitute the human meaning he cherishes. Zola's own dualities are evident in his description of Etienne's confused reactions to his inability to control the strikers.

> Who then was guilty? Posing the question, Etienne felt at an utter loss. In truth, was it his fault, this disease that sickened him as well, this misery of some, this slaughter of others, these women, these children, emaciated, without bread? He had had this mournful vision one evening, before these catastrophes. But even then a force was bearing him forward; he found himself being carried away just like his comrades. Besides, he had never directed them; they had led him; made him do things he would never have done were it not for the mob pressing him on. Each act of violence had left him stupified by events he had neither foreseen nor willed. . . . In each justification, in the reasons with which he tried to combat his remorse, there was a mute distress at having been unequal to his task—the incessant doubt and worry of the half-educated. But he felt at the end of his courage, no longer at one with his comrades; he was afraid of them . . . Little by little a repugnance set him off—the malaise of his refined taste, the slow ascent of all his being into a higher class. (III, 1521)

The abrupt movement from identity with Etienne's doubts to judgmental distance epitomizes Zola's central contradiction. One cannot pause to ponder while responding to the regenerative imperatives of force; self-questioning, indeed, is often a symptom of neurasthenia and decadence. Etienne's perplexity, like his character, is shunted aside. But the young man's quandry is much like that implicit in Zola's own estimate of force. Condemning such qualms as half-educated or as the selfish scruples of a bourgeois climber, Zola confounds the sickness that he wants purged with the moral discriminations that he believes must be preserved.

Despite the resonant concluding passage, Etienne's question remains. If moral judgment is at present wholly decayed, how is man to order those elemental forces that not only thrust us beyond good and evil but often seem to invite primordial chaos? The question arises precisely because Zola is not a neutral recorder; he does not want to lead his nation into a moral terra incognita. Versions of Etienne's bafflement are evident throughout the novels: in the opposing suggestions that the miners' misery is a painful phase in the history of progress and a monitory punishment called down by cultural disorder; in the hesitation between "fault" and "sin" in Serge's story; in the confusion between the characterization of Nana as an unconscious agent and as an accountable participant in decay.

The contending truths of new forces and old evaluations often lead such later writers as Gide and Conrad to a rich originality of characterization. But Zola's narratives and his dramatis personae are more often symptoms than projections of the conflict. The unclear alternation of humane pathos and thundered condemnation in *Germinal* undercuts both elements. The concluding symphony of hope is interrupted by echoes of the scene only fifty pages earlier when the Bakuninite anarchist Souvarine attacks the mine. Years before, tsarist tyrants put Souvarine's wife to death; he now believes that destruction is the only cure for social evil. Refusing all promptings of his humanity, of the human condition as it exists, he turns his back on his sympathy with Etienne's confused feelings of injustice and with the strikers' embattled cause. Risking his life, he lowers himself into the mine shaft and weakens the supports. When Etienne and the others descend, their elevator tears open the barriers holding back the underground sea.

> The mine drank this river; the flood would submerge the galleries for years to come. Soon the crater filled. What was once Le Voreux was now a muddy lake, like those beneath which slept the cities of the damned. In the terrified silence one heard only the pouring water booming into the bowels of the earth.
>
> Then, on the collapsed slag heap, Souvarine arose. He had recognized [the mother of Catherine and one of her sons] sobbing at the sight of this deluge, the weight of which pressed so heavily upon the heads of those unfortunate creatures down below. . . . without glancing behind him [he] set off into the deepening night. . . . He was heading yonder, somewhere into the unknown. With his tranquil air, he was bent on extermination, wherever dynamite could be found to blow up cities and men. It would be he, no doubt, whom the expiring bourgeoisie would hear beneath them as the very paving stones exploded under their feet. (III, 1547–48)

Zola's abhorrence is evident, but so too is his fear that the malaise he has described may court this fate. Unlike those who pervert the force flowing through them, Souvarine is a poison that cannot be composted. Anticipating Conrad's Russian absolutists in *Under Western Eyes*, the anarchist lays bare a nemesis resistant to civilizing hope. The character and the horror he represents are beyond the author's control.

And the similarity between the position of the annihilating devil beneath the pavement and the fecundating army beneath the soil renders the ending of the novel disturbingly equivocal.

Zola rejects society as a model for character and denies its capacity to mediate and order the absolute force Souvarine unleashes. But he can dramatize no convincing substitute. The élan vital that inspires the vibrant expressionism of the best portions of *Les Rougon-Macquart* enters character either as victimizing force or as an energy that turns human nature wolfish or worse. Yet the primal fertilities collected under the name of force are real; they contain truth; they hold the key to regeneration. Zola's positivistic belief separates him conclusively from the later writers who see a heart of darkness utterly at odds with traditional civilized values and definitions. His belief assumes energies amenable to progress. At the same time, its pervasive presence creates the contradictory directions that mark Zola as a typical Twilight novelist. Entering the fields of force, characters should be cleansed, strengthened, endowed with enduring substance. But those who should demonstrate the efficacy of faith remain mere fiats of hope. Hardy's strong women and his mayor intensify the inconsistencies and bewilderments that rule the modern condition; if more artistically than morally admirable, they are but larger examples of a general pattern. Zola's figures of decay, however—those whose lives are commandingly intersected by fevered sexuality, financial excess, mob psychosis, or mystic mania—are so much more impressive than his Paulines and Jean Macquarts that their potent presence casts damaging doubt upon the health the others are meant to advertise.

4

CHEKHOV'S CHARACTERS

True Tears, Real Things

*Is there really no "ideology" in the last story? You
once told me that my stories lack an element of
protest, that they have neither sympathies nor
antipathies. But doesn't the story protest against
lying from start to finish? Isn't that an ideology? It
isn't? Well, I guess that means either I don't know
how to bite or I'm a flea.*

Chekhov to Alexei Plescheyev, October 9, 1888

Responding to huge uncertainties, Hardy and Zola create
massive worlds populated by frequently oversized figures.
In the company of these baggy novelists Chekhov seems an
elegant alien. He is twenty years younger and from a distant land; his mature fiction is far closer to the aesthetic we
associate with Flaubert and James than it is to the judgmental, "ideological" omniscience of the Wessex and Rougon-
Macquart novels. Yet Chekhov's best work is a chamber
version of the sense of loss, threat, and bafflement that Hardy
and Zola orchestrate. Though Simon Karlinsky argues per-
suasively that Chekhov's joy in life and art sets him off from
the hypochondria of late-century exhaustion, his stories and
particularly his short novels deal repeatedly with nervous
people afflicted by a historical ailment akin to that suffered
by characters in the other writers.[1] The protagonists of the

[1] *Anton Chekhov's Life and Thought: Selected Letters and*

Russian's variegated plots typically experience feelings they cannot manage, ideas they cannot order. Chekhov insists that he himself is quite unlike the narrator of his first major short novel, *A Dull* [or *Dreary*] *Story*, who, approaching death, cannot "find what is called a general idea, or the god of a living man."[2] Such inability, however, is a common fate in his fiction. The stories are told with fine lucidity by an author who refuses for himself the distorting lenses of convention, formal ideology, metaphysics, or myth. But the men and women who inhabit the plots must frequently live out daily dilemmas arising from the absence of these organizing structures. Within the stories aesthetic clear-sightedness becomes an existential inability to achieve vision.

In a celebrated essay, Isaiah Berlin describes Tolstoy as combining the weighty sureness of the hedgehog, which knows one big thing, "a single, universal, organizing principle," with the cunning variousness of the fox, which knows many little things. Chekhov's fictions are the work of a committed fox, of one who pursues "many ends, often unrelated and even contradictory, connected, if at all, only in some *de facto* way, for some psychological or physiological cause, related by no moral or aesthetic principle."[3] As a man and as an artist, Chekhov is guided by deep convictions. But be-

---

Commentary, selection, introduction, and commentary by Simon Karlinsky, trans. Michael Henry Heim in collaboration with Simon Karlinsky (Berkeley: Univ. of California Press, 1975), passim. Karlinsky's extensive commentary constitutes the most accurate and sensitive account of Chekhov's life in English.

[2] *A Dull Story*, in *Ward Six and Other Stories*, trans. Ann Dunnigan (New York: Signet Classics, 1965), p. 216.

[3] Isaiah Berlin, *The Hedgehog and the Fox: An Essay on Tolstoy's View of History* (London: Weidenfeld & Nicholson, 1953), p. 1.

cause his creed refuses the prejudgments of abstract principle, his actors often seem abandoned on a stage devised by
their feelings and circumstances. Omniscience rarely extends a helping hand. Nor is the reader directed to understanding by the kind of evaluative comment common in
Hardy and Zola. Chekhov's sympathy expresses itself as
identity; it seldom suggests alternative modes of acting or
being. The impression we often receive resembles that produced by the protagonist of "An Attack of Nerves."

> One of Vasilyev's friends had once said of him that
> he was a talented man. There are all sorts of talents—
> talent for writing, talent for the stage, talent for art;
> but he had a peculiar talent—a talent for *humanity*. He
> possessed an extraordinary fine delicate scent for pain
> in general. As a good actor reflects in himself the move-
> ments and voice of others, so Vasilyev could reflect in
> his soul the sufferings of others. When he saw tears, he
> wept; beside a sick man, he felt sick himself and moaned;
> if he saw an act of violence, he felt as though he himself
> were the victim of it, he was frightened as a child, and
> in his fright ran to help. The pain of others worked on
> his nerves, excited him, roused him to a state of frenzy.[4]

Chekhov is no Vasilyev. Yet the art of this extremely active,
wholly engaged man of letters and of science often seems
both an objective defense against and a vehicle for a neurasthenic capability analogous to Vasilyev's.

In Chekhov's characters the internalized hierarchy of
social or cultural meanings central to the Balzacian tradition
collapses. The absence of any sustaining, authoritative con-

---

[4] "An Attack of Nerves," in *The Portable Chekhov*, ed. Avra-
ham Yarmolinsky, trans. Constance Garnett (New York: The Viking Press, 1947), p. 244.

viction—whether religious, social, or otherwise—brings with it a randomness of being. Those like the scientist von Koren in *The Duel* who can hold to a fixed scheme of life are presented as slightly inhuman, exempt from the warm indeterminacy of sentiments and ideas that marks most others. Characters meander in potentiality; the agent needed to make their lives fruitful is usually absent. In part because this dependent condition was commonly associated with femininity, Chekhov frequently portrays it in his women. Openness to external definition lies at the heart of Olenka's charm in "The Darling." Without force of self-definition, she forms herself upon the imprint of masculine preoccupations. "She was always in love with someone and could not live otherwise. First it had been her papa."[5] When her father dies, she marries the theater manager; "Whatever Kukin said about the theater and the actors she repeated" (277). After a few years, Kukin dies, and Olenka languishes until she meets, falls in love with, and marries Pustovalov, the manager of the local lumberyard. "It seemed to her that she had been in the lumber business for ages and ages, that lumber was the most important and essential thing in life, and she found something touching, dear to her, in such words as girder, beam, plank, batten, boxboard . . ." (279). Six years later, Pustovalov also dies. "It was clear that she could not live even a year without some attachment," so she becomes involved with an army veterinarian. "She repeated the ideas of the veterinarian, and now was of the same opinion as he about everything" (282). But he is posted elsewhere. "She

[5] "The Darling," in *Selected Stories*, trans. Ann Dunnigan (New York: Signet Classics, 1960), p. 276. Only first references to the stories and short novels are provided in the notes; subsequent quotations are followed by parenthetical page references in the text.

gazed indifferently into her empty courtyard, thought of nothing, wished for nothing, and later, when darkness fell, she went to bed and dreamed of the empty courtyard" (282–83). After a while, the veterinarian returns with a wife and son; Olenka persuades them to rent part of her house. As the story ends, we see her living through the boy, complaining to shopkeepers about the rigors of fifth-form tests.

Summarized in this way to underscore a point, the story can seem mechanical. It is not. The barren stretches of Olenka's life are less dwelt upon than the fulfilling joys of her attachments; her simplicity somehow expands into a vibrant mystery of being. Possible meanings crowd the brief text. Is Olenka a human chameleon? Does the portrait comment on female subservience? Is Olenka, like Flaubert's faithful Félicité in *Un Coeur simple*, a symbol of the artist who yields up his own character at each engagement with a new subject? The story resists specific interpretation. Yet unlike Kafka's parable-tales, to which several of Chekhov's works have been likened, no painful implication arises from the absence of indicated meaning. "The Darling" is quite without the harsh tonalities of enigma. Olenka is a type, but her typicality becomes uniqueness. Chekhov does not so much develop types into particularity as he enriches them through immersion in vivid representations of emotions all men share. Olenka conveys, not the data of her personal circumstances, but the necessity of her feelings. And Chekhov's empathic talent creates out of the clinging woman something as touching and dear to the reader as the types of lumber are to her.

The vagueness with which Chekhov renders Olenka's feelings—"the most important and essential *thing* in life," "some*thing* touching"—allows the reader to participate in an indeterminate emotional density. Cumulatively, the seeming looseness produces a taut clarity of sentiment. But the very compression of a life's emotions into so conclusive an impression has led some critics to label Chekhov a miniaturist or even to accuse him of artistic short-windedness. The perfect representation of felt moments and scenes does not require large organizing structures. Commenting on his progress with *The Steppe*, an early short novel, Chekhov was ruefully aware of the difficulty. "It's a good theme, and I'm enjoying writing about it, but unfortunately, since I'm not used to writing anything long and am afraid of writing to excess, I've gone to the other extreme: every page comes out as compact as a little story, and the scenes keep piling up, crowding each other, getting in each other's way, and ruining the general impression. Instead of a scene in which all the particulars merge into the whole like stars in the sky, I end up with an outline, a dry list of impressions."[6] Here and elsewhere the difficulty in achieving strong structure seems in part related to an uneasy sense that such structure might compromise the particular integrity of moments and details. Certainly in *The Steppe*, the theme, itself a cumulative impressionistic effect, never imposes itself firmly enough upon the individual impressions; the nine-year-old whose reactions should order the scenic values is kept too far in the background. Though *The Steppe* is a relatively immature work, the tension between precise representations of discrete reactions, relations, and scenes and the need for social or ideological frameworks that might give them greater scope and more purposeful shape recurs through Chekhov's career. Along with many of his contemporary commentators, he believes the particularities he dramatizes should coalesce

[6] Chekhov to Vladimir Korolenka, January 9, 1888, in Karlinsky, *Chekhov's Life and Thought*, pp. 89–90.

in what he considers novelistic breadth; private structures should intersect the pressing issues of public life. Writing about his cherished project for a full-length novel, "Stories from the Lives of my Friends," with which he struggled for two years before abandoning, he is keenly aware of the restrictions his kind of art entails. "The novel encompasses several families and an entire district—its forests, rivers, ferries and railroad. Two figures, one male and one female, form the district's focal point, and the pawns group themselves around them. I still lack a political, religious and philosophical world view—I change it every month—and so I'll have to limit myself to descriptions of how my heroes love, marry, give birth, die, and how they speak."[7] It requires no great leap to see this sense of limitation at work in *Three Years*, one of the most ambitious short novels, in which the circumstantial representation of a merchant world dangles from the account of unhappy love and marriage.

Chekhov's distrust of general organizing premises becomes a key to the frequent predicament of his characters. The disparateness experienced by many of his more fully developed figures is an almost bitter mirroring of the author's distrust of the prescriptive fixity of abstract positions, of his preference for the elusive truths of particular situations.

> The people I am afraid of are the ones who look for tendentiousness between the lines and are determined to see me as either liberal or conservative. I am neither liberal, nor conservative, nor gradualist, nor monk, nor indifferentist. I would like to be a free artist and nothing else, and I regret that God has not given me the strength to be one. I hate lies and violence in all of their forms. . . . Pharisaism, dullwittedness and tyranny reign not

[7] Chekhov to Dmitry Grigorovich, October 9, 1888, ibid., p. 115.

only in merchants' homes and police stations. I see them in science, in literature, among the younger generation. . . . I look upon tags and labels as prejudices. My holy of holies is the human body, health, intelligence, talent, inspiration, love and the most absolute freedom imaginable, freedom from violence and lies, no matter what form the latter two take. Such is the program I would adhere to if I were a major artist.[8]

As Karlinsky contends, Chekhov's convictions help explain why he emerges as the true artist who heroically liberates Russian literature from the divisive social, political, and ideological position-taking demanded of writers by the liberal critics of the age. The same creed establishes him as the heroic liberator of short fiction from the heavy hand of novelistic expectations. Both estimates are wholly accurate, but both play down the doubts and ambiguities surrounding the relation between Chekhov's movingly expressed beliefs and the damaged characters who are so often the results of these beliefs, between the artist's rejection of labels and his characters' frequent inability to give public definition to their lives.

It is not paradoxical that a creator of imaginary worlds should abhor lies, but Chekhov's insistence on a scrupulously honest realism complicates his presentation of the illusions, fictions, or lies that are the staff of bearable life for many of his characters. Talent for humanity would treat illusions with fellow feeling; dedication to good art must portray them as ill-conceived fictions; truth-telling demands that they be exposed as lies. In "At Home" (or "The Homecoming"), Vera, tormented by the dullness and hypocrisy of the provincial existence to which she returns from Moscow after

[8] Chekhov to Alexei Pleshcheyev, October 4, 1888, ibid., p. 109.

her parents' death, comes to realize that "Beautiful nature, dreams, music, told one story, but reality another."[9] Chekhov wants to express the full charm of the former story under the artistic key signature of the latter. However, the two bear an at best uncertain, at worst invidious, relation. The meaning of private imaginings alters when compelled to do public service. And even the private reliance on necessary fictions threatens the rational clarity Chekhov believes is our only sure guide in a murky universe.

The discrepancy between dream and fact is the traditional fare of realism. Yet Chekhov's commitment to both results in fictions that are at once pellucidly expressive and thematically opaque. As in Hardy and Zola, the inability to achieve a concord between individual needs and present realities becomes a symptom of the epoch's dilemma. But Chekhov's sense of impasse seems absolute. However ambiguous their positions, Hardy and Zola at times view the circumstances surrounding man as facts to which he not only must but can accommodate his life. For Chekhov, the outer and the human dimensions exist in permanent mutual exclusion: each is true; each can be beautiful or uncouth. The characters thus become less victims than aliens. Finding privacy incomplete, they enter spheres beyond themselves only to lose the truths that define and sustain them.

Though far less pointed and pontifical in his dismay, Chekhov shares the other writers' premise that social life as it exists cannot provide the fulfillments men need. Remembering that beneath Hardy's grey Wessex and Zola's French earth lie archetypal patterns that may in a coming time offset and correct humanity's present disarray, we might expect

[9] "At Home," in *The Duel and Other Stories*, trans. Constance Garnett (London: Chatto & Windus, 1916), p. 263.

Chekhov to seek solace or even solutions in nature. Certainly, he frequently contrasts human disorder with nature's bountiful beauty. But the contrast holds out no hope. Often, the solace of sky and landscape merely projects the human beholder's unreliable vision. In itself, nature is a thing apart, a separateness off which human desiring futilely rebounds. When in *The Steppe* Chekhov departs from the consciousness of his boy traveler to describe the heavens stretching above the sparse landscape, the passages make explicit the point of view that implicitly frames many of the later fictions.

> One glances at the pale green, star-spangled sky on which there is no cloudlet, no spot, and understands why the warm air is motionless, why nature is on her guard, afraid to stir: she is afraid and reluctant to lose one instant of life. Of the unfathomable depth and infinity of the sky one can only form a conception at sea and on the steppe by night when the moon is shining. It is terribly lonely and caressing; it looks down languid and alluring, and its caressing sweetness makes one giddy.
>
> . . . . .
>
> When you gaze a long while fixedly at the deep sky thoughts and feelings for some reason merge in a sense of loneliness. One begins to feel hopelessly solitary, and everything one used to look upon as near and akin becomes infinitely remote and valueless; the stars that have looked down from the sky thousands of years already, the mists and the incomprehensible sky itself, indifferent to the brief life of man, oppress the soul with their silence when one is left face to face with them and tries to grasp their significance. One is reminded of the

solitude awaiting each one of us in the grave, and the reality of life seems awful . . . full of despair. . . .[10]

Though in the later works Chekhov almost never repeats this kind of romantic conventionalism and rarely deals in such omniscient attitudinizing, his idea of nature pursuing an indifferent life of its own wholly removed from man's purposes is constant. In *Peasants*, published nine years afterwards—a long time in so intensely compacted a career—a sick waiter loses his job in Moscow and returns to his village with his wife. The first night home, they "watched the sky, crimson and gold, reflected in the river, in the church windows, and throughout the atmosphere, soft, peaceful, ineffably pure, as it never is in Moscow. And when the sun had set, the herd went by with bleating and lowing, the geese flew in from the far bank—and everything grew quiet; the gentle light faded from the air and the evening darkness descended swiftly."[11] Yet what appears to be a solace is only a chance encounter. Nature is a poem; the lives Chekhov narrates, a weary prose. The next day, the scene is as beautiful, but the relief it can provide proves futile.

> A shaky little log footbridge had been placed across the river, and directly under it, in the clear translucent water, swam schools of broadbrowed chub. The dew sparkled on the green bushes which gazed at themselves in the water. The air grew warmer and became pleasant. What a glorious morning! And how glorious life proba-

[10] *The Steppe*, in *The Bishop and Other Stories*, trans. Constance Garnett (London: Chatto & Windus, 1919), pp. 219, 251 (Chekhov's ellipses in second passage).

[11] *Peasants*, in *Seven Short Novels*, trans. Barbara Makanowitzky (New York: W. W. Norton, 1971), p. 367.

bly would be in this world if there were no want, terrible, inescapable want, from which there is no refuge. One had only to look back at the village now to remember all yesterday's happenings vividly—and the spell of happiness which seemed to ring them instantly dissolved. (371)

Chekhov's natural scenes almost always reflect, not external phenomena, but the sorcery of human need: the charm of happy moods, the disenchantment of pain. The emotions of the characters often seem equally deprived of objective meaning. Feelings are frequently expressed as poignantly as the glories of sunset or morning. But the force of Chekhov's evocations owes much to an accompanying implication of arbitrariness or unreality. The urgency of reconciliation and reborn affection at the conclusion of *The Name-Day Party* and *The Duel* is made pathetic as well as powerful by the note of impermanence. Just before he fights his duel, Layevsky discovers his mistress, Nadyezhda, in the arms of another man. After he is almost killed, he realizes the folly of his way of life and returns a chastened man.

> Nadyezhda Fyodorovna, pale and haggard, could not understand his gentle voice and unfamiliar bearing; she hurriedly told him everything that had happened to her. . . . It seemed to her that he scarcely heard and did not understand, and that if he knew everything he would curse her, kill her; but he listened, stroking her face and hair, and looked into her eyes.
> "I have no one but you . . ." he said.
> Then they sat in the garden for a long time, huddled together, saying nothing, or dreaming aloud in brief, broken phrases of a future happy life, and it

seemed to him that he had never before spoken at such length or so eloquently.[12]

Much of the power stems from an uneasy empathy with dreams so clearly remote from realities. Chekhov balances true emotion with the actors' incomprehension. The frequent use of *seems* suggests illusoriness. Even though *The Duel* ends with an apparent merging of feeling and fact —Layevsky and Nadyezhda do change their lives; their former selfish dreams pass, and they settle down into a respectable if faceless married life—the unexpectedness of this contentment after what we have seen of their haphazard temperaments insinuates uncertainty. The phrase repeated throughout the brief final section—"Nobody knows the truth"—makes the turnabout believable precisely by underscoring its vulnerability to future reversal.

Like Elizabeth-Jane's marriage in *The Mayor of Casterbridge*, Layevsky and Nadyezhda's seems to promise an accommodation between private desires and realistic options. Hardy's heroine, however, profited from the stringencies of fact and fate to chart a defensive strategy. By contrast, the sobered contentment of Chekhov's couple is made worrisomely fragile by its purely sentimental mode—by the reliance on elusive feelings to soften the hard contours of facts. But this mode is central to Chekhov's characterizations. The external determinants of human existence—social status, occupation, geographic setting—are always clearly demarcated. The private content of character, on the other hand, is often a turbid flux in which mood and feeling, dreams, oddments of perceptions, and bits of ideas distort the outlines of fact.

[12] *The Duel*, in *Ward Six and Other Stories*, p. 157 (Chekhov's ellipses).

This inner region operates much like the linguistic concept of purely connotative, "phatic" communication. Phatic speech conveys no empirically verifiable message; its meaning lies in emotional tonalities. Would-be lovers speak of current events, of the weather, of food; they are saying, "Look, we're together, we're empathizing." Such a mode requires the shelter of intimacy; it cannot tolerate the intrusion of declarative realities. Lives lived under the aegis of free-floating sentiment tend to be blind to the approaching traffic of events.

There are always painful, sometimes fatal, collisions. But these usually produce an effect quite different from the mechanical crushing of individuals by the juggernaut of a world they never made. Chekhov's generosity of tone pervades the portrait of each character's perspective and modifies the pessimism typical of naturalistic determinism. Moreover, though Chekhov rarely introduces his personal views, the hints of positivism in the letters and elsewhere (in the deacon's comments throughout *The Duel*; at the conclusion to *Uncle Vanya*) loosely approximate Hardy's and Zola's expectation of restored order. Chekhov's hopes are less clearly articulated, but he shares the allegiance to a progress that will revitalize and re-form the best values of nineteenth-century culture. Never does he present private life as a unique source of authenticity. Outside the enclaves built by individual dreams is the great globe itself, and the very facts that now violate dreams may some day fulfill them, may even render them unnecessary. The rare balance between inner and outer truths Chekhov achieves derives from this belief. The writer's task is to depict the conditions of present disorder with a rational clarity and an absence of bias as committed as the presence of fellow feeling.

In my opinion it is not the writer's job to solve such problems as God, pessimism, etc.; his job is merely to record who, under what conditions, said or thought what about God or pessimism. The artist is not meant to be a judge of his characters and what they say; his only job is to be an impartial witness. . . . Drawing conclusions is up to the jury, that is, the readers. . . . It's about time that everyone who writes—especially genuine literary artists—admitted that in this world you can't figure anything out. . . . if a writer whom the crowd believes takes it upon himself to declare he understands nothing of what he sees, that alone will constitute a major gain in the realm of thought and a major step forward.[13]

Continuing his battle against tendentiousness, Chekhov invokes an objectivity akin to Flaubert's *impassibilité* and a refusal to participate directly parallel to Henry James's insistence on authorial invisibility. However, Chekhov's impartiality goes beyond ambiguity to something approaching a final indeterminacy of meaning. Both James and Flaubert make use of ambiguity, but no one would compare their fiction—as some of Chekhov's has been compared—to Kafka's. Chekhov's highly personal positivism, his belief in joint scientific and spiritual progress, is a fact of his biography. But his authorial laissez-faire is often so complete as to obscure all evidence of his hopes. For his characters, there is scant sign of directions to follow or structures to imitate; for his readers, rational skepticism can appear to be existential uncertainty, and the unwillingness to impose understanding can

[13] Chekhov to Alexei Suvorin, May 30, 1888, in Karlinsky, *Chekhov's Life and Thought*, p. 104.

be confused with the loss of any dynamic, organizing vision.

Though Chekhov disclaims the superflousness and decadence of purpose that become chichés of the Twilight, he feels his scope circumscribed by the absence of vast structures of meaning that is also typical of the age.

> Tell me truthfully now, who among my contemporaries, that is, authors between thirty and forty-five, has given the world a single drop of alcohol? . . . They're nice, they're talented, you're delighted by them, but at the same time you can't forget your desire for a smoke. Science and technology are now going through a period of greatness, but for us this is a precarious, sour, dreary period. . . . The causes do not lie in our stupidity, our insolence or our lack of talent . . . but in a malady that for an artist is worse than syphilis or sexual impotence. We truly lack a certain something: if you lift up the skirts of our muse, all you see is a flat area. Keep in mind that the writers we call eternal or simply good, the writers who intoxicate us, have one highly important trait in common: they're moving toward something definite and beckon you to follow, and you feel with your entire being, not only with your mind, that they have a certain goal. . . . The best of them are realistic and describe life as it is, but because each line is saturated with the consciousness of its goal, you feel life as it should be in addition to life as it is, and you are captivated by it. But what about us? Us! We describe life as it is and stop dead right there. We wouldn't lift a hoof if you lit into us with a whip. We have neither immediate nor remote goals, and there is an emptiness in our souls. We have no politics, we don't believe in revolution, there is no God. . . . No one who wants nothing, hopes for nothing and fears nothing can be an artist. It

> may be a malady and it may not; what you call it is not what counts, but we must admit that we're in a real fix.[14]

The stylistic trenchancy and humanistic intelligence of this appraisal exempt its author from his own judgments. The characters in an art that so frequently embodies these qualities—not just central figures but such lesser actors as the fussily decent Doctor Samoilenko and the inconclusively innocent deacon in *The Duel*—are fully as memorable as the creations of an art "saturated with the consciousness of its goal." But the conviction of diminishment is no passing mood. Its shadow darkens the lives Chekhov recounts and merges into the realities that harm them. Chekhov is one of the first modern masters of the turmoil of identity in the throes of fragmentation, one of the first to view self-creation as an alternative to the crude determinisms and false emphases of the Twilight. But his protagonists cannot share the high purposes and accomplishments of the art that gives them being. Flawed inheritors of no longer sufficient dreams, they are without the strengths that the writers Chekhov calls eternal lend to at least some of their characters.

The short novels contain no equivalent to the sustained emphasis on cosmic law and temporal decay in Hardy and Zola. No less aware of modern hazards, Chekhov is far less judgmental. Not only does he refuse to dramatize possible answers, he is bent upon conveying the pathos of badly framed questions. His narratives deal with characters at those times when private fabrications wear thin, when the artifices that have become the modus operandi of selfhood cannot

[14] Chekhov to Alexei Suvorin, November 25, 1892, ibid., pp. 242–43.

protect their creators against the realities of "a precarious, sour, dreary period." Two modes of definition are always at war: the illusion each ego constructs and the external circumstances surrounding it. Illusion is necessary because culture and society no longer offer structures that can order and give stable value to individual aspiration. Compared to older faiths, illusions are arbitrary and short-lived. At best, in Chekhov's happier stories, the characters achieve only respite, moments when the impetus of fact is held at a standoff. And while the poignancy of fractured models and reductive distress is rarely held up for analysis or authorial comment, any representative collection of Chekhov's short novels will demonstrate the effects on character of a malady akin to Hardy's ache of modernism and Zola's malaise.

Private fictions cut one off from true relations with the world beyond the self. But when a character is unable to create such a fiction, his situation is desperate. He becomes a consciousness bandied about among indifferent forces. This is the predicament of the professor whose notebook we read in *A Dull Story*, the journal of an aging man whose sense of meaning and purpose is being paralyzed by what he takes to be the symptoms of approaching death. He begins: "There lives in Russia a certain Honored Professor Nikolai Stepanovich, privy councilor and knight, who has received so many decorations, both Russian and foreign, that when he has occasion to wear them all, his students call him 'the icon stand' " (163). The professor has valued public distinction, not for vanity's sake, but because his honors prove the reality of the private dream that is the ground of his being.

My conscience and my mind both tell me that the best thing I could do would be to deliver a farewell lecture . . . and yield my place to a younger, stronger man. But—God forgive me—I have not the courage to follow the dictates of my conscience.

Unfortunately, I am neither a philosopher nor a theologian. I know quite well that I have no more than six months to live; it would seem that now I ought to be concerned primarily with the mystery beyond the grave. . . . But for some reason my soul declines to face these questions, though my mind acknowledges them as all-important. Now, on the threshold of death, the only thing that interests me is what interested me twenty or thirty years ago—science. Even as I breathe my last, I shall go on believing that science is the most important, most beautiful, most essential thing in the life of man, that it always has been and always will be the highest manifestation of love, that by means of it alone will man conquer nature and himself. It may be that this belief is naive and fundamentally incorrect, but I cannot help believing as I do, and for me to overcome this belief of mine would be impossible. (173–74)

Emotionally and ideologically, Nikolai Stepanovich's faith is as deeply held as the experimental vision Zola's Doctor Pascal lives and dies for. But the professor's belief lacks the sustenance the doctor can draw from his. And this insufficiency provides the action of the short novel. Chekhov does not question the validity of a given faith; he shows the effects of a god that fails.

The humanity with which Chekhov invests the course of failure simply renders the emptiness that is its consequence available to sympathetic scrutiny. Unconnected with an inner order of dreams and sentiments, scientific rationality becomes a realistic clarity that drains the blood from all of life.

They say that philosophers and wise men are indifferent. This is not true. Indifference is a paralysis of the soul, a premature death.

. . . . .

"Know thyself" is excellent and useful advice; it is only a pity that the ancients failed to indicate a method for following it.

In the past when I wanted to understand someone, or even myself, I took into consideration, not actions, which are always conditional, but desires. Tell me what you want and I will tell you what you are.

And now I examine myself. What do I want?

I want our wives, children, friends, and students to love in us, not the fame, the label, the connections, but the ordinary man. What else? I should like to have assistants and successors. What else? I should like to wake up a hundred years from now and have a glimpse of what is going on in science. . . . Anything more?

No, nothing more. I think and think, but can think of nothing further. . . . there is nothing vital, nothing of great importance, in my desires. . . . there is no common element, nothing that would unify them into a whole. Each thought and feeling exists in isolation, and . . . in all the pictures my imagination paints, even the most skillful analyst would be unable to find what is called a general idea, or the god of a living man.

And without this there is nothing. (215–16)

As in "The Darling," typicality becomes uniqueness; a potential parody of the epoch's exhaustion becomes a suffering man. *A Dull Story*, Chekhov's first major short novel, announces what will be one of his central subjects. The professor's self-cauterizing objectivity, his stale inertia of mind and feeling, become the basis for a multidimensional portrait of the burden of flatness.

Nikolai Stepanovich wants those around him to love the private, ordinary man. But in the sense he intends, there is no such person. His failure to find or create meaning results in an offensive sourness; the cold eye he casts on himself and others reveals a petulant, ironic, and wholly negative version of scientific realism. His is the bitter truth-telling born of frustration. He sees life almost as a conspiracy of hypocrisies and unrealities.

> To describe our dinners nowadays would be as unappetizing as to eat them. Along with her usual worried look, my wife's face wears an expression of triumph and ostentatious dignity. . . . I look from [my daughter to my wife], and only now, at the dinner table, does it become clear to me that long ago their inner lives slipped from my control. I feel as if there had once been a time when I lived in my own home with a real family, and that now I am dining in the home of an unreal wife, looking at an unreal [daughter]. (187–88)

Yet even when life was real and Nikolai Stepanovich's beloved ward Katya formed part of it, he had been able to find "neither the time nor the inclination to follow the rise and development" of the girl's passionate interest in the theater. Though Katya was dearer to him than any other person, he refused to take her inner life seriously, to concede its reality. "When she felt a desire to share her enthusiasm with someone, she would come into my study and in a beseeching voice say to me: 'Nikolai Stepanovich, do let me talk to you about the theater!' I would point to the clock and say: 'I'll give you half an hour—go ahead!' " (179).

However understandable the professor's dislike for his

family's role-playing, the distaste for the theater that becomes clear in his attitude to Katya points to a maiming refusal ever to suspend disbelief. Neither of the three women, nor indeed anyone else in the narrative, is presented as humanly engaging. But it is really impossible to judge; Nikolai Stepanovich's corroding rationality destroys the warmth and charm that might belong to the characters people play at being. Artifice and blurring illusion are perhaps his missing "general idea." But the professor's unpleasantness is inseparable from the anguish of that "something altogether unendurable" (190) that occupies his soul. Standards of love, truth, and understanding exist. The reader is never allowed to forget that Nikolai Stepanovich is deeply wrong. Yet given his pathos, the standards seem beside the point; they are not allowed to cohere into a judgment. No external framework accounts for the terrible unreality that has overcome the narrator. The professor's situation realizes Huysmans's description of naturalism in *Là-Bas*: a valuable, necessary precision of detail and a denotative accuracy of reference accompany an inability to plumb the soul's depths.[15] Joy in science has become inhuman scientism. It is as if the professor's incompleteness had reduced the grand contemporary achievements in science to the impotence of principle and sour dreariness that Chekhov believes to have overtaken creative literature.

Such corrosive insufficiency becomes a hallmark of Chekhov's characters. Even when a protagonist embraces a general idea, the direction his life follows is similar. Inner hollowness collaborates with an indeterminate malady in the outer world. Misail, the narrator of *My Life*, asserts a Tolstoyan simplicity, a belief in equality, justice, and truth, on

---

[15] See J.-K. Huysmans, *Là-Bas* (Paris: Librairie Plon, 1942), pp. 4–5.

the basis of which he abandons his rank among the provincial gentry. To the disgust of his father, a complacent tyrant and the architect responsible for the town's ugliness, he takes up the life of a workman. He wants to be free of the pretentious mediocrity, myopic egotism, and spiritual vacuity of his father's class. He inveighs repeatedly against the town's crudeness.

> I did not understand what these sixty-five thousand people lived for, or how they lived. I knew that in Kimry people lived from the manufacture of boots, that in Tula they made samovars and guns, that Odessa was a seaport, but what our town was and what it did—I did not know. [Our street] and the other two decent streets lived on investments and official salaries; but what supported the other eight streets . . . had always been an insoluble riddle to me. And I hate to say how these people lived! No park, no theater, no decent orchestra; . . . rich and educated people slept in close, stuffy rooms on bug-ridden beds, their children were kept in disgustingly filthy rooms called nurseries, and the servants, even those who were old and respected, slept on the floor in the kitchen covered with rags. On ordinary days the houses smelled of borscht, and on fast days of sturgeon cooked in sunflower oil. The food was unsavory and the water unwholesome.[16]

Nothing in the story invalidates these observations. Indeed, Misail's clear-sighted attack is perfectly in line with Chekhov's continual exposure of provincial meagerness. Yet Misail's truth-telling, like the professor's, is a symptom of his own limitations.

Critics have commented that Misail espouses a Tol-

[16] *My Life*, in *Ward Six and Other Stories*, pp. 230–31.

stoyan passivity that Chekhov, by the mid-nineties, severely distrusts. Chekhov's misgivings certainly help shape the story, but Misail's principles are no more a primary issue than the professor's belief in science. Again, the psychology of a common attitude broadens into an existential ambiguity. The incomprehension that finds the town's way of life "an insoluble riddle" derives originally from Misail's rebellion against his father's grasping practicality, against the selfish overlordship that the architect wants to impose upon the lives of his son and his daughter, Kleopatra. Misail is no fool; his naive simplicity is cultivated. Rejecting all that his father stands for and going to the other extreme, he marries an unconventional woman, a singer, and departs to lead a life outside the town. Problems immediately arise. Trying to refurbish their ramshackle house and to practice good works by starting a village school, the couple is frustrated at every turn by the local inhabitants.

> She was outraged, and resentment was beginning to seethe in her soul, while I, on the other hand, was growing used to the peasants and felt more and more drawn to them. For the most part they were nervous, irritable, humiliated people; they were people whose imaginations had been stifled, who were ignorant, whose outlook on life was meager and drab, with always the same thoughts of gray earth, gray days, and black bread, people whose cunning was like that of the birds . . . they were incapable of calculating. . . . They were, indeed, dirty, drunken, foolish, and dishonest, but for all that, one felt that peasant life on the whole was healthy and sound at the core. However crude a peasant might appear . . . one felt that there was something vital, something great in him, . . . namely, his belief that the principal thing on earth was truth, that his salvation and that

of all people lay in truth alone; and this made him love justice above all else in the world. (281)

As Chekhov's own portraits of peasant life show us, Misail's attitude is a sentimental oversimplification. Yet the beauty of Misail's commitment more than balances the shallowness of his conclusions. That the psychological roots of his appraisal manifest an almost point-by-point reversal of all his father represents leads us, not to reductive analysis, but to the kind of comprehending awareness we might have of the motives of a dear friend.

Sympathy with Misail's needs is a precondition for any larger perspective on his typical predicament. His decent desire for meaning, for truthful selfhood, like that of so many others in the short novels, is thwarted by the general inconclusiveness of life. Even more centrally than in *A Dull Story*, this bitter development is suggested through theatrical references. The key item in Misail's brief catalog of the amenities his town lacks is a theater. He loves the amateur theatricals for which he helps build sets. When he abandons his class, he is excluded from these performances. His delight in theater and well-plotted roles must exist in a world that refuses to be a stage. His situation is one that Chekhov often examines in both his fiction and his own plays—the uncomfortable open-endedness of direction resulting from the disappearance of that orderly faith that Scribean and Ostrovskian drama imitated in its neat structures. Characters craving such conventional conclusiveness confront a *deus ex machina absconditus*. They are compelled to search for an author, to improvise a habitable plot. Misail's rejection of the uninspired but clear part his father would have him play forces the young man to invent his own play. And he is not a talented artist.

Misail's stage-struck temperament does lead to his most active role: his love and marriage. Marya Viktorovna, his beloved, is herself in search of a satisfactory part. Her desire for novelty and excitement sets her apart from the townspeople. Brought up on the larger stage of St. Petersburg, a singer and performer of talent, she embodies for Misail a real-life drama. She in turn views his refusal of the town's lackluster ways as real-life heroism. His need for illusion, however, is greater than hers; it survives her departure for America and its more glamorous opportunities. Like his belief in the peasants, his love must transform the facts Chekhov provides. Marya resembles the flighty wife in "The Grasshopper," an earlier short story. The latter's trendy dabbling in the world and lives of artists blinds her to the worth of her brilliant but socially naive doctor husband. Marya is more fully and sympathetically drawn than the shallow wife Chekhov clearly expects his readers to see through, but her unconventionality is no less a social artifice, akin to those Misail condemns in his father's world. His failure to see her for what she is springs not only from a lover's illusionism but also from the necessities of his own drama.

Invariably, private fictions distort vision. Misail's self-creation blinds him to contradictory evidence. More seriously, it prevents him from seeing the necessary complexity of the roles others choose or are forced to enact. Chekhov surrounds Misail with a rich roundedness of setting and supporting cast and poignantly conveys the young man's struggle to do away with his own multidimensionality. Acting out his principles, Misail flattens others and himself. His attitude toward his sister recalls the professor's toward Katya. Kleopatra has been tormented into ugly clumsiness by her father. Her need to make a life of her own is as great as Misail's. Yet when she rebels from the housekeeping duties her father exacts by venturing to take part in the theatricals, her brother's report focuses on the naked charmlessness beneath the facade of hope.

> She wore a black dress with a string of coral round her neck, a brooch which from a distance looked like a little puff pastry, and big earrings sparkling with brilliants. It made me uncomfortable to look at her: I was shocked by her lack of taste. The others also noticed that she was oddly dressed and that her jewelry was out of place; I saw their smiles and heard someone say with a laugh: "Kleopatra of the Nile."
>
> She was trying to be worldly, unconstrained, at ease, which only made her seem mannered and odd. Her simplicity and sweetness deserted her.
>
> "I told Father just now that I was going to a rehearsal . . . and he shouted at me, saying he would deprive me of his blessing, and he actually came very near striking me. . . . Well, the die is cast. . . ."
>
> She felt that everyone was looking at her, that they were all astounded at the momentous step she had taken and were expecting something special from her, and it was impossible to convince her that nobody paid any attention to such unimportant and uninteresting people as herself and me. (291–92)

Kleopatra forgets her few lines and breaks down in despair; she collapses, is discovered to be pregnant, and is ejected in disgrace. Misail's account of the scene is perfectly precise; his reactions clearly rest on love and sympathy. Yet his tone has an acidulous clarity as well as a touch of the moralistic "I told you so." Kleopatra offends the image of abstract sweetness and simplicity he desires for her; she violates the role he has assigned her in his private drama. Misail's clear-sighted estimate of her tasteless bungling is as denuding as her father's cruelty or the town's mockery.

Though Chekhov had unaccustomed trouble settling on a title, being particularly unsatisfied with the *my*, the pronoun is fittingly restrictive.[17] Misail's illusion holds him off from those he cares for. His damaging limitation emerges pointedly in his attitude toward Radish, the workman on whom he attempts to model himself. He presents Radish as a conclusive instance of peasant worth and truth. But what we read is an account of peasant grayness. Improvident, mildly grasping, Radish rises from the sickbed on which he spends the winter months to labor with excellent craft but dour spirit. His relations with employers and even with his own men are often clouded by incomprehension; his conversation—consisting mainly of bleak formulae such as "Anything can happen!"—verbalizes some opaque inner sense of dreary difficulty and leaden endurance. Seeking to absorb what he considers Radish's virtues, Misail gradually takes on the peasant's sourness. "I am now considered a good worker and the best contractor after Radish. . . . I have aged and grown silent, stern, austere; I rarely laugh and they say I have become like Radish, that like him I bore the men with my useless admonitions" (304). This concluding colorlessness seems but a declassed version of the dull vacuity Misail had originally condemned in the town. He has become his nickname, "Better-than-Nothing." His sympathetic, decent qualities remain, but his voice, initially vibrant, is muffled by his seemingly senseless refusal of roundedness, depth, glitter, and joy.

While the plentiful life that Chekhov allows to sound

[17] See Gleb Struve, Preface to *My Life*, in *Seven Short Novels*, p. 279.

through Misail's narrative never destroys our sense of the speaker's appeal, it does imply the existence of a radically richer perspective. Like several others in the short novels, Misail tries to enforce his private fiction by employing what seems a parody of his author's demandingly delicate objectivity. The moral imperative to which Chekhov's aesthetic responds—the hope that sympathetic yet impartial truth-telling may bring rational order to human muddlement—is distorted, if not lost, in the character's selective clarity. Chekhov's unwillingness to intervene with comment allows Misail full scope to construct his dream. But because, in the absence of a thematic goal, the very art of the author's narration impinges on the story being narrated as the only real-life, positive option in evidence, Misail's parody of this unique value comes to seem a terrifying betrayal. And the human incompleteness that here and elsewhere brings this about becomes in its way more final than the obvious decadence at work in Hardy's Wessex and Zola's Second Empire.

The counterpoint between the limitations of a first-person narrator and the full-bodied art that expresses them recurs in many of the third person stories in a different but no less foreboding relation between character and art. Chekhov's use of the indirect free style, of narrated consciousness, mirrors the flailing attempts of separate lives to escape their hermetic plight. Immersing himself first in one consciousness and then in another, often without omniscient transition, Chekhov dramatizes self-imprisonment and the immense difficulty of transposing private melodies even into duets—let alone into social orchestration. The principle laid down by Rebecca West in one of her short novels some thirty years later provides an appropriate epigraph. "There is no such thing as conversation. It is an illusion. There are intersecting monologues, that is all. We speak; we spread round with sounds, with words, an emanation from ourselves. Sometimes they overlap the circles others are spreading round themselves. Then they are affected by these other circles, to be sure, but not because of any real conversation that has taken place."[18]

In *My Life*, Misail's illusion of Marya marries her illusion of him. But since Misail is narrating, the vulnerable illusionism is implied rather than stressed. Such intersections occur more pointedly in the third-person accounts. *Three Years*, one of the most nearly novelistic narratives, is typical. Laptev, deeply in love, marries a girl who, though indifferent to him, hopes to find freedom in his wealth. As the years pass, his frustrated love sours into cold bitterness. When, near the end, the wife belatedly realizes his virtues and falls deeply in love with him, Laptev no longer cares. This ambitious story is by no means schematic. But in it—as in *The Name-Day Party* and elsewhere—the incomprehensions, bad timings, and cross-purposes associated with difficult marriages or loves in novels of manners become the depressingly familiar setting for Chekhov's theme.

Even on the infrequent occasions when two narrated consciousnesses coalesce in one voice, there is scant hope. The shared note is drowned by external noise. In "The Lady with the Dog" the middle-aged, unsuccessfully married Dmitri Gurov encounters the lady at a summer resort. He senses that she is available, and they begin what he thinks will be but another in the series of brief affairs with which he occu-

[18] Rebecca West, *There Is No Conversation*, in *The Harsh Voice: Four Short Novels* (New York: Doubleday, Doran & Co., 1936), p. 67.

pies his time. He learns that she too is caught in an unrewarding marriage, though their similar situation does not seem of great interest to him. However, when her stay ends and she leaves, he discovers that he is in love for the first time. He goes home, then suddenly goes to seek her out in her town. To his joy, she returns his love. In the last paragraphs they have begun a life of clandestine meetings.

> Then they spent a long while taking counsel together, talked of how to avoid the necessity for secrecy, for deception, for living in different towns and not seeing each other for long at a time. How could they be free from this intolerable bondage?
> "How? How?" he asked, clutching his head. "How?"
> And it seemed as though in a little while the solution would be found, and then a new and splendid life would begin; and it was clear to both of them that they had still a long, long way to go, and that the most complicated and difficult part of it was only just beginning.[19]

Private poetry shades into prosaic limitation. The use of *to seem* is more pointedly ominous than in *The Duel*; it permits us to sense the forbidding territory of fact. The story concludes with the bleak suggestion that the lovers' shared dream is stranded between their past failed marriages and a future that can have no clear shape at all.

The intense psychological empathy and understanding that distinguish Chekhov from Hardy and Zola are transformed within the content of his characters' lives into an intense

[19] "The Lady with the Dog," in *The Lady with the Dog and Other Stories*, trans. Constance Garnett (London: Chatto & Windus, 1917), p. 28.

self-absorption resembling modern Laodiceanism and Empire neurasthenia. In several of the major short novels, moreover, the social bad faith and indifferent universal law typical of the other two writers enter the foreground of Chekhov's presentation. Edmund Wilson's contention that the stories and plays of Chekhov's later years "constitute a kind of analysis of Russian society, a miniature *Comédie Humaine*," clearly points to a more than psychological focus.[20] The social, natural, and cosmic forces that intrude upon individuals are central to at least two of the studies of middle-class character, *Ward Six* and *An Anonymous Story*—both written slightly before the period Wilson specifies—and to two accounts of peasant life, *Peasants* and *In the Ravine*.

Ward Six, the narrative of a provincial madhouse that deeply moved Lenin, derives some of its great power from apparent artistic flaws. Chekhov himself judged the short novel rather harshly, thought it hastily conceived and not wholly coherent.[21] Yet the unresolved technical problems have the effect of showing the subject to be in part unmanageable, and the atypical uncertainty of focus endows the action with a parable-like fluidity of meaning. The tone and viewpoint of the first-person introduction confuse our sense of the direction to be followed. Our first encounter with the ward takes place under the auspices of a particularizing indignation that appears to demand the reform of a social sore —a possibility for temporal cure that will be negated by the absolute human plight in the main action of the story. The opening paragraph, after a grim glance at the hospital yard,

[20] Edmund Wilson, Preface to *Peasants and Other Stories* (New York: Doubleday Anchor Books, 1956), p. vii.
[21] See Gleb Struve, Preface to *Ward No. 6*, in *Seven Short Novels*, p. 106.

presses beyond simple descriptive intent: "These spikes, the fence, and the annex itself [Ward Six] all have that peculiarly desolate, Godforsaken look characteristic of our hospital and prison buildings." The speaker challenges the reader to enter: "If you are not afraid of being stung by nettles, come with me . . . and let us see what is going on inside."[22] Within, we see a handful of "lunatics" dressed in shapeless regulation pajamas, the tyrannical guard Nikita, and piles of rubbish. "The place stinks of sauerkraut, smoldering wicks, bedbugs, and ammonia, and for the first moment this stench gives you the impression that you are entering a menagerie" (8).

Soon, however, the Dickensian picture of unnecessary, corrigible misery gives way to a different view. The guiding narrator now acts as a humanizing bridge across this noxious filth. The inmate to whom he draws attention requires the mediation of a sympathetic voice if his story is to be rescued from our predictable response to foulness and madness.

> I like his broad pale face with its high cheekbones, an unhappy face in which a soul tormented by perpetual struggle and fear is reflected as in a mirror. His grimaces are queer and morbid, but the fine lines drawn on his face by deep and genuine suffering denote sensibility and culture. . . . I like the man himself, always courteous, obliging, and extremely considerate. . . . his madness expresses itself in the following ways. Sometimes in the evenings . . . trembling all over, his teeth chattering, [he] begins rapidly pacing up and down like a man in a high fever. . . . it is clear that he wants to say something very important, but evidently realizing that nobody will listen to him or understand him, he impatiently shakes

[22] *Ward Six*, in *Ward Six and Other Stories*, p. 7.

his head and continues pacing. Soon, however, the desire to speak overrules all other considerations, and he lets himself go and talks feverishly, passionately. His speech, as in a delirium, is frenzied, spasmodic, disordered, and not always understandable, yet one detects something singularly fine in the words and in his voice. When he talks, both the lunatic and the man are distinguishable in him. . . . He discourses on human baseness, on violence vanquishing truth, on the glorious life that one day will appear on earth, on the iron grilles on the windows which constantly remind him of the stupidity and cruelty of the oppressors. It makes for a confused and incoherent potpourri of songs which, though old, have yet to be sung to the end. (9–10)

Ivan Dmitrich Gromov is Chekhovian man in extremis; he conclusively epitomizes the discord between private selves and public realities. The purposes, generous perceptions, and truths that so often mark the former have been fractured by the alienating pressures of the latter into a lunatic word salad. What ought to be a mutually beneficial relation between inner and outer has taken the form of "persecution mania." Chekhov's subject is one man, not an allegory of the world as madhouse or of mankind as mad. But the narrator's affection and respect present Gromov as an outgrowth of the seemingly endemic distress afflicting contemporary Russia.

In the sections that follow, the brief, now third-person, outline of Gromov's early life both continues this emphasis and, in the context of the story as a whole, lengthens the long preparation for the entrance of the protagonist, Doctor Ragin, who will sing the song to its bitter end. In Gromov's youth, his wealthy father went bankrupt, was convicted of forgery, and died in prison. "The whole series of misfortunes which suddenly rained down" on the family warped the young man's nature (10). He became acutely nervous, his speech marked by an irritable enthusiasm for absolute values —beauty, justice, truth. Lacking the resilience to cope with the demands of life in his small town, a provincial slough even grayer than Misail's home, Gromov sensed a general tyranny and began to cower. Some workmen came to reset his stove; he believed they were policemen in disguise. Feeling somehow guilty of something, he fled: "it seemed to Ivan Dmitrich that all the violence in the world had gathered together in pursuit of him" (15). He is institutionalized, as truly insane as the town is vacuous and the ward vile.

Gromov's fate—character as imprisoned monologue—is comprehensible, though apparently irremediable. The town is little-minded, but not vicious. Conditions in the ward are grim, but might be reformed. Neither in themselves nor in their interrelationships are the three subjects truly mysterious. But the relation between Gromov, town, and ward on the one hand and Doctor Ragin on the other is opaque, frightening. The organizing concern with madness connects all of them, but taken together they do not cohere into the unity of action we expect from Chekhov's best work. In particular, Gromov and Ward Six seem almost random nemeses spawned by the Doctor's way of life. Unlike Tolstoy's "superfluous" details and scenes, which come together in a general impression of lifelike density, Chekhov's confusing environment of process and event appears to be out of focus, uncontrolled by artistic symmetry. The variegated emphases of the introductory sections seem at times to lead their own lives, as inexplicable as the floating balls that appear in the commonplace apartment of Kafka's "Blumfield, An Elderly Bachelor." Gromov receives an attention that outweighs his plot function—the luring of the doctor into the ward—and then creates abruptness, even awkwardness, when Chekhov shifts his focus onto the doctor:

> Of late, however, a rather strange rumor has been spreading through the hospital. It is reported that the doctor has been visiting Ward Six.

V

> A strange rumor!
> Dr. Andrei Yefimych Ragin is a remarkable man in his way. He is said to have been very religious in his early youth . . . but it seems that his father, a doctor of medicine and a surgeon, was virulent in his ridicule and categorically announced that he would no longer consider him his son if he became a priest. How true this is I do not know, but on more than one occasion Andrei Yefimych himself confessed that he had never felt a vocation for medicine or for the exact sciences in general.
> However that may be, after graduating from medical school he did not take Orders. He evinced no special devoutness and was no more like an ecclesiastic at the beginning of his medical career than he is now. (17)

The speaker is presumably the original narrator, now discovered to be a fellow townsman and acquaintance. The indignation initially aroused by the hospital now shifts to the irresponsible doctor. Andrei Yefimych's lazy self-satisfaction, his provincial pretentions to sensibility and culture, are laid bare with a rancor unusual in Chekhov. Deeming conditions in the hospital and ward of which he is supervisor to be hopeless, Ragin retreats into his smugly sanguine "philosophy." He reasons that no reform should be undertaken; there is no point in saving lives, "since death is normal, the decreed end for everyone." Why alleviate suffering? "In the first place, suffering is said to lead to self-perfection, and in the second place, if man learns to ease his suffering with pills and drops he will completely abandon religion and philosophy, wherein till now he has found not only a defense against every adversity, but happiness itself" (20). Debased misapplications of his early religious training, the doctor's ideas are morally outrageous.

But just when Ragin seems wholly condemned, the perspective changes again. The comforting banalities that make up his conversation and the undemanding routine of his simple contentment begin to manifest the charm Chekhov often accords the fictions that make life bearable. The emphasis on complacency and hollowness gives way to a picture of appealing eccentricity. We are introduced to a pleasant delusion of private worth. "I often dream about intelligent people and conversations with them," Andrei Yefimych explains to his one friend, the postmaster:

> under the influence of the ideas of the sixties, [my father] forced me to become a doctor. I sometimes think that if I had not obeyed him I would now be in the very center of some intellectual movement. . . . Of course, intellect too is transitory, not immortal, but you know why I have an inclination for it. Life is a miserable trap. . . . a trap from which there is no escape. . . . If [a thinking man] tries to find out the meaning and purpose of his existence he either gets no answer or is told all sorts of absurdities. . . . And just as men in prison, united by their common misfortune, feel better when they are together, so in life people with a turn for analysis and generalizations do not notice that they are in a trap when they come together and pass the time in the exchange of free and elevating ideas. (24)

However clichéd, Ragin's views are as tenable as the professor's and Misail's. But whereas with the first-person narrators we inhabit a private perspective and only gradually come to sense its public shortcomings, with the doctor we begin by seeing from the outside and only gradually enter the shelter of illusions he has tried to build against "common misfortune." The different approach creates an uncertainty of location and reaction on the reader's part that Chekhov will exploit later in the work. But both techniques stress the fact of divided character.

The sloth deserving indignation belongs to one dimension; the sentimental achievement of Ragin's dreams and ideas to another. The latter is presented with increasing seriousness. The thinness of the doctor's thought comes to seem beside the point. However weak his intellectual grasp, his desire for meaningful conversation and for freedom is estimable, and its frustration painful. His efforts toward an exchange of ideas are better than the postmaster's appreciative grunts. The two men share a companionly routine. But the doctor's craving for something more leads him to the ward and to Gromov. He does not ask much—indeed, his minimal expectations recall those of many of Hardy's and Zola's victims. Yet to ask at all proves fatal. On one of his infrequent visits to the hospital annex, he is struck just as the narrator was by Gromov's "voice and his youthful face, intelligent despite his grimacing" (30). Here at last is someone with whom he can converse. He advocates the need for stoicism; Gromov counters:

> "A convenient philosophy: you have nothing to do, your conscience is clear, and you feel you're a sage. . . . No, sir, this is not philosophy, not thought, not breadth

of vision, but laziness, pretense, mental torpor. . . . Yes!"
Ivan Dmitrich grew angry again. "You despise suffering, but if you pinched your little finger in that door,
you'd probably start howling at the top of your voice."

"Perhaps I wouldn't howl," said Andrei Yefimych
with a gentle smile. (37; Chekhov's ellipses)

Both Gromov and Ragin speak with the sincerity, truthful-
ness, and logic that often mark the inner worlds of Chekhov's
characters. But they are conversing on the wrong side of the
looking glass of public expectations. Ragin's conviction that
he has found a true interlocutor and a serious stage is the prelude to the howl that will end his life's song.

He goes so often to visit Gromov that the townspeople
become suspicious. His hospital assistant, hoping to get his
job, convinces the authorities that the doctor should submit
to an examination for sanity. He answers the rote questions
normally, but when asked "whether it was true that there
was a remarkable prophet living in Ward Six," he replies:
"Yes, he is ill, but he is an interesting young man." "There
were no more questions after that" (41). Ragin is relieved
of his place; his friend, the postmaster, thinking that distraction will help him recover his old self, proposes that they
take a trip.

> To go somewhere for no reason, without his books,
> without [his maid] and his beer, suddenly to disturb a
> routine of life that had been set for twenty years, at
> first struck him as a wild, fantastic idea. But then he
> recalled the conversation in the town hall, the feeling of
> depression he had experienced as he returned home, and
> the thought of a brief absence from a town where stupid
> people regarded him as a madman suddenly appealed
> to him. (42)

Ragin's reactions are now treated with complete sympathy. Within the small province of his feelings and ideas, an education is taking place. Pleasant habits are infiltrated by strange threats. And the consequent depression nurtures perceptions that isolate him even further. Indeed, the birth of something genuine, of the kind of stern understanding we have seen in the professor, Misail, and Gromov, begins to qualify Andrei Yefimych as another of Chekhov's examples of Twilight alienation.

As Ragin develops, the world around him takes clearer form as an environment of meanness. Closer acquaintance shows the postmaster to be a typical provincial egotist. On the trip he whisks his companion along, bombasticating, bullying, boring. The doctor knows neither how nor on what grounds to resist. He retreats to the hotel room, thinking: "True happiness is impossible without solitude. The fallen angel probably betrayed God out of a longing for that solitude which is denied to angels" (45). The idea has more force and is truer to Ragin's experience than the earlier platitudes. The trip is a constant misery; it also swallows Andrei Yefimych's meager savings. The postmaster and townspeople had believed that the doctor's irresponsibility included the usual amount of peculation, but in this, as in most other matters, he has been naive. On his return, he has to move from his cherished quarters into a dingy boarding-house, where he sinks rapidly into irritable inertia. The postmaster, promising a new journey for the coming year, and the medical assistant, hypocritically offering bromine drops, visit him. "Get out, both of you! . . . Stupid people! Fools! I don't want your friendship—nor your medicine, you blockhead! The vulgarity—sickening!" (51). The exacerbated nerves of defeated dreams have developed along with Ragin's new perceptions. Later that day, on the pretext of wanting his advice, the assistant takes him to Ward Six, and leaves him there, a new inmate.

"All this seemed strange, even incomprehensible, at first. But Andrei Yefimych was convinced even now that there was no difference between [the boardinghouse] and Ward No. 6, that everything in this world was nonsense, vanity of vanities; and yet his hands trembled, his feet were cold, and the thought that Ivan Dmitrich would soon get up and see him in a hospital robe filled him with dread" (54). With nightfall, his fear increases. He turns to Gromov for consolation only to be told: "Try philosophizing." His noisy demands to be let out bring the brutish Nikita, who beats him.

> Then all was quiet. The moon shed its pale light through the bars. . . . It was terrible. Andrei Yefimych lay still, holding his breath, waiting in terror to be struck again. . . . He bit the pillow and clenched his teeth with pain; and all of a sudden out of the chaos there clearly flashed through his mind the dreadful, unbearable thought that these people . . . must have experienced this same pain day in and day out for years. How could it have happened that in the course of more than twenty years he had not known, had refused to know this? Having no conception of pain, he could not possibly have known it, so he was not guilty, but his conscience, no less obdurate and implacable than Nikita, made him turn cold from head to foot. He jumped up, wanting to shout at the top of his lungs, to rush out and kill Nikita, . . . the superintendent, the medical assistant, and then himself, but no sound came from his mouth and his legs would not obey him . . . [he] fell back on the bed unconscious. (58)

The speaker of free and elevating ideas is struck dumb. Chekhov abhors lies, and Ragin has lived a lie. Chekhov detests bad doctors, and Ragin's refusal even to try to alleviate pain is abominable. Yet the violence of Ragin's fate far transcends any sense of just deserts; even were Chekhov prone to judgmental moralism, no man could earn this horror. The doctor's lie, delusion, or fiction is his identity. He cannot survive the ward because no private fiction can shut out the omnipotent onslaught of such realities. The next day he is ill, beyond any solace of "philosophy."

> Toward evening Andrei Yefimych died of an apoplectic stroke. He first suffered violent chills and nausea; something loathsome seemed to permeate his entire body even to his finger tips; it rose from his stomach to his head and flooded his eyes and ears. Everything turned green before him. Andrei Yefimych realized that the end had come and remembered that Ivan Dmitrich, [the postmaster], and millions of others believed in immortality. And what if they were right? But he felt no desire for immortality, and gave it only momentary thought. A herd of reindeer, about which he had been reading the day before, extraordinarily beautiful and graceful, ran by him; a peasant woman held out a registered letter to him. . . . [The postmaster] said something. . . . Then all was gone, and Andrei Yefimych lost consciousness forever. (59; Chekhov's ellipses)

The ending carries Ragin's story past social indignation, past his faults, into the tragic clarity of the tears of things. Not only are individuals imprisoned within the identities they dream; even if they did not dream, they would be prisoners within social and perhaps cosmic bonds. Gromov's and Ragin's narrative belongs to Chekhov's repeatedly re-staged drama of the contemporary predicament; the plot is as somber as any conceived by Hardy and Zola at their most pessimistic. The warmth and appeal of the dramatis personae go for nothing. Characters exhibit a random course of thoughts and emotions, a fox's fate. Once unraveled from their illusions or dreams, men flounder in alien and alienating actualities. At the conclusion of Ragin's life, no memory survives of the initial suggestions of reform. What happens is as obdurate and implacable as Nikita's fists. No matter how engendered, the "desolate, Godforsaken look characteristic of our hospital and prison buildings" is no mere appearance, but a real token of fundamental blight. Somewhere beyond, apart from men's flaws and life's violence, may lie the field of reindeer. But there seems no way to earn so fragilely hinted a grace; indeed, no way to survive until it might descend.

The action of *Ward Six*—developing from the initial concern with its milieu—proceeds rapidly toward the inwardness of individuality that is Chekhov's essential subject. This mild sensation of imbalance recurs in several of the other stories that follow a similar course. Setting becomes a symptom of late-century malady, which then becomes the private predicament of a given character. Despite extreme differences in the social framework that forms the point of departure, and despite the uniqueness of the individual temperaments portrayed, the symptoms and predicament all draw our attention to the epoch's lack of purposeful direction. Hence, *An Anonymous Story* (or *An Unknown Man's Story*) provides another version of Gromov's and Ragin's fate. The short novel is not one of Chekhov's best. It is marred not so much by a dissonant development from its framing milieu, conspiratorial revolutionism, into its portrait of the anonymous revolutionist narrator as by too blatant a parallel between public and private malady. Historical situation and individual character become indistinguishable, so that the narrator's situation seems so clear an epitome of Chekhov's appraisal of the Twilight as to be a caricature.

Like Misail, the narrator is a member of the gentry whose search for truth and a goal has led him to break with his class. He turns to utopian revolutionism, and when his narrative opens, he has just entered as a servant into the household of a blasé bachelor, Orlov, in order to get at his employer's father, an important government official. Even at the beginning, radicalism seems insufficient as a source of meaning.

> I had incipient tuberculosis. . . . Whether it was the effect of illness, or of some new change of outlook which eluded my notice at the time, I was obsessed day in day out by a passionate, hypersensitive craving for ordinary, everyday life. I yearned for peace of mind, health, fresh air, plenty to eat. I was becoming a daydreamer, and as such I did not know exactly what I wanted. . . . I would imagine myself buying a dozen acres and settling down as a country squire. Or else I would swear to take up academic work and make a point of becoming a professor at a provincial university. As a retired naval lieutenant I had visions of the sea . . . I wanted to experience once again the indescribable sensation of walking in a tropical forest, or of gazing at the sunset in the Bay of Bengal, when you swoon with ecstasy and feel homesick: both at the same time. I dreamt of mountains, women, music. With childlike curiosity I scrutinized people's faces and hung on their voices. . . .

> I felt less like a servant than a man for whom everything on earth, even an Orlov, held some interest.[23]

The passage strikingly parallels aspects of Chekhov's life: consumption, Eastern memories, omniverous openness to and curiosity about the world, desire for an ordinary existence. And these similarities suggest the theme. At one time or another each fact or trait occurs in Chekhov's letters as a threat to the vocation of art; each relates to the competing goals and lack of overriding direction about which he sometimes complains. *An Anonymous Story* projects the situation of a man wholly without its author's compelling vocation, it relates the anonymity of one who cannot subordinate his ideas and impulses to a single principle of action.

Though the narrator's revolutionism no longer provides a compelling goal, the indignation at complacency and injustice that originally nurtured it finds ample scope in the home of a philanderer. Condemnation requires no action— a fact that suits both the writer's weakened health and the passivity born of his uncertain purpose. Righteous scorn is a reasonable response to Orlov, but, divorced from any effort to change things, it resembles a peeping Tom's insistence that those he spies on act in good faith. The servant watches with disgust as, in the story's main action, Orlov's egocentric routines are upset by the arrival of his current love, who has suddenly decided to leave her husband. Zinaida asserts the brave joys of free life and love. An extravagant sentimentalist, she expects an equal display of feeling from the bachelor. But Orlov, whose character expands the social conventionalism and human shortsightedness of the postmaster in *Ward Six*,

[23] *An Anonymous Story*, in *Seven Stories*, trans. Ronald Hingley (London: Oxford Univ. Press, 1974), pp. 160–61.

cannot stand the vagaries of enthusiasm. Zinaida weeps; he remonstrates, becomes exasperated. At last, pretending that he must take a business trip, he sneaks off to stay with his like-minded friends. Discovering his perfidy, Zinaida prepares to leave. But unwilling to return to her husband, she has no place to go. At this point, the narrator—as moved by her predicament as he is enraged at Orlov—feels that he must act. He reveals his true, highborn identity and decides to depart with and save the young woman.

Idealism is all that remains of revolutionism. A few days earlier, Orlov's father, the official whom the writer had wanted to destroy, had stopped by to collect some papers. The two men were alone in the apartment. "I spurred myself on, clenching my fists, searching my heart for some particle at least of my former loathing. . . . But it is hard to strike a match on crumbling stone. The sad old face . . . evoked in me only trivial, cheap, futile thoughts about the transiency of all things terrestrial and the proximity of death. . . . I had changed, I had become a new man. . . . But what kind of man was I now? What should I think about? What should I do? What was my goal in life?" (198–99). The questions belong to the traditional Russian rhetoric of dilemma that figures so often in Dostoevsky and Tolstoy. But those novelists have visions that dissolve the impasse their cherished characters confront. Seen coldly, the narrator's questioning appears trivial because the generalizing dimension contained in a Raskolnikov's or a Pierre's perplexity has been reduced to the measure of purely individual confusion. The anonymous man shares the talent for humanity common to Chekhov's protagonists. He feels deeply for others' pain. But no form—except the awkward imitation of art, perhaps—is available to give his talent some shape and direction. Like his questions, his decent impulses become incoherent and merely personal. In the intensity of his confusion, he reaches out for any word or act that may blunt his sense of transiency. Revolution being no longer a goal, he fixes on Zinaida.

The substitution of sentimental relations for religious, cultural, or ideological order—an inchoate version of a displacement that will recur often in modern fiction—dominates the last sections of the work. Despite his worsening health, the narrator persuades Zinaida to accompany him to Italy. Sympathy, not love or lust, is his program. He wants to give her what she is giving him: something to live for. His efforts to convert his companion to an idealistic activism in which he himself no longer believes are both brittle and compulsively high-pitched. The incompleteness and shilly-shallying that Hardy often depicts in his modern men render the anonymous writer's attentions not only inappropriate and abstract but also offensive. Zinaida is bewildered, then angry. In desperation, she lashes out at his "lack of intention," contrasting him bitterly with Orlov who "at least didn't tag any ideas to his betrayal" (220).

> I wanted to go on talking about mercy and forgiveness, but my voice suddenly rang false and I felt confused.
>
> "I feel such zest for life!" I said sincerely. "Oh, to live, to live! I want peace and quiet, I want warmth, I want this sea, I want you near me. Oh, if only I could instil this passionate craving for life in you! You spoke of love just now, but I would be content just to have you near me, to hear your voice and see the look on your face—" (220–21)

However sincere, sentiments are not what Zinaida wants or needs. She dismisses the narrator and retreats to her room, where she dies giving birth to Orlov's daughter. The narrator has been too taken up in his good works to be aware that she was pregnant.

Almost at once the function Zinaida was to perform is transferred to the child, Sonya. The narrator carries her back to Russia. "My craving for ordinary commonplace life became more and more powerful and insistent in course of time, but my sweeping fantasies stopped short at Sonya as if in her they had at last found just what I needed. I loved this little girl insanely. In her I saw the continuation of my own life. This was more than just an impression, it was something I felt, something I had faith in, almost . . ." (222). Reallizing that he has not long to live, that Sonya must be provided for, he turns to Orlov, who is, after all, her father. Ever rationally attentive, Orlov treats this potential obstacle to his well-ordered life as a problem to be solved expeditiously. He writes that he has found a lady who runs "a kind of kindergarten where she took quite small children. The woman was completely reliable, but before settling things with her it might be as well to talk to [the lawyer], as the formalities required." In the last lines, as the narrator reads Orlov's note, "Sonya sat on the table looking at me most attentively, without blinking, as if she knew that her fate was being decided" (226).

Like Ragin, the unknown protagonist and Orlov both evade responsibility. Orlov's comfortable egotism is clear; his behavior more obviously reprehensible. In his fluid adaptation of social utility to personal interest he recalls Farfrae in *The Mayor of Casterbridge*—though he has none of the Scotsman's decency and rectitude. Though the narrator's deficiencies weaken the effect of the condemnation, it is clear that for Chekhov the bachelor is a reduction to unpleasant absurdity of the Balzacian ideal: not a mixture of public actualities with private needs, but a purely social creature whose very dreams are external. However, Zinaida's would-be savior seems a more dangerous type. His dream of an "ordinary, commonplace life" neuters his judgments and behavior. His weak ideal of well-intentioned forcelessness carries Chekhov's hatred of violence into a flaccid meaninglessness. Artistically, the portrait of this impotent selfhood, of a man whose muse has been unsexed, is too neat; moral fiasco is more evident than the warmth of being it defeats. Yet the lack of subtlety highlights Chekhov's theme. Like his numerous kin, the narrator utters sincere judgments, sheds true tears. If the erosion of truth and meaning by general malady is always implicit, here it is overt. Chekhov's point is underscored by the baldness of the damage. Zinaida's silliness is transformed into genuine, if melodramatic, distress, not by Orlov's predictable deviousness, but by the anonymity that cannot come to her aid. And lest the judgment be missed, the orphan's fate that awaits Sonya provides a thematic exclamation point.

Neither moral-pointing nor the subtle delineation of flawed selfhood is pertinent to the short novels of peasant life. Bourgeois comforts and delusions are absent. The unemphatic clarity of misery explains why genteel culture averts its gaze. The dream of individuality is replaced by the merging of separateness into larger units or movements. Sentiment is no longer quite private, but often a generic emanation of time, place, and circumstance. Pathos is condensed into grains of data. Near the beginning of *In the Ravine*, written toward the close of Chekhov's life, preparations are under way for the marriage of the elder son of Tsybukin, a wealthy peasant trader.

In the village of Shikalova lived two dressmakers, sisters, who belonged to the Flagellant sect. The new clothes for the wedding had been ordered from them, and they frequently came for fittings and then stayed a long time drinking tea. For Varvara they made a brown dress trimmed with black lace and bugles, and for Aksinya a dress of light green with a yellow bodice and a train. When the dressmakers had finished their work Tsybukin paid them not in money but in goods from the shop, and they went away dejectedly, carrying parcels of candles and sardines, which they did not in the least need, and when they got out of the village and into the fields, they sat down on a knoll and wept.[24]

Tsybukin is a mean, miserly man, but the sisters' tears are called forth less by his dealings than by the nature of their lives. The two never reappear, yet Chekhov's vignette comprehends in its counterpoint of detail and feeling the tone of their existence. The subsequent action follows the logic of this correlation of dresses, candles, and sardines with the *lacrimae rerum*.

There is no raisonneur such as the doctor in *Jude the Obscure* or Zola's Doctor Pascal to explicate the social or cosmic causes of what is. The vitality of peasant truth that Misail asserts in *My Life* may exist, but it is not what we see in *Peasants*. The short novel begins:

A waiter at the Moscow hotel Slavonic Bazaar, Nikolai Chikildeyev, fell ill. His legs became numb and his gait so altered that as he was walking down the corridor one day he stumbled and fell with a tray of ham and green peas. He was forced to leave his job. Whatever money he and his wife had saved, he spent on treatment; there was nothing left to live on, it be-

[24] *In the Ravine*, in *Ward Six and Other Stories*, p. 346.

came tedious being without work, and he decided that, probably, he should go home to his village. It is easier to be at home when you are sick, and it is cheaper to live there. How truly is it said that the walls of home are a help. (366)

Chekhov's laconic factuality contradicts the mild hopefulness of the proverb. Elemental human need inhabits a world that lumps together illness, spilled ham and green peas, poverty, and home. The decency that lifts Gervaise above anonymous victimization in *L'Assommoir* has here no meaning. Since Nikolai is deadened by constant pain, his gentle wife Olga bears the burden of their new situation. She fears the crudeness of Nikolai's home, of his domineering, nearly senile mother; she fears the drink-besotted violence of her brother-in-law and the villagers who also drink and fight. When she arrives in the village, the beauty of nature seems to promise her peace. But as we have seen, nature is simply there, of no human avail. Wherever Olga turns, her timorous piety trembles before raucous fact.

> On the meadow below, young girls were doing a round dance and singing. A harmonica was playing. And on the far side of the river, too, a kiln was burning and girls were singing, and from a distance this singing sounded harmonious and delicate. In and around the tavern, the peasant men were raising an uproar; some were singing in drunken voices, each separately, and they swore so that Olga just shuddered, and kept saying: "Ah, holy saints! . . ." (374; Chekhov's ellipsis)

Village life is too loud; the details of home too brutally immediate. Olga's faith does little more than preserve her to endure continuing violations. Shortly before the story ends, Nikolai dies, a local healer having covered him with leeches.

Olga and their daughter are left to the flux of things.

> Oh, what a hard, what a long winter!
>
> They had had no grain of their own since Christmas. . . . Kiryak [the brother-in-law], who was now living at home, raised an uproar in the evenings, horrifying everyone, and suffered from headaches and shame and was pitiful to see in the mornings. The cattle shed resounded day and night with the lowing of the hungry cow. . . . And as if on purpose, the frosts continued to be bitter, the snowdrifts piled high, and the winter dragged on: at Annunciation, a real winter blizzard blew, and snow fell at Eastertime.
>
> But however that may be, winter did come to an end. . . . one warm day won out at last—and the rivulets flowed; the birds began to sing. The whole meadow and the bushes bordering the river wallowed in spring floods. . . . The spring sunset, fiery, with magnificent clouds, invented something unusual, new, and unbelievable every morning, the sort of thing one does not believe afterward on seeing the same colors and clouds in a picture.
>
> The cranes flew swiftly, swiftly, and called plaintively as though inviting company. Standing on the edge of the bluff, Olga gazed for a long time at the flood, at the sun, at the bright, seemingly rejuvenated church, and the tears flowed, and she was breathless with a passionate longing to go away, to follow her gaze, even to the edge of the world. And it had already been decided that she would go to Moscow again as a chambermaid, and that Kiryak would be sent with her to be placed as a porter or something. Oh, to get away quickly! (393)

Expressed through Olga's consciousness, winter harshness and spring beauty take on human dimension. But at the same time, the narrated consciousness is not altogether hers, and she is carried about, even flatteningly generalized, by the momentum of needs and seasons.

The sun invents a magnificence beyond Olga's scope, conveying something of the vitality and sublimity Chekhov's sophisticated protagonists crave. The splendor recalls Schiller's "naive," his concept of the concord between man and his surroundings that antecedes civil history. However, Schiller finally preferred the complex and taxing present. Chekhov agrees. The cruelty and lack of freedom that he hates are far more naked in Olga's and the dressmakers' experience than in the professor's or Misail's. The steppe, ravine, and village are set off from the environments of genteel life by a barrier built by moral culture and rational enlightenment. Inexplicable decay now weakens this bulwark; those who should repair and maintain it are somehow paralyzed. Fissures open, and through them rushes the random violence that claims Ragin. The doctor's fate is tragic, and Chekhov holds no one accountable for tragedy. Yet Ragin is still typical of the many protagonists who, instead of acting to shore up their blessings, luxuriate in dreams and dismiss responsibilities with spiteful irritation.

The contrast between peasant life and bourgeois well-being suggests something of Chekhov's fundamental faith. Set against the belittling conditions of peasant existence, not only the circumstances but also the dreams of the cultured characters represent an achievement. In themselves, and particularly in the general diminishment of the Twilight, these touches of civilization are "better-than-nothing." Chekhov's view seems close to that of the deacon in *The Duel* when he muses on the quarrel between the utilitarian scientist von Koren and the self-styled "superfluous" gentleman Layevsky.

"A splendid mind!" he thought of von Koren as he stretched out on the straw. "A fine mind, God grant him health. Only there's something cruel about him. . . ."

Why did he and Layevsky hate each other? Why were they going to fight a duel? If they had known the poverty he had known since childhood, if they had grown up among ignorant, hard-hearted, grasping, coarse and ill-mannered people who grudged you a crust of bread, spat on the floor and belched at dinner and at prayers; if, from childhood, they had not been spoiled by pleasant surroundings and a select group of friends, how they would have reached out to each other, how readily forgiven one another's shortcomings, valuing what was good in the other. Why, there were so few even outwardly decent people in the world! True, Layevsky was flighty, dissipated, and strange, but, after all, he didn't steal, didn't spit loudly on the floor, or abuse his wife, saying: "You'll eat till you burst, but you won't work"; nor would he beat a child with harness reins, nor feed his servants putrid salt meat—surely this was reason enough to treat him with forbearance? Besides, he was the first to suffer from his failings, like a sick man from his sores. Instead of being induced, either by boredom or some sort of misunderstanding, to look for degeneracy, extinction, heredity, and other such incomprehensible things in one another, would it not be better to stoop a little lower and direct their hatred and anger to where whole streets were groaning with gross ignorance, greed, impurity, cursing and screaming? . . . (148–49; Chekhov's ellipses)

The deacon understandably overstates the power of outward decency. What is freshly valuable to him is stale to Layevsky, who has indeed been spoiled by an affluent mother. Though he shares the deacon's esteem for material progress, Chekhov surely sees further. Escape from the world the deacon describes is a blessing, but no solution. Like his many characters who possess physical comforts, Chekhov craves something more.

The desire for this something pervades the artificing lives Chekhov narrates, endowing dreams and failures with roots in authentic need. The characters try to invent equivalents to goals now lost. The author's equivalent is his art, save for which he too is in the dark. As in the portraits of Olga and the deacon, he treats religious feeling with deep sympathy. But he himself does not believe. He agrees that civilized existence is far better than the rawness of peasant life. But though he is happy with the progress of science and technology, he presents the contemporary condition of humanity as static, sometimes as cruelly stricken. He describes nature as often beautiful. But he portrays its beauty as unreachable. The lovingly impartial artistic parenthood he does believe in is dearer and more touching to us than the ways in which Hardy and Zola approach their creations. It determines the intimacy and intensity of expectation that preside over each new story; it explains the hopeful sense that surrounds the characters, as if they might be able to contradict their appearance of dimmed promise. Yet we remember the art more often than we do its characters, few of whom even approach the wholeness that Chekhov, like Hardy and Zola, desires to see reborn. The ethos of such wholeness, the synthesis of personality and cultural purpose that I have associated with the Balzacian model, does not survive the Twilight. Hardy, Zola, and Chekhov would find much to admire in the beliefs and techniques that enter into modern novelistic character, but they would deplore the passing of the moral imperatives they equated with their craft.

INDEX

Index

This first comparative study of Hardy, Zola, and Chekhov is an essay in practical criticism. The author compares the idea of character in these late-nineteenth-century writers to the Balzacian model that preceded them and then to modernist notions that have followed. He questions the validity of recent semiotic, structuralist, Marxist, and psychophilosophical criticism by his emphasis on the importance of the historical configurations that shaped Hardy's Wessex, Zola's Second Empire, and Chekhov's Russia.

The Balzacian idea of character as a synthesis of private needs and public circumstances was not adequate as a framework for the Twilight authors. They attempted to form a new type of character to challenge, or at least to survive, new situations. Neither Hardy, Chekhov, nor Zola grants that character can develop out of itself, absolved of the need for cultural definition, but they do shift their focus inward. Major components of this effort include: a renewed interest in cosmic rather than social determinants of human life; an attempt to substitute archetypal patterns for the goals of present culture; an emphasis on nature instead of social nurture. For these reasons, these authors are considered precursors of modern fiction.

VARIETIES OF DRAMATIC STRUCTURE

A Study of Theory and Practice

Edward Murray

UNIVERSITY
PRESS OF
AMERICA

Lanham • New York • London

Copyright © 1990 by
University Press of America®, Inc.
4720 Boston Way
Lanham, Maryland 20706

3 Henrietta Street
London WC2E 8LU England

Library of Congress Cataloging-in-Publication Data

Murray, Edward.
Varieties of dramatic structure : a study of theory and practice /
Edward Murray.
p.   cm.
Includes bibliographical references (p.   ).
1. Drama—History and criticism.   2. Drama—Technique.
3. Tragedy—History and criticism.   4. Tragedy—Technique.
I. Title.
PN1661.M85   1990   809.2—dc20   90–12170 CIP

ISBN 0–8191–7785–7 (alk. paper)
ISBN 0–8191–7786–5 (pbk. : alk. paper)

 The paper used in this publication meets the minimum requirements of
American National Standard for Information Sciences—Permanence
of Paper for Printed Library Materials, ANSI Z39.48–1984.

For My Son, Michael

"Form is the expression of necessity,"
I say in a critical piece.
    Best definition: Content presents
the task; form, the solution.

                        --Friedrich Hebbel,
                        <u>Journals</u>
                        (trans. Eric Bentley)

Contents

Contents

Contents

Prologue

Love and hate, ecstasy and sorrow, triumph and defeat, free will and determinism--most of us would prefer to talk about these subjects as they are expressed in great drama, instead of concerning ourselves with bipartite structure or Freytag's pyramid. Structural analysis sounds dry, architectonical . . . And yet, how can we claim to understand <u>Oedipus</u> or <u>Hamlet</u> if we do not attend to the shape of these masterpieces? Structure is basic. Without it, the characters in a play are prevented from going anywhere; even in "anti-plays" there exists a poetic or pictorial framework of meanings. There is no way out of it. Structure, character, and theme are--except for purposes of analysis--inseparable.

But the moment we turn to a consideration of structure, we discover that some theorist has arrived before us and has erected a theory between us and the play. Now, the trouble with theories of dramatic structure--and there have been many of them from Aristotle down to the present--is that the theorist generally attempts to convince us that there is one ideal or characteristic or inclusive structure in all drama; or at the very least that all plays of a certain period or by a certain dramatist are identical in structure. Of course most working critics realize--however dimly--that generalizations about <u>the</u> structure of Greek tragedy, say, or <u>the</u> structure of Shakespearean tragedy are largely nonsense.

Nevertheless such generalizations about dramatic structure persist. Why? Because they spare us the necessity of looking at the plays with our own eyes and, on the basis of the evidence, thinking for ourselves; because they make life easier for busy historians and over-worked teachers; because they retain, even in our iconoclastic age, a prestige value ("As Hegel says. . ."); because--in short--they are con-venient, transmittable, authoritative. Unfor-tunately, they are also too often misleading, ir-relevant, and downright wrong.

This study does not pretend to be a comprehen-sive survey of dramatic structures. Nor does it advance still another theory of dramatic form. My scope has been considerably more modest. The focus has been restricted to the major tragedies of Aeschylus, Sophocles, and Euripides, five tragedies by Shakespeare, one neo-classical tragedy by Dryden, and several modern plays by Ib-sen, Chekhov, Brecht, and Ionesco. It is my in-tention to distinguish the structure of a play by one dramatist from that of another; to dis-criminate, in some cases, among the various kinds of structure in the plays of a single dramatist; and to analyze, wherever I think it instructive, the different kinds of structure in a single play by a great dramatist.

By "structure," I mean--quite simply--the ar-rangement and interrelation of all the parts of a whole. It is the overall plan or form or shape or outline of a play. It is the division of the ac-tion in terms of both the sequence of scenes and acts and the handling of conflict, movement, and theme. But what structure is can best be under-stood, not in the abstract, not through generalizations, but by looking at specific ex-amples from the work of renowned playwrights.

If, in the pages that follow, theories of dramatic structure frequently come off badly when exposed to the actual practice of dramatists--well, so much the worse for the theories. I would prefer to be accused of irreverence towards a theory than to be charged with presumption in respect to a play by a master dramatist. It is my hope that the reader will return to the plays with a greater appreciation for the different formal orderings in their complex perceptions of life.

STRUCTURE IN GREEK TRAGEDY

1. Aristotle on Structure

One can hardly speak of Greek tragedy without reference to the _Poetics_. When authors of books on dramatic technique discuss the structure of ancient tragedy, they invariably use _Oedipus_ as their model. All the "typical" features of classical playwriting are supposedly present in Sophocles's masterpiece, which Aristotle judged to come closest to what he conceived to be the ideal tragedy. Since there are many people who cannot see Greek tragedy except through Aristotle's eyes, some summary remarks on what he had to say about dramatic structure are in order before turning to the plays themselves.

According to Aristotle, the plot--or "the structure of the incidents"--is the most important part of a play (the other parts being character, diction, thought, spectacle, and song). Aristotle's reason for elevating structure above the other elements lies in his approach to tragedy. "For tragedy is an imitation, not of men, but of an action and of life, and life consists in action, and its end is a mode of action, not a quality," he says. "Now character determines men's qualities, but it is by their actions that they are happy or the reverse. Dramatic action, therefore, is not with a view to the representation of character: character comes in as subsidiary to the actions. Hence the incidents and the plot are the end of a tragedy; and the end is the chief thing of all."[1]

VARIETIES OF DRAMATIC STRUCTURE

After defining plot as "the arrangement of the incidents" and "the structure of the incidents"-- why does Aristotle go on to distinguish the incidents from the plot? The reason is that for Aristotle plot is also "the first principle, and, as it were, the soul of a tragedy."[2] Through his mastery of form, the playwright aims for a "proper purgation" or "catharsis" (depending on the translator)[3] of pity and fear. It is not clear what, exactly, Aristotle intends here. For some scholars "proper purgation" or "catharsis" takes place emotionally for the audience; for others it occurs on stage and is worked out thematically between the tragic hero and the subordinate characters. Within each main group of interpreters there are many subgroups, and the controversy goes on.

The proper dramatic structure consists, in Aristotle's opinion, of a single as opposed to a double action and is unified into a whole which has a beginning, a middle, and an end. Emphasis is placed on the logical development of the action-- the latter being the one "unity" the philosopher requires. About unity of place Aristotle says nothing; in respect to unity of time he simply observes that "tragedy endeavors, as far as possible, to confine itself to a single revolution of the sun, or but slightly to exceed this limit."[4] The unity of the hero is rejected outright. Dramatic action is governed by the law of probability or necessity; hence Aristotle also rejects episodic structure, or those plots "in which the episodes or acts succeed one another without probable or necessary sequence."[5] Unless the structure is ample enough to allow for a change from bad fortune to good, or from good fortune to bad, the plot will fail for want of "proper magnitude."[6]

Aristotle lays particular stress on two features of what he considers good plot structure-- namely, "reversal" and "recognition." By "reversal" the philosopher intends "a change by which the action veers round to its opposite"; by "recognition" he means "a change from ignorance to knowledge, producing love or hate between the persons destined by the poet for good or bad fortune." Plots are most satisfactory when "recognition is

2

coincident with a reversal of the situation"--as in, according to Aristotle, Oedipus.[7] Although simple plots provide for a change of fortune, they unfortunately lack reversal and recognition; however, complex plots include one or both. Aristotle also has ideas about how dramatic structures should end. "The change of fortune should not be from bad to good," he declares, "but, reversely, from good to bad." The Oresteia appeared in 458 B.C.; all the same, Aristotle--in 330 B.C. or thereabouts--adds that the practice of the stage supports what he says.[8] Now, even if some lost plays had an influence on Aristotle's judgment, his ignoring the Oresteia seems odd.

Finally, Aristotle says that every tragedy can be divided into two parts. The first part is called the "complication"--or that part which extends from the beginning of the action to the part which marks the turning point to good or bad fortune. The second part is called the "unraveling"--or that part which extends from the beginning of the change to the end.[9]

Few books have enjoyed so much authority, or have been quoted so piously, as the Poetics. Too often we have been told that Aristotle's method was an inductive one. But if we look at the plays instead of the Poetics, we find that the structure of Greek tragedy tends to refute much of Aristotle's dicta about play construction. Even some modern Aristotelians have recognized this fact. "Typically, only after the generalizations does [Aristotle] cite specific works; and when they are cited they are almost always used as examples that confirm the theory," observes O. B. Hardison, Jr. "If the inductive method is to begin with particulars and to move backward to ever larger generalizations, Aristotle's method must be labeled deductive."[10]

The chief aim of this chapter is to establish to what extent the structure of Oedipus is typical of Greek tragedy, and to what extent it remains atypical. After examining Oedipus in the light of Aristotle's analysis, together with other critical and theoretical approaches, we will look at the remainder of the Sophoclean canon before moving on to a consideration of form in Aeschylus and Euripides. But before doing so, a few words are in order on one of the important conventions of Greek tragedy.

2. The External Structure of Greek Tragedy

A distinction is made in the Poetics between the elements of the whole and the "quantitative parts," or the separate sections into which the elements are divided. (Many scholars regard section twelve of the Poetics, where the quantitative parts are discussed, as an interpolation.) Let us substitute "internal structure" for the elements of the whole and "external structure" for the quantitative parts.

Viewed externally, the structure of a Greek play begins with a prologue. This scene can involve either a single character (man or god) or a dialogue. Normally, the function of the prologue is exposition and foreshadowing. In some of Euripides's plays, the entire plot is summarized in the prologue.

Next comes the parodos. Here the chorus makes its initial appearance. In some plays the chorus is closely involved in the action; in other plays it simply offers inter-scene commentary, which may or may not have thematic relevance. At its best, the chorus serves many purposes: it reminds the audience of past events; it prepares the audience for future events; it bridges time lapses; it gives voice to what Aristotle calls the "thought" element in the play;[11] it provides a sounding board for the tragic hero; and it can even take an active part in the conflict, or the progress of events. Donald Clive Stuart estimates that in Aeschylus the average choral part constitutes about two-fifths of the total play, whereas in Sophocles and Euripides the average drops to about one-fifth of the total.[12] After the parodos is over, the chorus generally remains in view for the entire play.

Following the parodos is the first episode. Since most Greek plays are about the length of a modern one-act play, the episode roughly corresponds to what we today would call a scene, a logical or thematic unit in the development of the action. In general, most episodes are limited to alternations of two characters confronting each other, one of the characters sometimes being the leader of the chorus. After each chorus comes a choral ode, or stasimon. Occasionally, a commus (a lyric passage sung by one or more actors together with the chorus) is substituted for the stasimon. Although there are four episodes in Aeschylus's The Persians and seven in Sophocles's Oedipus at Coloneus, the average Greek tragedy contains five episodes and as many choral odes. The last episode --during which the chorus delivers its final commentary before departing--is the exodus.

Admittedly, the mold is a rigid one. Yet the wonder of Greek drama is that Aeschylus, Sophocles, and Euripides could manage the internal structure of their plays in such a way as to express their individual and varied projections of the tragic with a splendor that has not faded since the fifth century B.C. Let us turn now to a study of their achievements.

3. Sophocles and the Structure of Oedipus

Externally, Oedipus contains--in addition to the standard prologue, parodos, and exodus--four episodes and four choral odes. Internally, the play is distinguished by extreme concentration, economy, and power.

The action starts late, or close in time to the ending. When Oedipus begins his search for the sinner who has brought a plague upon Thebes, Aristotle's "complication" is set in motion. The ability of Sophocles to fuse exposition with the forward movement of the plot--his weaving together of past and present--represents an unsurpassable feat of construction. In the course of just a few hours Oedipus's eyes are opened to his terrible fate. Progression is relentless, as one character after the other confronts the hero, and the moment of truth looms nearer and nearer. During the last three episodes the tempo accelerates, each succeeding scene being shorter than the previous one. Since it is twice as long as the fourth episode, the exodus balances in length the prologue and parodos. Hence formal symmetry in Oedipus remains high.

The turning point in the action occurs about sixty lines short of the play's middle. As Jocasta gives an account of Laius's death, Oedipus reveals the first signs of self-doubt. Perhaps he himself is the sinner for whom he is searching. His speech appears two-thirds of the way through the second episode. All the rest of the play constitutes the "unraveling."

According to Aristotle, the reader will recall, the "best form of recognition is coincident with a reversal of the situation, as in the Oedipus." The reader will also recall that Aristotle defines the reversal as "a change by which the action veers round to its opposite." Aristotle concludes: "Thus in the Oedipus, the messenger comes to cheer Oedipus and free him from his alarms about his mother, but by revealing who he is, he produces the opposite effect."[13] Actually, the messenger comes to report the death of Polybus. It is only after Oedipus expresses fear of incest with Merope that the messenger, seeking to cheer the hero, informs him that the couple in Corinth were not really his parents. Far from saving Oedipus, the revelation carries him closer to ruin.

Aristotle is correct in describing this action as the reversal; however, it can scarcely be considered as occurring simultaneously with the recognition. The reversal begins in the third episode. It is not until the last lines of the fourth episode, when the herdsman reveals that Oedipus is already guilty of parricide and incest, that the hero's recognition occurs. After experiencing his moment of truth, Oedipus rushes into the palace. It can be seen that the larger framework of action

6

also involves a reversal, in that Oedipus starts out to find the sinner who is defiling the land-- and finds that sinner to be himself.

When Oedipus next appears in the exodus he is blind, having gouged out his eyeballs. Although it was Apollo who brought woe upon him, he says, he himself shares responsibility for what occurred. This idea is expressed several times in the last episode. Having brought the audience up to a high emotional peak, Sophocles seems intent on easing it down so that the thought embodied in the previous action will not be lost in the violent rush of events. As usual, the chorus ends the play by reminding the audience that no one can be adjudged to be happy until he is safely dead and beyond the possibility of pain.

Oedipus is not without its improbabilities. For example, it seems incredible that Jocasta--who has been married to Oedipus long enough to give birth to four children--had never, previous to the second episode of the play, discussed the cir- cumstances surrounding the murder of her first hus- band. "Realism" (in the narrow sense), however, was hardly Sophocles's aim in writing the play; for he had his eye on a larger truth, which the tight- ness of his structure underscores. As H.D.F. Kitto observes: "The admired logic of Sophocles's plots is not merely a dramatic merit--it is the reflec- tion of the logic that he sees in the universe; this is the way in which _dike_ works."[14] In short, form equals content.

The Cambridge School of Classical Anthro- pologists have tried to improve on Aristotle's method of analysis. Following Nietzsche's lead in _The Birth of Tragedy_, Gilbert Murray in _The Classi- cal Tradition in Poetry_ chides Aristotle for treat- ing Greek tragedy simply as an artistic performance and overlooking the fact that drama had a ritual origin. As Murray sees it, the plot structure of a play like _Oedipus_ is a reworking of the old ritual purification pattern, which still endures as a sub- structure of the action. The essential tragic idea, according to this view, is a disguised enact- ment of the death of the Year-Spirit. Structurally, the external and internal features of Greek tragedy--choral odes, recognition scenes, and the like--correspond to the primal dance involving the death and resurrection of Dionysus. In his influential book The Idea of a Theater, Francis Fergusson applies the speculations of the Cambridge school to Oedipus (as well as to a restricted number of other plays), and argues that the "real meaning" of the tragedy resides in its structure. Borrowing terms from Kenneth Burke, Fergusson labels the stages in the action as Purpose, Passion, and Perception. Thus Oedipus commences with the title character's "reasoned purpose" of locating the murderer of Laius. Encountering great difficulty in his search, Oedipus suffers terribly, and this suffering is his passion. Finally a "new perception" emerges, thus redefining the purpose and helping to give shape to the structure of action as a whole. When Oedipus sees that he is the guilty one, the play comes to a close. For Fergusson the hero of Sophocles's great play is a "scapegoat," a "dismembered king or god-figure."[15]

Although Fergusson admits: "Experts in classical anthropology, like experts in other fields, dispute innumerable questions of fact and interpretation which the layman can only pass over in respectful silence,"[16] he still advances his "ritual" interpretation of Oedipus as if the grounds for doing so were based on fact, or at the very least on a consensus among classical scholars. But any analysis of structure which depends for its authority on agreement about the birth of tragedy has to be based on theory and not on fact. Gerald F. Else makes a similar point in The Origin and Early Form of Greek Tragedy, and he goes on to argue: "Gilbert Murray never demonstrated either the existence of . . . a ritual sequence in preclassical Greece or its survival in the extant tragedies. This was shown in detail by Pickard-Cambridge [in Dithyramb, Tragedy, and Comedy back in 1927], and the theory is not now held, at least in its strict form, by any leading scholar." Else adds that apparently Fergusson was unaware of the best classical scholarship, and this was indeed unfortunate. "The notion that Sophocles's audience approached his tragedies in a spirit of 'ritual expectancy,'" Else concludes, "does serious damage to our interpretation of the plays...."[17]

Like Fergusson, many critics assume that their theories are based on more or less hard evidence concerning the ritual origin of Greek tragedy. But since, as Richard Schechner rightly points out, there "is no primal ritual extant; the connections between surviving rituals and the dithyramb are doubtful; and the connections between the dithyramb and Greek theater are unproven,"[18] it would seem prudent not to insist too much on the ritual basis underlying the structure of <u>Oedipus</u>, or of any other play. Herbert Muller makes the sensible observation that at the end of Sophocles's masterpiece there is no reference to or suggestion of a happier state in Thebes resulting from the alleged ritual purification; instead, the emphasis seems to be on the suffering hero and his daughters. And those in the audience watching Sophocles's play would have known that all Thebes had to look forward to was more suffering as Oedipus's sons fought for power.[19]

Even if it could be shown that Greek tragedy did evolve from a primal ritual, or perhaps from a later stage of religious development, one would be guilty of the genetic fallacy by declaring that the structure of a play like <u>Oedipus</u> is an imitation of a primitive religious action. Drama would seem to come into its own at the point where it dissociates itself from worship (as in the medieval period, where the link between liturgy and drama seems more than a matter of guesswork). Clearly, then, Fergusson's explanation of dramatic structure rests on a shaky foundation. In addition, the Burkean triad has a tendency to become, in Fergusson's hands, a Procrustean bed upon which play structures are measured. Like Aristotle, Fergusson uses <u>Oedipus</u> as a touchstone--and with predictable results. Hence any play whose structure fails to measure up is not, according to Fergusson, a "true tragedy."

4. Electra and Four Other Plays by Sophocles

The only other extant play by Sophocles which resembles Oedipus in tautness of plot construction is Electra; however, the two plays are by no means identical. In Oedipus the past becomes the present, as exposition and progression combine to reveal how the tragic hero has not been able to escape his fate. We are inclined to regard this extreme retrospective method as characteristic of Greek tragedy; but, in fact, it is not even characteristic of Sophoclean tragedy.

In Electra, Sophocles treats the legendary material that Aeschylus has left to us in the Choephori, the second play of his great trilogy, the Oresteia, which will be discussed in due course. Once the preliminary background information is given in Electra--the murder of Agamemnon after his victorious return to Argos from Troy by his wife Clytemnestra and her lover Aegisthus, and their fear that Orestes, son of Agamemnon and Clytemnestra, will return to punish them for what they have done--then the action moves steadily forward through the present to the ending. The focus is on Electra, who has long awaited the appearance of her brother Orestes. Tension builds towards the moment when Orestes avenges the murder of Agamemnon by killing Clytemnestra and Aegisthus. Instead of being retrospective in technique, Electra is largely "prospective."

Although both plays center on a single character, Oedipus ends in bad fortune for the hero, whereas Electra concludes with good fortune, the chorus rejoicing with the heroine in the destruction of the two murderers. Both plays are tightly joined and unified. Oedipus, however, is much more complicated structurally and thematically. Electra has a complex plot only in the Aristotelian sense, including in its action both reversal and recognition. Indeed, Electra would have served Aristotle better than Oedipus as an example of a play in which reversal and recognition occur coincidentally. I refer, of course, to the scene where

Electra--believing at one point Orestes to be dead--discovers that she is actually talking to him.

Sophocles's remaining extant plays resemble the form of Oedipus even less closely than Electra. Three of the plays--Ajax, Antigone, and The Trachiniae--have a split or diptych structure.

In the Ajax, which takes place at a time between the events described by Homer in the Iliad and the Odyssey, Sophocles contrasts the heroic but arrogant character of Ajax with the shy but noble and generous character of Odysseus. After the death of Achilles, the Greek leaders had selected Odysseus as his successor. Feeling that he should have been chosen, Ajax wanted to kill those who had decided against him. Because of his hubris, the goddess Athena visited upon Ajax the affliction of madness; consequently, he killed some sheep attached to the army, thinking in his deranged state that they were his enemies. So much for exposition. In the course of the play, the sane again, but now further humiliated, Ajax commits suicide. Structurally, Ajax breaks into two parts, inasmuch as the title character dies two-thirds of the way through the play. The remaining portion--focusing as it does on a prolonged debate over the propriety of giving Ajax a ritual interment, and on Odysseus's magnanimity towards the corpse--seems anticlimactic.

Antigone will be analyzed in the next section.

The Trachiniae is a study of a jealous wife, Deianeira, who learns that her husband, the middle-aged Heracles, is having an affair with a younger woman. Distraught, the heroine kills herself. Afterwards Heracles gives up his mistress, accepts the fact that he is aging, and marries the young woman off to his son. Clearly, the focus of attention shifts from one character to another. Deianeira is central in the design for the first 812 lines; Heracles, who first appears at line 970, assumes the commanding position until the play ends on line 1278. Although Heracles is presumably the tragic hero, his sufferings appear rather insignificant compared to the fate of Deianeira. Most critics have concluded that The Trachiniae remains Sophocles least impressive achievement.

Philoctetes and Oedipus at Coloneus are more highly regarded than Ajax or The Trachiniae. Neither of the later plays has much in common, however, with Oedipus, the alleged paradigm of Greek tragic structure. As Walter Kaufmann points out, Philoctetes--although it does not divide into two parts--raises the problem whether Neoptolemus is not the hero instead of Philoctetes.[20] Nor would Muller seem amiss in his assertion that Philoctetes is, on the whole, as non-Sophoclean as it is non-Aristotelian.[21]

After being attacked by a poisonous snake, Philoctetes is abandoned on a lonely island by the Greeks. But now, because they need his bow in their war against the Trojans, the Greeks have sent Neoptolemus to entice Philoctetes back to their ship. Once he has gotten the bow, however, Neoptolemus reveals the truth to Philoctetes, who is thrown into a frenzy of impotent anger. Pitying him, Neoptolemus returns the bow. Suddenly Heracles (a character in this play, too) appears and commands Philoctetes to forgive the Greeks and rejoin them in their assault on Troy. Structurally, it is never clear who is at the center of Philoctetes. There is no final tragic reversal in which the hero--whoever he may be--falls to his doom. Indeed, as John Gassner has suggested, Philoctetes sometimes seems more like a pastoral than a tragedy.[22]

In Oedipus at Coloneus, probably Sophocles final play, the great dramatist focuses on the last hours before the death of the title character. Some twenty years have gone by since Oedipus. When the play begins an Argive force is poised to attack Thebes; however, an oracle has declared that Thebes can avert ruin if Oedipus is allowed out of exile to be buried in Theban ground. But Oedipus does not plan to get involved in the political intrigues of Thebes. Another oracle persuades him to head for Athens now, and along the way--against a background of lightning and thunder--he is mysteriously changed from a blind and groping old man into an erect and sure one who can lead his companions to his final resting place.

Although some critics see in <u>Oedipus at Coloneus</u> evidence of Sophocles's best work, the play is generally regarded as static and episodic in construction. There is no way <u>Oedipus at Coloneus</u> can be made to conform with Aristotle's view of ideal dramatic structure, or with what many scholars routinely describe as <u>the</u> form of Sophoclean drama.

5. Antigone

With the exception of <u>Oedipus</u>, <u>Antigone</u> remains Sophocles's most highly regarded play, in spite of the fact that its structure has prompted a good deal of critical discussion.

<u>Antigone</u> is divided into five episodes. At the end of the fourth episode--line 942--Antigone is led away to her death and the play continues for another nearly 400 lines; in other words, the title character disappears after only two-thirds of the action has taken place. It could be argued that the focus shifts from Antigone to Creon even earlier; that is, by the end of the second episode, or roughly half-way through the play.

If we analyze <u>Antigone</u> in the light of Aristotle's formula for tragic structure, the results are far from gratifying. The complication begins with Antigone's decision to bury her brother, Polyneices, in defiance of Creon's edict. At the conclusion of episode four, Antigone is taken away by guards to be punished. This is the turning point in the action because it leads to bad fortune for both Antigone and Creon.

Now it is here--in the last third of the play--that the structural problem begins for many critics, Aristotelian and otherwise. During the unraveling Sophocles not only centers attention on Creon, but he also makes him the subject of the reversal and recognition. Before exiting from the play Antigone says that if her judges are at fault, may they suffer the same bad fortune as she is about to experience at their hands. These words become a prophecy of doom for Creon.

In the exodus Creon learns that his stiff-necked course of behavior has resulted in the suicide of his son Haemon, who loved Antigone, and of his wife Eurydice, who was heartbroken over the death of her son. Creon's tragedy is summed up by the chorus when it says that wisdom remains the better part of happiness, and that the gods must be revered. Fate pounds wisdom into the proud hearts of old men.

Gustav Freytag--whose method of structural analysis in <u>Technique of the Drama</u> is basically Aristotelian--attempts to meet the challenge of the play by simply asserting that Antigone is continued in the person of Tiresias and the messenger in the final third of the action.[23] But how many readers would agree that either of these characters are adequate substitutes for the charming young woman named in the title?

Critics who favor the Cambridge ritual approach to structure have also had their problems with <u>Antigone</u>. For example, Robert Hogan and Sven Eric Molin come up with the ingenious assertion that "the structure of <u>Antigone</u> shows its complexity, for the character of the hero is actually split in two. Antigone is the sacrificial victim, but Creon gets the recognition . . . Although it seems on the level of plot that Antigone and Creon are antagonists, more deeply they are alike in their pride that knows no moderation and recognizes no counsel. While the play is thus somewhat unusual in having a dual hero, its structure is typical of tragedy . . . [T]he parts are, of course, always the same, in the same place and in the same proportion."[24] Observe that Antigone's character must be made as blameworthy as Creon's in order to force the play into conformity with the ritual pattern. (Similarly, Aristotelian critics have been diligent in their search for Antigone's "tragic flaw.") If plays were packaged like sausages, then perhaps all tragedies would be "always the same."

Hegel believed that dramatic structure could best be understood in terms of force, opposing force, and resolution (thesis, antithesis, and synthesis). In Antigone he saw the supreme example of tragedy: a collision between two moral powers. Specifically, Hegel argued that the structure of Antigone is polarized into, on the one hand, family love, the sacred, the domain of spiritual life, feeling--in short, the law of the gods; and, on the other, the law of the State. Both sides represented by Antigone and Creon have, according to Hegel, an equal validity. Tragedy enters only when one or both sides claim all of an individual's allegiance.[25]

Although some critics have found Hegel's theory of dramatic structure persuasive, the Hegelian approach simply fails to work when applied to Antigone. Creon's edict is not legitimate--the structure of the play proves this, for the gods punish Creon and vindicate Antigone. It is not that Creon's claims are merely one-sided: they are intrinsically wrong. In forbidding the burial of Polyneices, Creon does not speak for the State--he speaks for himself. When Creon tells Haemon that the city belongs to the ruler, the son replies that his father would make an excellent potentate of an island with only one inhabitant on it.

Kaufmann follows Hegel in suggesting that there are two separate kinds of tragic structure: one kind involving a single hero, the other kind representing a collision.[26] But do we really have two mutually exclusive forms here? A play with a single hero (such as Oedipus) can also include a collision (and if Oedipus's encounter with fate isn't a collision, I think we will be hard pressed to say what else it is). If a playwright followed Hegel's thinking, he might produce a thrilling tragedy. But how many existing tragedies actually fall into the Hegelian pattern?

It would be silly to dismiss <u>Antigone</u> just because a single hero does not dominate the action. There is room in drama for various kinds of structure. If a single hero is a criterion of excellence, then what is to be said about the <u>Oresteia</u>? Nor can it be affirmed that <u>Antigone</u> lacks unity of action. Although there is a break in the structure, the two parts are interdependent; neither part is complete without the other. There is also unity of theme: the thought expressed by the chorus at the conclusion of the play pervades the entire action. No doubt about it, <u>Antigone</u> remains a coherent whole.

This is not to say, however, that <u>Antigone</u> is perfect. Kitto believes that the old criticism was naive in assuming that the piece was really about the title character. <u>Antigone</u> has two central characters, Kitto argues, but the more important one is Creon. "It is simply," says Kitto, "a matter of looking at the dramatic facts."[27] But if we <u>do</u> look at the dramatic facts, we find that the second part of <u>Antigone</u> is less satisfactory than the first part, simply because for most people Creon is a less interesting creation than the heroine. It could also be said that Haemon's and Eurydice's suicides are insufficiently foreshadowed, and their deaths, following immediately one upon the other, result in <u>too</u> <u>much</u> tragedy.

Nevertheless <u>Antigone</u> is a great play. Structure--for all its importance--is not the sole factor in evaluating drama. If it were, then the well-made play might represent the supreme achievement of Western theater. However one chooses to judge the form of <u>Antigone</u>, the fact remains that the play succeeds in spite of whatever shortcomings one might find in its construction. In <u>Oedipus</u> Sophocles dazzles us through his mastery of structure; in <u>Antigone</u> he thrills us through the image he creates of an unforgettable character. And that character--together with the theme of the play--has proved sufficient to account for the durability of <u>Antigone</u> over the centuries.

6. Bipartite Structure in Greek Tragedy

Kitto--who insists that Sophocles's use of the diptych form represents a stage in the development of the playwright's tragic vision--is prone to explain away every problem related to bipartite structure, whereas Waldock contends that the diptych form always results in a loss of power and unity because of the division in focus. Kitto sees bipartite structure in terms of a particular transient vision of the tragic by Sophocles, whereas Waldock maintains that the whole of Greek drama shows an inclination towards this form of patterning.[28]

By Waldock's reckoning, at least four of Sophocles's lost plays--<u>Assembly of Achaeans</u>, <u>Epigoni</u>, <u>Odysseus Acanthoplex</u>, and <u>Tereus</u>--take the diptych form, in addition to <u>Ajax</u>, <u>Antigone</u>, and <u>The Trachiniae</u>. At least four of Euripides's extant plays--<u>Hippolytus</u>, <u>Hecuba</u>, <u>Andromache</u>, and <u>Heracles</u>--are, according to Waldock, diptychs. (Indeed, <u>Heracles</u> may even be considered a triptych.) Of the lost plays by Euripides, <u>Chrysippus</u> and <u>Phaethon</u> both seem to Waldock bipartite in structure.

Sophocles wrote between 124 and 130 plays; Euripides is credited with ninety-two. Thirteen plays out of a total of roughly 222 plays does not seem to be a very high proportion of diptychs. Furthermore, it could be argued that at least one of the plays--namely, <u>Hippolytus</u>--is not split in structure. In my judgment, bipartite form is not necessarily or inherently defective; for example, if Creon was as great a character as Antigone few critics would find fault with Sophocles's play, since it has both unity of action and unity of theme.

As Waldock sees it, Greek tragedy was prone to the diptych form because of its single line of action--a line of action which begins on a high level of tension and close in time to the conclusion. The single line of development precluded the introduction of complicating factors by way of a

17

subplot. By starting with a bang, the Greek playwright was faced with the possibility of using up his material too rapidly. Consequently, the dramatist felt obliged to replace the initial thrust of the play--which threatened to fall considerably short of the ending--with a second thrust about midway in the action.

But did Greek tragedy really have a bias towards the diptych form? Or did that form simply result from an individual playwright's handling, or mishandling, of his material in a specific play? Ibsen used a form similar to the one developed by the Greeks. His plays also begin close to the ending, and also move along a single line of action. Yet none of his plays could be described as bipartite in construction. If we begin counting with Ibsen's A Doll's House, the first important play in the distinctly "Ibsenian" form, we find that the dramatist wrote only eleven works for the stage between 1879 and 1899. Perhaps the law of averages was at work against Sophocles and Euripides, both of whom wrote about ten times as many plays as Ibsen did using a similar type structure.

7. Structure in the Plays of Aeschylus

If Oedipus is unique in Sophocles's canon, and if only Electra resembles it in tightness of plot development, Aeschylus's plays reveal even less evidence that would warrant describing Oedipus as "typical" of Greek tragic structure.

Not much is known about the form of pre-Aeschylean drama, except that it involved a chorus and a single actor; of the two, the chorus was paramount in importance. Thespis probably developed the structure of "lyrical tragedy" (as pre-Aeschylean drama is called by some scholars) about as far as it could go, but unfortunately none of his work has come down to us. Aeschylus is the first writer of Greek tragedy whose output has survived, and he arrived on the scene about thirty

years after the death of Thespis. In all, Aeschylus wrote approximately 90 plays, of which total
only seven have survived.

Aeschylus's earliest extant work, The Suppliants, no doubt owes much to previous models.
Aristotle says that Aeschylus added a second
actor.[29] Now the obvious advantage of a second actor in a play structure is that he allows for a
dramatic confrontation between the protagonist and
the antagonist. But in The Suppliants--though the
second actor is already present--Aeschylus does not
utilize to the full the potential inherent in the
expanded form. The structure which Aeschylus inherited from Thespis guaranteed that the subject
matter of the play would be sung or recited, inasmuch as it was impossible for two characters to
clash in an individual scene. And, on the whole,
this is the situation that we find in The Suppliants. The chorus still maintains its dominant
position; when dialogue does occur, it consists almost entirely of an exchange between the chorus and
a single character. Scarcely any "action" in the
ordinary sense is present--the structure is simple,
lyrical, static. The Suppliants further differs
from Sophoclean models in that it is the first part
of a trilogy, the second and third parts of which
have vanished.

The Persians--Aeschylus's next extant play--was
written about twenty years after The Suppliants.
Once again, the plot remains slight, progression
almost non-existent; instead of enactment there is
narration. The Persians, however, does reveal a
somewhat diminished role for the chorus and a
resultant increase in dialogue.

In The Seven Against Thebes, Aeschylus borrows
the same myth that Sophocles uses in Oedipus. The
Seven Against Thebes is the final and only extant
play of a trilogy, the first and second plays, entitled Laius and Oedipus, having been lost. Unlike
Sophocles's Oedipus, The Seven Against Thebes is
constructed in a simple, straightforward manner.
Aeschylus continues to prefer the heightening of a
tragic situation--the intensification of a tragic

mood--to complicated plotting.   Most of the "action" remains descriptive and lyrical; in other words, the chorus is still vital to the structure.

Nevertheless some important differences appear in the design of <u>The Seven Against Thebes</u> as compared to <u>The Suppliants</u> and <u>The Persians</u>.   For the first time in an Aeschylean prologue there is a dialogue between characters instead of a song by the chorus; furthermore, one of the characters who appears in the prologue--namely, Eteocles--is also the chief personage in the tragedy and remains on stage throughout most of the play.   In the <u>Poetics</u>, Aristotle argues that unity of plot and unity of the hero are not the same.   One person's life is too complex to be reduced to unity, and there are too many actions in that life to be formed into a single action.[30]   However, if one does not share Aristotle's bias for plot--and for a specific ideal plot at that--one could speak of Eteocles as the first tragic hero in Greek drama and regard Aeschylus's focus on him as a source of structural cohesion.

In his next play, <u>Prometheus Bound</u>, Aeschylus carries the method of <u>The Seven Against Thebes</u> further.   Not even Sophocles--at least not in any of his extant plays--ever kept one character continuously on stage; yet this is exactly what Aeschylus does with his title character.   Of course the reason for the technique is obvious: Prometheus <u>is</u> bound.   Having defied Zeus by teaching man the use of fire, Prometheus is punished by being chained to a rock.   The hero remains in this fixed position until the end of the play, at which point he sinks from sight into Tartarus.

Although continuity and focus are achieved through the person of Prometheus, there is--not surprisingly--little progression.   True, the choral part has dwindled still further in importance; moreover, the resolution occurs on stage--that is, it is enacted rather than reported.   Between the prologue (which, like the previous play, involves dialogue) and the ending, however, there is mostly narration and description.   The technique here does not seem calculated to provide the most lively form of "action." True, there is conflict between Prometheus as the protagonist and Zeus as the antagonist; yet Zeus nowhere puts in an appearance. Whatever reality the antagonist assumes is created indirectly through the introduction of his servants, who confront the protagonist in the course of the play.

There is tension in Prometheus Bound, but there is almost no movement. We are given a picture of the hero's situation and state of mind; we are not given a plot in any meaningful sense of the word.

Consequently, it would be a serious mistake to assume that by concentrating on a single hero in The Seven Against Thebes and Prometheus Bound, Aeschylus was inching his way ever closer towards Aristotle's notion of form. The structural pattern apotheosized in the Poetics remains largely irrelevant to the dramaturgy of Aeschylus. As Kitto points out, the order of scenes in Prometheus Bound does not adhere to what Aristotle (or, one might add, Sophocles) would consider an inevitable or probable sequence. Kitto also makes the shrewd observation that the structure of Prometheus Bound probably has more in common with music than with logic.[31]

To prove that Aeschylus had his own ideas about dramatic structure, the Oresteia--his masterpiece --stands witness. For in this play we find the great artist "regressing" in his development and abandoning his concentration on a single tragic hero.

8. The Oresteia

The Oresteia--composed of Agamemnon, The Choephori, and The Eumenides--remains the only Greek trilogy that has come down to us intact. It is believed to be the last work written by Aeschylus.

21

Of the three plays, Agamemnon is the most favored--at least by modern readers; so much so, in fact, that it often appears alone in anthologies of plays. In Tragedy and the Theory of Drama Elder Olson devotes an entire chapter to Agamemnon, with barely a reference to The Choephori or The Eumenides. Says Olson: "there is a difference between a succession of three complete wholes and a succession of parts. The three plays of the Oresteia are complete plays; the Acts which make up a Shakespearean tragedy are not."[32] Olson arrives at this curious judgment by stressing the fact that each play of the trilogy centers on one deed or event: in Agamemnon the killing of the title character by his wife, Clytemnestra; in The Choephori Orestes's avenging of his father's death by slaying Clytemnestra; and in The Eumenides the acquittal of Orestes on the charge of matricide through the creation of the Athenian court of the Areopagus. There is no doubt that each of the three plays can be enjoyed to some degree separately. Nevertheless Aeschylus designed the trilogy as a single tragedy on the problem of justice. And to the extent that we limit our concern to Agamemnon, we impoverish Aeschylus's tragic art.

Although it is correct to say that the Oresteia is structurally and thematically unified, one hesitates to agree with Kaufmann in his contention[33] that the trilogy comprises a single plot. Plot--if by "plot" Kaufmann means the causal progression found in Oedipus and praised in the Poetics--was never, as we have seen, Aeschylus's burning concern. Certainly Muller is right when he says of Aeschylus: "His interest was in a doom-- what necessarily happened, not so much in just how it happened, still less in any possibility that it might have happened otherwise."[34] At the start of an Aeschylean tragedy a certain fate is pronounced, and the remainder of the piece is simply an increment of tension as we wait for the doom to materialize.

If we tried to fit the Oresteia into an Aristotelian mold, we would surely be in a difficult situation. For then we would have to argue that the complication involves the slaying of Agamemnon

and Clylemnestra, and that it takes up all of the
first two plays; that the turning point for the
tragic hero, Orestes, comes in The Eumenides when
it is decided that Athena will judge his case; and
that the unraveling occurs in the last two-thirds
of the final play--which ends, not in catastrophe,
and not in the way Aristotle preferred, but in good
fortune for all the living.

The Aristotelian schema works, however, only if
it be allowed that Orestes is the central character
in the trilogy--a technical point which, if true,
Aeschylus was at great pains to conceal. Orestes
does not appear at all in Agamemnon; and he departs
before The Eumenides is over, leaving the stage to
Athena and the chorus of Furies who conclude the
play. No wonder Aristotle all but completely ignores Aeschylus in the Poetics.

Plot and tragic heroes were less important to
the author of the Oresteia than idea. This doesn't
mean, of course, that Aeschylus's trilogy is
without structure. No play, however crudely put
together, is lacking in structure of some kind.
And the Oresteia is far from being crude in either
conception or execution. Actually, what we find in
the trilogy is a controlling thematic structure.[35]

Aeschylus is intent on showing that the injunction "an eye for an eye" (an injunction which most
men act upon with little or no prodding from Zeus
or any other god) solves nothing. Indeed, such
behavior--even if divinely inspired--only leads to
a crime worse than the one it is supposed to
avenge. This is why we cannot separate one play
from another in the trilogy. Although each play is
constructed around a single event, the three
events--the murder of Agamemnon, the murder of
Clytemnestra, and the pardoning of Orestes--are interdependent. Throughout Agamemnon and The
Choephori we are made to see the folly of blood
lust in order to fully appreciate the fusion of
justice and mercy based on understanding which is
achieved in The Eumenides.

VARIETIES OF DRAMATIC STRUCTURE

The Oresteia is both lyrical and dramatic in structure. Agamemnon has a short prologue given over to a watchman who looks for a signal that Troy has been defeated and that the title character is coming home. Through several ominous references to the past, the watchman prepares us for the doom awaiting Agamemnon upon his arrival in Argos. The parodos is extremely long--seven times as long, in fact, as the same section of Oedipus; but, on the whole, Aeschylus subordinates the chorus throughout the trilogy to the actors. And even where the chorus assumes added importance, such as in The Eumenides where its members become the Furies, it seems more like a group of actors than mere recitators, inasmuch as developments take place directly in front of the audience. Furthermore, a third actor (a convention which Sophocles had by this time established) is used effectively, if sparingly, by Aeschylus during the entire action.

And there is "action" in Agamemnon, by anyone's definition. For at the heart of the play's construction lies the confrontation between Clytemnestra and Agamemnon. Here--shortly before the midpoint of the piece--Aeschylus shows that he can dramatize an episode as well as any playwright who ever lived. Not that we are surprised by what happens. The lyrical, or narrative, portions of the play have foreshadowed the slaying again and again by reminding us of the curse on the House of Atreus and of Agamemnon's own sins. Throughout Agamemnon the lyrical and the dramatic are complementary.

Agamemnon ends on a high level of tension as Clytemnestra and Aegisthus seek to assert their claims of authority against the chorus. Although Clytemnestra naively believes that there will be no more killing, the chorus looks forward to the coming of Orestes and his avenging of Agamemnon's murder. Thus the first play in the trilogy concludes with a "curtain" that would make any dramatist in the three-act form proud.

Roughly the first half of The Choephori is lyrical and rather static: Orestes, Electra, and the chorus stand fixed before Agamemnon's tomb, bewailing the loss of the king, praying for strength

24

to avenge his death, and reminding us of the dark past. Repetition is used to create a sense of impending doom. The technique is reminiscent of music, where a theme is played over and over in order to evoke a strong emotional reaction in the listener. Finally, Aeschylus presents Orestes's slaying of Aegisthus and Clytemnestra in a scene of dramatic power to rival the second part of Agamemnon. And once again, Aeschylus leaves the audience in a state of expectancy. The Furies have already made their appearance before Orestes to avenge the matricide; and the chorus asks, Where will doom strike next? Clearly, The Choephori demands The Eumenides as "an inevitable sequel" (Eugene O'Neill, see note 32), for what remains at stake is not only the fate of Orestes, but also the whole question of justice.

The Eumenides is somewhat different in its structural technique from the two previous plays. In Agamemnon and The Choephori, Aeschylus follows the lyrical with the dramatic; in The Eumenides, he more nearly integrates the two elements. There is more movement than usual in Aeschylean drama, even in terms of place changes. During the first episode, for example, the scene shifts abruptly from Delphi to Athens. The Eumenides is also rich in spectacle, a part of tragedy which Aristotle undervalued, feeling that it was not really artistic or intrinsic to poetry but had more to do with stage gimmickry.[36] From the prologue--which shows Orestes clinging to Apollo's altar for protection against the Furies who lie slumbering a short distance from him--to the closing scene--which reveals the Furies transformed into the Eumenides, or Goddesses of Mercy, and exiting from the stage in processional form--the play is noteworthy for its striking pictorial effects. What Aristotle calls spectacle is actually integrated with structure in The Eumenides, so tightly has Aeschylus drawn together the various elements of his play.

It should be clear by now that any discussion of structure in Greek tragedy which ignores the work of Aeschylus--especially the Oresteia--cannot be said to be worth much as a guide to ancient drama.

25

9. Euripides and the Structure of <u>Medea</u>

Aristotle dismissed Euripides's general management of his subject as faulty; at the same time, however, he considered the dramatist the most tragic of the poets because so many of his plays ended in bad fortune for the hero.[37] Since Aristotle's time, Euripides has often been described as a slipshod technician in one sentence and praised as one of the world's greatest playwrights in the next. Perhaps the wrong yardstick is too often used to measure Euripides's accomplishment.

It is not possible to discuss here--even summarily--all the extant works of Euripides. A combined total of fourteen plays by Aeschylus and Sophocles survive, but nineteen of Euripides's plays have been preserved. Although it seems doubtful whether Aeschylus or Sophocles wrote anything superior to, or even as good as, their extant plays, there is reason to believe that several masterpieces by Euripides (<u>Andromeda</u>, <u>Antiope</u>, and <u>Cresphontes</u>) have been lost. However that might be, it will serve the aims of this study to limit analysis of structure to three of Euripides's best-known surviving works: <u>Medea</u>, <u>Hippolytus</u>, and <u>The Trojan Women</u>.

Can <u>Medea</u> be squeezed into the Aristotelian mold? Let us see. Medea is certainly the main character and driving force within the action. So there is no division of interest, no bipartite structure here. The complication is announced in the prologue when Medea's nurse informs us that Jason has deserted her mistress and married the daughter of Creon, King of Corinth. Before the prologue ends an attendant tells the nurse that Creon plans to banish Medea and the two sons she has given Jason. That the title character is scheming some terrible revenge upon her enemies is plain.

The turning point occurs when Medea encounters the King of Athens, Aegeus, who is passing through Corinth, and who has made a pilgrimage to Artemis in the hope that children might be born to him. After Medea explains her unhappy situation to Aegeus, he promises her a sanctuary in his own land. Now Medea decides to act. In the unraveling, she slays Creon, Jason's bride, and her two sons. Then--after having thus triumphed over her enemies--she is carried off to Athens in a chariot drawn by dragons.

There are, however, a number of difficulties attendant upon an Aristotelian reading of structure in Medea--difficulties which point up major differences of a formal nature between the practice of Sophocles and that of Euripides. In Oedipus, the reader will recall, the title character begins with perfect confidence in himself and only gradually moves toward catastrophe. The turning point is reached when Jocasta, in her narration of Laius's murder, first speaks words which put doubts about himself in the hero's mind. The situation is otherwise in Medea. In the prologue, the nurse tells us that her mistress hates her children now. She is afraid Medea will take out her anger on them by putting a sword through their hearts. Or else she might find some means of killing the bride and bridegroom in their bedchamber. One thing is certain: No man will find it easy to triumph over Medea.

Clearly, almost the whole future course of action is presented to us at the start. All that remains is for Euripides to dilate the tragic mood and actualize the catastrophe. The structural technique here calls to mind the dramaturgy of Aeschylus more than it does that of Sophocles.

In Oedipus, the turning point seems to grow logically out of character and story--seems, because we question the fact, as noted, why Jocasta has waited so long to tell Oedipus about the circumstances surrounding the death of Laius. In the course of the action, however, we do not pause to object at the turning point, so expert is the skill of Sophocles in maintaining our interest.

27

Yet critics have deplored the way Euripides introduces Aegeus. The King of Athens, who bears no
integral relationship to the plot, just happens to
be passing through Corinth, and just happens to offer the heroine a refuge in his country. Even
during the action we are conscious of how for-
tuitous all this appears. Medea's encounter with
Aegeus constitutes a turning point only in the
sense that the man's childlessness crystallizes the
heroine's thought of killing her sons as a way of
punishing Jason (a possibility foreshadowed, as we
have seen, in the prologue) and that his offer of
sanctuary allows her to escape the wrath of her
former lover. But the turning point in Medea is
not in any sense harmonious with some law of probability or necessity.

Aristotle was not happy with the unraveling in
Medea, and he compared it unfavorably to the design
of Oedipus. Like the complication, the unraveling
should flow naturally from the plot; the conclusion
must not be brought about by the deux ex machina.
The irrational can occur before or after the play
proper, but within the action itself the irrational
must be excluded. If the irrational has an integral relationship to the story, then it should be
kept outside the structure of action, as in
Oedipus, and not used to end the play, as in
Medea.[38]

Without doubt, Aristotle also lamented the absence of reversal and recognition in Medea. And
probably the ambiguous ending of the piece also
troubled him. For to the extent that Medea triumphs over Jason and escapes to Athens, she enjoys
good fortune; but since she has killed her own
children and forever separated herself from the man
she loves, her fortune seems bad indeed.

No, Medea does not really conform to
Aristotle's notion of tragic structure . . . But
then, is there any reason why it should? The Aristotelian pattern is a good one for those dramatists
who view the world in terms of order. F. W.
Bateson is surely unfair to Aristotle when he accuses him of being exclusively concerned with
plots, or well-made plays.[39] For Aristotle, the

28

plot of a play _is_ its meaning--or a large part of it--and not a mere excrescence. Not all playwrights, however, see life the same way; consequently, why should they mirror life with the same kind of structure?

The action of _Medea_ is practically given away in the prologue because Euripides cares little for either causality or character development. His interest lies in tragic passion, the irrational. Does the appearance of Aegeus violate our ideas of probability? But in a world where all is not reasonable, why shouldn't the King of Athens chance to pass by and offer Medea a haven? Castigating Euripides's craftsmanship, Muller says: "The notorious _deus_ _ex_ _machina_ is only symptomatic of the mechanical quality that pervades his drama, and that appears as well in the mere cleverness, the rhetoric, the sensationalism, the artificial or illogical actions, the extreme or inconsistent characterizations. These faults are more disturbing because they appear to be due to sheer perversity rather than incompetence." Most of these "faults"--perhaps all of them--could be explained in terms of the playwright's ironic treatment of an absurd or irrational world. Even Muller concedes that all of Euripides's plays suggest that the governing powers of the universe are irrational-- although it does not seem to have occurred to him that such a view might render the playwright's forms different from those of Sophocles.[40]

Some have argued that the heroine's escape in a chariot is bad structuring because Euripides fails to prepare us for it. Such criticism misses the point. The sudden appearance of the dragon-chariot remains of a piece with the impression of life which Euripides wishes to convey. Aristotle says that the irrational must be kept out of the action. Euripides does not agree. Just as playwrights in the Theater of the Absurd revolted against the logic of Ibsenian structure, just so Euripides seems to have wanted to embrace _within_ the form of his plays more of the irrational than Sophocles was disposed to admit. Hence it is foolish to expect

Medea to duplicate the logical progression of _Oedipus_, or to adhere to the rational pronouncements of the _Poetics_.

10. Hippolytus

If the structure of _Medea_ is unified less by plot and character than by theme, the same is true of _Hippolytus_, which most critics regard as Euripides's finest play. Like _Medea_--and so unlike _Oedipus_--the past has little bearing on the design of _Hippolytus_; therefore, scant exposition is required, and the spectator's attention can be directed to events unfolding in the present.

This does not mean, however, that suspense plays a greater part in _Hippolytus_ than in _Medea_. Although the Greek audience knew the story of Oedipus, they could deceive themselves during the performance into believing that the end might turn out differently for the hero. In _Hippolytus_, Euripides arouses no such vain hopes. Right from the start, in the prologue, Aphrodite informs the audience that she has made Phaedra fall in love with her stepson, Hippolytus, because the young man worships Artemis, the virgin goddess of the hunt, instead of revering the goddess of love. Furthermore, Aphrodite foretells that Hippolytus will reject Phaedra, that the latter will die, and that the youth will be falsely accused before his father, Theseus, who will then slay his son.

Obviously, Euripides's interest is not in "what happens"--but in "why it happens." Whatever the playwright might have thought of his two goddesses (and to a modern audience they seem petty and vindictive), he makes clear that Hippolytus suffers from vanity and coldness. Indeed the title character's lack of passion leads to his destruction through Phaedra's and Theseus's excess of it.

Waldock believes, as noted earlier, that _Hippolytus_ has a diptych structure. And Muller, who argues that Phaedra is the main source of interest, agrees: "Many readers feel a let-down after she kills herself, well before the end, and all have to recognize a shift of interest to the tragedy of Hippolytus and Theseus."[41]

Both critics are, I believe, in error. An analysis of structure in Hippolytus reveals that Phaedra is not central to the design. As G.M.A. Grube has pointed out, the main character is clearly the title character. He remains the one over whom the goddesses quarrel. Aphrodite remarks that to her Phaedra is unimportant; likewise, Artemis treats her with a complete lack of concern. Hippolytus's part is extended over most of the play and he spends more time on stage than any other character except Theseus.[42]

Like Medea, Hippolytus could be hammered into the Aristotelian pattern. The complication is set forth in the prologue; the turning point occurs when Phaedra--having been rejected by Hippolytus--decides, before killing herself, to leave a note for Theseus accusing his son of having attacked her, thus starting the movement toward the hero's bad fortune; and the unraveling shows Theseus putting a curse on Hippolytus, whom the god Poseidon then destroys.

But the Aristotelian analysis is, of course, all wrong here. Oedipus is the driving force in the structure of Sophocles's play; Oedipus is a doer. Hippolytus does nothing. True, he is central to the design, and he is more significant than either Phaedra or Theseus. Nevertheless he remains more acted upon than acting. And while it is also true that Phaedra acts, the play does not belong to her: she is merely an instrument of an avenging goddess, a vehicle to express passion and the irrational.

Once again, the basic Euripidean structural principal lies not in this or that character, not in a logical ordering of a plot cut to the precise dimensions of "Greek Tragedy" or some philosopher's ideal tragedy--but in an idea, a theme, about the destructive effects of strong emotion. Hippolytus has no scene comparable to the one involving Aegeus in Medea. Nor does the later play have any magic

31

chariots floating about the premises. There are, however, gods and goddesses working their mischief; a great bull that issues out of the sea; and a _deux ex machina_, in that Artemis appears overhead in the exodus to explain the tragedy to Theseus. In short, the irrational is again a dominant force _within_ the Euripidean structure.

11. The Trojan Women

Plot--as normally understood--is not overly significant in _Medea_ and _Hippolytus_; but in _The Trojan Women_ Euripides dispenses with it entirely and succeeds in writing great drama.

The Trojan Women is based on an Athenian atrocity perpetrated against Melos during the Peloponnesian War. In the prologue, the god Poseidon and the goddess Pallas Athena appear on stage to sketch in the background of the play. The scene is a recent battlefield near the walls of Troy. As in Melos, the males of Troy have been slaughtered by the Greeks, who are now preparing to carry off the women and children. Poseidon condemns the passionate and irrational excesses of the Greeks, for they have also destroyed the temples and the graves where the venerable dead lie buried. Poseidon agrees with Athena that the Greek fleet, on its homeward journey, must be destroyed as a form of punishment.

After a brief parodos, there follows four episodes, the chief focus in each being on the sufferings of the women named in the title. Andromache, Cassandra, and Hecuba receive most of the attention (the latter is present continuously); but no single character dominates the play. Structurally, _The Trojan Women_ breaks all the "rules." Since the women are caught in a trap from which escape is impossible, there is no problem to be worked out.

We learn that Hecuba, Queen of Troy, has been awarded as a spoil to Odysseus; that her daughter, Cassandra, has been given to Agamemnon; that

32

another daughter, Polyxenia, is to be sacrificed at the tomb of Achilles; and that Hector's infant son, Astyanax, is to be taken from his mother, Andromache, and thrown from the wall of Troy. There is no conflict between the women, or within them. Nor are the women in conflict with the Greeks. Indeed, except for the herald, Talthybius, and some supernumeraries, no Greek even appears in the play. Consequently, there is little "movement." The play opens with the women already doomed; it closes with the women walking out into the darkness--their homes burning behind them--to embrace their fate. As in Medea and Hippolytus--as well as in the plays of Aeschylus--there is neither reversal nor recognition. There is a gradual intensification of a tragic situation; there is no tragic development.

The Trojan Women is more lyrical than Medea and Hippolytus, and in this respect Euripides is nearer than ever to Aeschylus (even as he is further removed from Sophocles). Because there is no logical framework to the "action," some commentators feel that the individual episodes could be reshuffled. The authority of Aristotle is often invoked here: "so the plot, being an imitation of an action, must imitate one action and that a whole, the structural union of the parts being such that, if any one of them is displaced or removed, the whole will be disjointed and disturbed. For a thing whose presence or absence makes no visible difference is not an organic part of the whole."[43] The Trojan Women is a whole; but it does not have a beginning, a middle, and an end in the Aristotelian sense. In view of the emotional effects arising from the organization of the play, however, the thematic structure would be irretrievably damaged by any play doctor who was impudent enough to believe that he could improve upon Euripides.

The majority of critics are agreed that The Trojan Women is outstanding drama. However, some of them--because of their preconceptions about structure--have difficulty classifying it. John Gassner says: "Although The Trojan Women is a rather static, long-drawn out lament (even Euripides's greatest modern champion, Gilbert Mur-

33

ray, concedes that judged by common standards 'it is scarcely even a good play'), this tragedy has a greatness all its own."[44] But how can a mediocre play be at the same time a great play? And what "common standards" are being used to judge Euripides's work?

One can easily see why The Trojan Women might trouble Gilbert Murray, for its structure hardly conforms to his ritual thesis. Other critics have taken refuge in meaningless semantic distinctions. For example, Whitney J. Oates remarks: "The Trojan Women perhaps from the point of view of structure is not strictly speaking a play [!], but rather is a tragic pageant which presents one facet of that far greater tragedy, war itself."[45] Similarly, Waldock asserts that Euripides's play is not a tragedy, but a "dramatic pageant."[46] Structurally speaking, what is the difference between a "play" or a "tragedy" and a "tragic pageant"--or between a "tragedy" and a "dramatic pageant"? Kitto declares that Euripides, in The Trojan Women, "is not putting together a play but presenting a tragic idea."[47] How can a "tragic idea" be expressed without achieving a form of some kind? And what transcendental ordinance prevents us from calling that form a play? Stuart rightly observes: "the plot of The Trojan Women arouses little interest; but after seeing the play one never forgets the heart-rending scenes in which the child Astyanax is torn from his mother and is brought back dead to the grief-stricken woman."[48]

Now what do we want--a plot or great drama?

12. Structure in Greek Tragedy

A study unhampered by ideas derived from Aristotle, Hegel, and the Cambridge School of Classical Anthropologists shows that there is no typical structure for Greek tragedy--let alone all tragedy.

Sophocles's plays are far less consistent in design than is generally believed. Three of his plays are bipartite in structure; one is episodic; and another is at least fuzzy in its focus on a central character. Only two plays--Electra and Oedipus--are tightly organized. But it is no exaggeration to say that, in terms of dramaturgy, Oedipus has more in common with Ghosts than with Electra.

Aristotle's assertion that every tragedy can be divided into two parts is wrong. How illuminating is it to analyze the Oresteia, Medea, Hippolytus, and The Trojan Women in the light of "complication," "turning point," and "unraveling"? Furthermore, the majority of Greek plays fail to reveal evidence of a "reversal" and/or "recognition" (Aristotle himself gave only two examples of "reversal"--one from Oedipus, the other from Theodectes's Lynceus); therefore, according to Aristotle's way of thinking, the structure of most Greek plays is "simple," not "complex." Each reader will have to decide for himself whether "simple" structure (again, in Aristotle's sense) is inferior to "complex" structure, and if so, why.

Plot is not very important--indeed, at times it is non-existent--in the plays of Aeschylus and Euripides. Alan S. Downer claims that the unity of Greek drama comes from the structural concentration on the main character.[49] This is a common assumption. As we have seen, however, some of the best Greek plays do not have a central figure--nor do they appear any the worse for it. Aeschylus and Euripides depend less on plot and character for structural cohesion than on theme. Both playwrights tend to ignore causal development in favor of intensification. Structure in some plays by Aeschylus and Euripides resembles a musical pattern, inasmuch as the form inclines toward the vertical.

Non-linear form--as the Theater of the Absurd has shown--can be just as dramatic as linear. But we also want to remember that linear and non-linear, horizontal and vertical, are not mutually exclusive categories. They are a matter of artistic emphasis. Lyrical passages, set orations, descriptive and narrative speeches can be found in the plays of all three dramatists, just as enact-

35

ment can be found in them. Oedipus is certainly horizontal; however, as Kitto observes, Sophocles adopts a vertical strategy when he thrusts the Corinthian messenger--an ordinary man, and a minor character--into the action.[50] Similarly, to the extent that the Oresteia is repetitive, it is vertical; to the degree that events do occur in it, it is horizontal.

Naturally, the circular shape of the Greek orchestra--with its tightly restricted acting space--was bound to influence the form of any play designed to be enacted before as many as seventeen thousand spectators. The action, if everyone present was expected to follow it, had to remain clear. There was no room for sub-plots or parallel movements. What has come to be called the three unities were observed by Aeschylus, Sophocles, and Euripides because their theater virtually demanded it. Only two extant plays have a major place change: Ajax and The Eumenides; only two obviously exceed a twenty-four-hour time span: The Trachiniae and The Suppliants. A few plays, it is true, stretch credibility by drastically telescoping events. But the immense majority of Greek tragedies convincingly persuade us that their action is occurring within a brief period of time.

The most important unity--and, as noted earlier, the only one Aristotle stressed--is unity of action. Each playwright approached the idea of dramatic action differently (plot is important in Oedipus but absent entirely in The Trojan Women). Each playwright, however, aimed for thematic unity (Oedipus has a unified plot structure and thematic structure, but The Trojan Women has only a unified thematic structure). Here the physical shape of the theater was not the only factor conducive to the observance of unity. The external structure (or the quantitative parts) that remained a fixed convention of the form also contributed to an orderliness and symmetry in the internal structure, in spite of the differences in treatment by each playwright.

It is this highly patterned aspect of Greek dramaturgy that often deceives us into thinking that all the plays of the age are tightly plotted, when in fact the action of some remains episodic. But whether the scenes are part of a causally arranged plot (as in <u>Electra</u>) or merely comments on a thematically organized whole (as in <u>Prometheus Bound</u>)--that is to say, whether the approach is predominantly horizontal or predominantly vertical--the internal structure almost invariably remains restricted to a single story or subject. Even a diptych play like <u>Antigone</u> has its two parts unified by a single theme.

To repeat: Neither <u>Oedipus</u> nor any other single play can be described as typical of Greek tragedy. There is simply too much formal variety in the genre for that to be possible. Any generalizations about structure in the plays of Aeschylus, Sophocles, and Euripides have to be ample enough to do justice to masterpieces as diverse in form as <u>Prometheus Bound</u>, the <u>Orestia</u>, <u>Oedipus</u>, <u>Antigone</u>, <u>Medea</u>, <u>Hippolytus</u>, and <u>The Trojan Women</u>.

Notes

[1]The <u>Poetics</u>, in S. H. Butcher, <u>Aristotle's Theory of Poetry and Fine Art: With a Critical Text and Translation</u> (New York: Dover, 1951), pp. 25 and 27.

[2]Ibid, pp. 27 and 29.

[3]Butcher uses "proper purgation" (p. 23), whereas Leon Golden opts for "catharsis" in his translation. See <u>Aristotle's Poetics</u> (Englewood Cliffs, N.J.: Prentice-Hall, 1968), p. 11. The commentary in this edition is supplied by O. B. Hardison, Jr., who follows Golden and also uses the word "catharsis."

[4]The <u>Poetics</u>, in Butcher, p. 23.

[5]Ibid, p. 39.

[6]Ibid, p. 33.

[7]Ibid, p. 41.

[8]Ibid, p. 47.

[9]Ibid, p. 65.

[10]Hardison, _Aristotle's Poetics_, p. 62.

[11]The _Poetics_, in Butcher, p. 25.

[12]Donald Clive Stuart, _The Development of Dramatic Art_ (New York: Dover, 1960), p. 97.

[13]The _Poetics_, in Butcher, p. 41.

[14]H. D. F. Kitto, _Greek Tragedy_ (New York: Anchor, 1954), p. 153.

[15]Francis Fergusson, _The Idea of a Theater_ (New York: Anchor, n.d.), p. 39.

[16]Ibid, p. 39.

[17]Gerald F. Else, _The Origin and Early Form of Greek Tragedy_ (New York: Norton, 1972), pp. vii and 3-4.

[18]Richard Schechner, "Approaches to Theory/Criticism," _Tulane Drama Review_, 10, Summer 1966, p. 10.

[19]See Herbert Muller, _The Spirit of Tragedy_ (New York: Washington Square Press, 1966), p. 77.

[20]Walter Kaufmann, _Tragedy and Philosophy_ (New York: Anchor, 1969), p. 261.

[21]Muller, p. 83.

[22]John Gassner, _Masters of the Drama_ (New York: Dover, 1940), p. 50.

[23]Gustav Freytag, Technique of the Drama, trans. Elias J. MacEwan (Chicago: Scott, Foresman, 1904), p. 171.

[24]Robert Hogan and Sven Eric Molin, ed. Drama: The Major Genres (New York: Dodd, Mead & Co., 1966), pp. 61-62.

[25]See Anne and Henry Paolucci, ed., Hegel on Tragedy (New York: Anchor, 1962), pp. 178, 325, and 49.

[26]See Kaufmann, pp. 234-248.

[27]Kitto, p. 130.

[28]Kitto, pp. 131-132, and elsewhere; A. J. A. Waldock, Sophocles the Dramatist (London: Cambridge, 1951), pp. 49-59.

[29]The Poetics, in Butcher, p. 19.

[30]Ibid, p. 33.

[31]Kitto, pp. 61 and 65.

[32]Elder Olson, Tragedy and the Theory of Drama (Detroit: Wayne State University Press, 1966), p. 182. Eugene O'Neill seems to have shared Olson's view of Aeschylus's trilogy. After finishing Mourning Becomes Electra--his Freudian updating of the Oresteia--O'Neill noted in his diary: "I flatter myself it is unique thing in dramaturgy--each play complete episode completely realized but at the same time, which is the important point, not complete in that its end begins following play and demands that play as an inevitable sequel--few trilogies in existence in drama of all time and none of them has this quality which, in any time under any conditions, could not have failed to prove an asset--if gained without harm to the separate play, of course, as I believe I have done." O'Neill's description of structure in Mourning Becomes Electra, however, also fits the Oresteia. See Eugene O'Neill, "Working Notes and

Extracts from a Fragmentary Work Diary," in
American Playwrights on Drama, ed. Horst Frenz (New
York: Hill & Wang, 1965), p. 14.

[33]Kaufmann, p. 214.

[34]Muller, p. 56.

[35]Thomas G. Rosenmeyer makes a similar point in
The Art of Aeschylus: "It was Sophocles who chose
to assimilate the dramatic plot to the hiagraphical
curve of growth, disenchantment, despair, and sal-
vation. The fractured life of the Sophoclean hero
furnishes the model for the dramatic plot. Not so
in Aeschylus, who celebrates no heroes, but narrates and analyzes the fates of houses or cities,
or whole worlds: embattled universes draw strength
from the largeness of the setting. But the structure of the action which defines them answers to no
one pattern and resists a shapely organization.
Faced by a choice between the virtues of clarity
and articulation and the fullness of unremitting
conceptualization, Aeschylus preferred the latter."
See Thomas G. Rosenmeyer, _The Art of Aeschylus_
(Berkeley: University of California, 1982), p. 335.

[36]As David Seale points out, Sophocles--
Aristotle's idol--is not "reluctant to employ the
aid of spectacle for his own dramatic purposes. To
believe this would be to overlook the intricacy of
his stage craft and to exclude the spectacular element from his work altogether." See David Seale,
Vision and Stagecraft in Sophocles (Chicago:
University of Chicago Press, 1982), p. 12. For
Aristotle's remarks on spectacle, see the _Poetics_,
in Butcher, pp. 29 and 31.

[37]For Aristotle on Euripides, see the _Poetics_,
in Butcher, p. 47.

[38]For Aristotle on _Medea_, see the _Poetics_, in
Butcher, pp. 55 and 57.

[39]F. W. Bateson, "Catharsis," in _Tragedy:
Modern Essays in Criticism_, ed. Laurence Michel and
Richard B. Sewall (Englewood Cliffs, N.J.:
Prentice-Hall, 1963), p. 295. Bateson is even more

unfair to Sophocles, calling <u>Oedipus</u> "the model of the well-made play" and "as much a melodrama as a tragedy."

[40]Muller, pp. 88 and 95.

[41]Ibid, p. 100.

[42]·G. M. A. Grube, <u>The Drama of Euripides</u> (New York: Barnes & Noble, 1961), p. 177.

[43]The <u>Poetics</u>, in Butcher, p. 35.

[44]Gassner, p. 69.

[45]Whitney J. Oates, <u>The Complete Greek Drama</u>, vol 1, ed. Oates and Eugene O'Neill, Jr. (New York: Random House, 1938), p. 957.

[46]Waldock, p. 35.

[47]Kitto, p. 223.

[48]Stuart, p. 92.

[49]Alan S. Downer, <u>The Art of the Play</u> (New York: Holt, 1955), p. 176.

[50]Kitto, pp. 191-192.

II

Structure in Shakespearean Tragedy

1. Structure in Shakespearean Tragedy and the
   Elizabethan Playhouse

If, as we have seen, the physical conditions of
the Greek theater helped to shape the formal
qualities of plays by Aeschylus, Sophocles, and
Euripides, the same relationship between playhouse
and play structure also remains a factor in the
great tragedies of Shakespeare. No one can fully
appreciate the structure of Hamlet or King Lear
without knowing something about the structure of
the Elizabethan playhouse, for one clearly influenced the other. But it also needs to be added
here that the public playhouse of Shakespeare's
London was itself influenced by medieval stage
production. Indeed, it is fair to say that the
structures of Hamlet and King Lear with their multiple actions owe more, say, to the Wakefield drama
festival of the fourteenth century than to the
practice of Sophocles in Oedipus or to the theoriz-
ing of Aristotle in the Poetics.

Four methods of staging plays in the medieval
period can be enumerated. One way was to use a
"round," an elevation of earth or stone large
enough to permit a number of playing areas. The
"round" was on the edge of a plain, which sometimes
was also used for the actors, providing the
audience remained close to the raised stage and did
not spread out into this wider area. A second
method was to disperse the acting areas over a town
square on level ground. There was no linear struc-

turing of the action; instead of arranging the stages in a straight line, the playing areas were placed here and there in such a way as to integrate the actors with the townspeople. Another method involved lining up a series of "mansions"--actually, boxes or platforms representing scenes--in a straight line or semicircle before an open space designated for enactment. One such play in 1501, John Gassner informs us, went on for over a week and had nearly seventy different scenes.[1] And lastly, there was the method of mounting the mansions on wheels and rolling them or drawing them by horses to the audience at specific locations in the town. The individual plays constituted a cycle and were acted by specific crafts in the community; each craft built a wagon--called a "pageant"--and the wagon became that craft's stage. Each pageant accommodated a number of related stories. This method of staging was especially popular in England. And, as Alan S. Downer correctly points out, it was the progenitor of Shakespeare's theater with its many place changes and shifts in time.[2]

What the four methods of staging plays in the Middle Ages had in common was an ability to present multiple enactments. On the medieval stage, unlike the Greek, there was considerable freedom of movement and an opportunity to use dozens of actors.

The staging of plays in the Middle Ages cannot be separated from the kind of material enacted. Medieval drama was a religious drama which probably grew out of the Christian Church.[3] The mystery plays were based on the Scriptures and were enacted in great cycles; the miracle plays were devoted to the lives of the saints. Both genres called for a structure much more extensive in scope than that provided by the physical conditions of the Greek theater.

Whether the religious drama of the Middle Ages evolved in a straight line into the secular drama of the Renaissance, or whether Shakespeare and his contemporaries merely continued medieval ways of looking at life (with modifications, of course, otherwise there would be no identifiable change in the historical process called the Renaissance), is

44

unimportant for our purposes. Suffice it to observe that structure in Renaissance drama is
similar to that in medieval drama, and that in many
important respects the theater of each is different
from the theater of Aeschylus, Sophocles, and
Euripides.

The English public theater seems to have been
designed for largely uninterrupted action. There
were multiple playing areas, including a main stage
which extended into the spectator area, an inner
stage (an alcove behind the main stage), an upper
stage (a balcony above the inner stage), windows
above the stage doors which led into the main platform, and a room in the turret on top of the building. Although there was more than one playing area
in the Greek theater, most of the action took place
in the middle of the orchestra; and, because of the
convention involving the "quantitative parts"--that
is, enactment regularly followed by choral ode--
dramatic action was not continuous. Like the
medieval theater, the playhouse of Shakespeare's
day allowed for a large cast and fluid movement in
time and space.

Thanks to the various stages, action in
Shakespearean structure flows almost continuously
with few intermissions. The Elizabethan dramatist
had great latitude where scene placement was concerned; a scene in Rome could be followed by one in
Actium, followed by another in Alexandria, then on
to Egypt, back to Alexandria, and so forth. Because of the multiple playing areas, Shakespeare's
structures--long by modern standards--played much
more rapidly for an Elizabethan audience--generally
taking some two and a half hours, or about the same
length of time for one of our much shorter contemporary plays.

Since there was no scenery on Shakespeare's
stage, the audience was never distracted from the
action. In this, the Elizabethan theater resembled
that of the Greeks, which was also void of back-
drops, screens, or other illusionistic trappings.
However, the Elizabethan thrust stage, and the
seating arrangement which limited the audience to
no more than three thousand, made for an intimacy

45

(relatively speaking) lacking in the theater of ancient Greece. An Othello, consumed by rage, thun-
dering from scene to scene--at times almost touching the audience (some important people actually
sat on the stage itself occasionally)--would possess a dramatic quality different in kind from that
afforded the ancient Greek in the "bleachers," one
of seventeen thousand or more spectators looking
down at Oedipus or Antigone.

The episodic narrative material of medieval
drama established a tradition which led Elizabethan
playwrights and their audiences to think of theater
in terms of what Madeleine Doran calls
"multiplicity and sequential action." I have already commented on "multiplicity." By "sequential
action," Doran means "action ab ovo developed in
historical sequence or natural order as opposed to
the 'crisis' action or artificial order, beginning
in medias res, of Greek drama."[4] The physical
properties of the public stage, together with the
narrative conventions dating from the Middle Ages,
impelled Elizabethan dramatists away from "the
three unities." Hence some writers have tried to
differentiate the formal qualities of Greek and
Elizabethan drama by using contrasting terms. It
was Heinrich Wolfflin, I believe, who introduced
"closed" and "open" as descriptive categories for
artistic styles. Over the years, "closed" has often been applied to Greek tragedy, "open" to
Elizabethan drama. Alan S. Downer, however,
prefers "focused" (Greek) and "panoramic"
(Elizabethan); Marvin Rosenberg likes "linear"
(Greek) and "contextual" (Elizabethan); and Bernard
Beckerman favors "intensive" (Greek) and
"extensive" (Elizabethan).[5] I will comment on the
utility of such an approach in due course.

In a form where action "begins at the beginning" and often proceeds along two or more lines of
development, the structural unity is bound to be
non-Aristotelian. Until the twentieth century,
though, most writers were unable to accommodate
Elizabethan form within their theories of dramatic
structure.

46

French theorists in the century following Shakespeare's death asserted that English Renaissance drama lacked form. In vain did John Dryden declare Shakespeare's greatness and elevate him above all other dramatists.[6] And when French neoclassical drama and the later Scribean well-made play had each made their historical exit, Ibsenian structure made its entrance. In other words, the tight, single-action model dominated the drama.

True, the romantic writers adored Shakespeare, and even the French learned to speak of Voltaire, Scribe, and the author of Hamlet in the same breath. But few nineteenth-century critics praised the great English playwright qua playwright. And even today, one often gets the impression that many theorists regard Shakespearean structure as some kind of artistic sport, a perverse variation from an Aristotelian norm. For example, Jackson G. Barry in Dramatic Structure: The Shaping of Experience tells us: "the typical dramatic structure orders its incidents in a causal chain--as opposed to a poetic structure, which might arrange its parts according to the contrast or likeness of the themes or images."[7] But as we discovered in the last chapter, the Aristotelian formula is irrelevant even to the structure of most Greek plays, which tend to be much more episodic (in spite of their adherence to the three unities) than is generally realized.

It is not hard to understand why Euripides, and not Sophocles, was the most popular Greek playwright during the Elizabethan period; for an episodic play like The Trojan Women--unlike Oedipus--bears a resemblance in structure to a play by Shakespeare. Nevertheless this obvious fact has not prevented theorists from writing books in which they endeavor to squeeze Shakespeare's tragedies into a shape that would elicit an imprimatur from the author of the Poetics.

VARIETIES OF DRAMATIC STRUCTURE

2. Freytag on Structure

If it is true that one can scarcely write about Greek tragedy without discussing Aristotle's _Poetics_, it remains only a little less true that one can scarcely undertake a study of structure in Shakespearean tragedy without consideration of Gustav Freytag and his famous "pyramid." Freytag's _Technique of the Drama_, published in 1863, has been extremely influential and has more or less colored our view of structure in Shakespearean tragedy ever since. Indeed, even those who have never heard of Freytag still tend to measure _Hamlet, Othello, King Lear, Macbeth_ and Shakespeare's other tragedies in Freytagian terms.

Like Aristotle, Freytag begins by dividing the structure of a play in half. According to the Freytagian formula, structure in the drama takes the shape of a pyramid, falling into two equal parts called the "play" and "counterplay." With characteristic Teutonic thoroughness, however, Freytag goes far beyond his master in mapping out plot structure.

Freytag subdivides the two parts into five movements: 1) the "introduction" (or exposition); 2) the "rising action" (which includes an "exciting force"--the beginning of which is dubbed the "complication," "where, in the soul of the hero, there arises a feeling or volition which becomes the occasion of what follows; or where the counterplay resolves to use its lever to set the hero in motion"); 3) the "climax" (or "the place in the piece where the results of the rising movement come out strong and decisively; it is almost always the crowning point of a great, amplified scene, enclosed by the smaller connecting scenes of the rising, and of the falling action"); 4) the "falling action" (sometimes initiated by a "tragic force"--not to be confused with the "climax," to which it is closely related; nor is the "tragic force" to be mixed up with the "force of the final suspense"--that deceptive ray of sunshine just before the final movement in Freytag's "counterplay"); and 5) the "catastrophe" (or "the

48

closing action; it is what the ancient stage called the exodus. In it the embarrassment of the chief characters is relieved through a great deed. The more profound the strife which has gone forward in the hero's soul, the more noble its purpose has been, so much more logical will the destruction of the succumbing hero be").[8]

The same objections which were raised against Aristotle's and Hegel's analyses of structure can also be leveled at Freytag's pyramid. How many plays actually fall into such a precise pattern? At least Aristotle's complication, turning point, and unraveling has the benefit of simplicity; Freytag's multiplication of terms is Gothic. Yet he admits that not all plays have a tragic force. Since the tragic force is not essential to the pyramid, the question arises whether any play really has such an isolable element. The climax is the turning point in the action--that is, it starts, by definition, the falling action. Consequently, what purpose is served in positing a tragic force?

Freytag seems to blueprint plays with meticulous precision; however, he is often inexact and even slipshod. The catastrophe in Greek plays is not always identical with the exodus. For instance, most critics would agree that the catastrophe in Oedipus occurs at the moment when the title character recognizes that he has killed his father and married his mother. This is the moment towards which the structure of the play has been building--this is the moment of truth. But it falls at the conclusion of episode four, not in the exodus. In his description of Oedipus, Freytag divides the catastrophe into three parts, lumping together episode four and the exodus. The division hardly results in either clarity or consistency.

It is important to note that Freytag, again following Aristotle, makes Sophocles the touchstone of Greek tragedy. A whole chapter in Technique of the Drama is devoted to Sophocles's dramaturgy; no such extended treatment, however, is accorded to either Aeschylus or Euripides. Perhaps Freytag sensed a difficulty in any attempt to apply his formula to the work of Sophocles's peers. Actually, the Freytagian pattern does not clarify the structure of Sophocles's plays too well, either—although the critic is at great pains to stretch each of them to the dimensions of his pyramid. We have already noted how, in his analysis of Antigone, Freytag covers the disappearance of the title character after the climax by postulating her continued existence in the person of Tiresias. Hence the difficult problems attendant upon a painstaking critique of Antigone are by-passed so that the play will serve to exemplify, still again, the construction of the drama. Freytag believed that his five movements were reflected in a five-act structure. Once more, we would seem justified in asking a pertinent question: How many plays in the five-act form adhere to a pattern involving an act of exposition, an act of rising action, an act with a climax, an act of falling action, and an act leading to catastrophe?

In the sections of this chapter devoted to specific Shakespearean tragedies, I will return to Freytag and his pyramid. First, however, the problem of act division in Elizabethan drama must be addressed.

3. Act Division in the Structure of Shakespearean Tragedy

Since the average Greek play was divided into five episodes, the number five took on a mythical significance in the minds of later commentators. In The Art of Poetry, Horace informs the would-be Latin playwright: "Let a play which would be inquired after, and though seen, represented anew, be neither shorter nor longer than the fifth act."[9] We can be fairly certain that Horace's injunction was not based on any custom prevailing among playwrights in his own time. In the medieval period, however, Donatus sliced Terence's plays like so much baloney into the prescribed number of acts—although many scholars today believe that Terence, like most Roman dramatists, did not divide his plays into acts at all. Minturno, Scaliger,

Trissino, Robortello, and Castelvetro also accepted the supposed classical practice. Probably the only Latin playwright who segmented his work into five parts was Seneca; and, ironically, his "plays" were not, so far as we know, staged in the usual sense but merely recited by a single actor.

Today most editions of Shakespeare's plays are still divided into five acts. This in spite of Samuel Johnson's warning in his preface of 1765 that such a division is "in almost all the plays void of authority,"[10] and in spite of excellent modern studies that confirm the truth of Johnson's judgment. As James E. Hirsh puts it in his criticism of T. W. Baldwin's _William Shakespeare's Five-Act Structure_: "That an apple pie--to use a homely metaphor--can be divided into five pieces does not mean that an apple pie has a five-part structure."[11]

Hirsh argues that Shakespeare's plays should be divided into scenes, not acts, because the latter "obscure the actual structure of the plays":

> The interval between one entrance or exit and the next such change has for a long time been recognized as an important structural unit in classical French drama, and the term _scene_ has been applied to it . . . Act divisions in the classical French theater usually occur, in turn, at those points when the stage is entirely cleared of characters and, in this respect, correspond to scene divisions in Shakespearean drama. Though there are many more scenes in a given play by Shakespeare than acts in a French play, the scene is nevertheless the largest structural subdivision that is unquestionably to be found in every play by Shakespeare, and the _liaison des scenes_ within an act in the French theater corresponds to the continuity within a Shakespearean scene.[12]

Hirsh isn't saying Shakespeare's structures are "classical," for he emphasizes--following Doran--that "multiplicity of detail" found in Elizabethan drama.

With the exception of Ben Jonson, Elizabethan dramatists for the public stage before 1607 ignored act division (writers for the private stage, however, heeded Horace and his later Italian disciples). The plays for the public stage were performed without intervals, except perhaps in the case of exceptionally long pieces where the audience might be given a brief rest.

After 1607 the number of divided plays began to increase, and by 1616 the practice was just about followed universally on the public stage. Wilfred T. Jewkes accounts for the change in terms of "the infusion of new blood into the ranks of the major dramatists, in the persons of Middleton, Fletcher, Beaumont, and Field, who joined with Jonson in the practice of act division, since most of them wrote equally as many plays, if not more, for the private theaters."[13]

With few possible exceptions, the act divisions in Shakespeare's plays are a result of later editorial work on the texts. Apparently, the only divisions Shakespeare wrote into the structure of his plays were of a scenic nature; that is, he indicated dividing points in a play where the stage is temporarily vacated in the course of the action to allow for a shift in time and/or place. The length and number of such scenic divisions varies greatly.

By dividing all of Shakespeare's plays into five acts, editors convey the false impression that two structurally dissimilar plays--for example, Hamlet and Othello--are alike in form. As Alfred Harbage observes, the reader is then likely to miss "the original effect of the juxtaposition of two actions when the first now appears at the end of one 'act' and the second at the beginning of the next 'act'."[14]

In the sections of this chapter which follow, I intend to examine five of Shakespeare's tragedies--namely, Hamlet,Othello, King Lear, Macbeth, and Antony and Cleopatra--in an attempt to refute the still prevalent assumption that there exists a typical Shakespearean pattern.

4. Hamlet

Hamlet is the only play by Shakespeare which Freytag analyzes completely in terms of his five-step construction of the drama. According to Freytag the introduction occurs in Act I, Scenes 1, 2, and 3, wherein we learn about Hamlet's grief over his father's death and his indignation over his mother's hasty marriage to the new king, Claudius. The exciting force makes an appearance in Scenes 4 and 5 when Hamlet meets his father's ghost, and is directed to avenge his father's murder at the hands of Claudius. (Freytag makes no distinction between the complication and the exciting force.) The rising action takes up all of Act II, and Scenes 1 and 2 of Act III, culminating in the Player's Scene in which Hamlet's suspicions of Claudius are confirmed.

When Hamlet spares the king at his prayers in Act III, Scene III, the climax is reached. The tragic force follows in Scene 4 when Hamlet stabs Polonius in the queen's closet. (Freytag seems to include the first three scenes of Act IV under the tragic force heading, too.) The falling action--or the counterplay--in which fortune turns against the hero, takes place in the last four scenes of Act IV and the first scene of Act V. Finally, the catastrophe occurs in the last scene of the play: Hamlet destroys his enemies, but is himself slain, too.[15]

If we focus on Hamlet as the central character in the action, we find that Freytag's analysis (like Aristotle's method as applied to Oedipus) works fairly well. Most critics have concurred, for example, that the climax or turning point in the action arrives when Hamlet neglects to kill

Claudius in Act III, Scene 3; for the hero's decision allows the king time to set in motion the
counterplay, which inevitably results in
catastrophe. The Players's Scene is sometimes
cited as the turning point, but critics who interpret the action in such a way reveal that their
mind is not on Hamlet's death at the hands of his
enemies. Thus Francis Fergusson--whose interest
lies in ritual--views the Players's Scene as "the
climax and peripety of the whole complex plot-
scheme."[16] Similarly, Charles R. Forker--whose
concern is with theatrical symbolism--believes that
the Players's Scene constitutes the climax or turning point of the plot.[17]

Shakespeare's structures are rich, and they
move on many levels. It only confuses matters,
however, to transfer the terminology proper to one
level to another where it does not belong. Although G. Wilson Knight stresses the spatial nature
of dramatic structure as opposed to its temporal or
Aristotelian-Freytagian aspect, he nonetheless uses
the language appropriate to the latter category to
make the following announcement: "_Hamlet_ begins
with an explosion in the first act; the rest of the
play is the reverberation thereof . . . The usual
process is reversed and the climax is at the
start."[18] By any ordinary definition of climax--as
Freytag's turning point, or as the point where the
audience makes its greatest emotional response, or
as the answer to the dramatic question in the
resolution of an Ibsenian play--Knight's application of the term is surely bewildering.

Freytag's insistence on the importance of the
tragic force is also puzzling. Since the tragic
error was committed at the climax, it seems redun-
dant to assume (as Freytag _appears_ _to_--he fails to
justify _any_ of his choices) that when Hamlet stabs
Polonius Shakespeare has invented a tragic force,
because now Hamlet must leave the court just as he
is about to succeed in his revenge. The scene in
the queen's closet is important for the light it
throws on the hero's character, but it is not
decisive in terms of the pyramid as described by
Freytag himself. Furthermore, the Freytagian
analysis only accounts for one line of action in

the play; therefore, as a description of dramatic structure the method remains woefully incomplete. It seems significant that Hamlet, as noted, is the only Shakespearean tragedy analyzed in its entirety by Freytag. The reader may recall that Freytag also ignores, for the most part, Aeschylus and Euripides, and that his method does not succeed convincingly when applied to any of Sophocles's plays, with the exception of Oedipus. Since the Freytagian approach is basically Aristotelian, it could not be made to square with the Oresteia, Medea, and The Trojan Women, or at least not without a good deal of Procrustean chopping and sawing.

As we shall see when the time comes to look at Shakespeare's other great tragedies, Freytag is no more helpful than Aristotle as a guide to the variety of structures found in drama.

Historically, Hamlet is in the tradition of the Revenge Play. One school of thought traces the genre back to Seneca; a second argues with Howard Baker that the Revenge Play owes more to medieval drama than it does to the Roman playwright.[19] Since influences are complex and difficult to isolate, it is safe to say that some merit resides in both views. The Elizabethans liked Seneca even better than Euripides, probably because Seneca, who modeled his work on that of Euripides, was even less chary than his master about violating Aristotelian ideas of action. As we have seen, the medieval theater had also prepared the Elizabethan age to view dramatic form in a non-Aristotelian way.

Whatever its derivation, the structure of the Revenge Play typically involves intrigue, strong action, and hesitation on the part of the hero, who may be a father avenging the death of a son, or vice versa, with the ghost of the deceased guiding the avenger. Thomas Kyd's The Spanish Tragedy, John Marston's Antonio's Revenge, and Cyril Tourneur's The Atheist's Tragedy are examples of the type. T.S. Eliot argued that "there are verbal parallels [in Hamlet] so close to The Spanish Tragedy as to leave no doubt that in places

55

Shakespeare was merely <u>revising</u> the text of Kyd."[20]
Both plays include the device of a play-within-a-
play. Scholars agree that Kyd also wrote a piece
about Hamlet similar to <u>The Spanish Tragedy</u>, although he reversed the situation of the earlier
play in which a father avenges the death of a son.
Kyd's version of the Hamlet story has disappeared;
however, the consensus is that certain structural
details in Shakespeare's play derive from the earlier, more melodramatic, version.

Even though <u>Hamlet</u> derives its form, or a large
part of it, from the tradition of the Revenge Play,
it transcends the limitations of the original
genre. Shakespeare could not help but change
whatever he touched. In altering the old form to
allow for the expression of his individual genius,
however, Shakespeare created not only a masterpiece
but a problem. "Why does Hamlet hesitate in seeking to avenge his father's murder?" : that is the
question which has helped to make Hamlet the most
written about play in the history of the drama.
The problem is relevant to a consideration of
structure.

In the neo-classical period, Johnson touched on
the subject. He found evidence in <u>Hamlet</u> of what
he conceived to be inconsequential plotting. He
pointed out that the hero is more of "an instrument
than an agent"; and he objected to the ending because "the exchange of weapons is rather an ex-
pedient of necessity than a stroke of art."[21]
Johnson was no slave to neo-classical rules; for
instance, he did not hold in high esteem the
pseudo-Aristotelian unities of time and place. All
the same, we can detect in Johnson's criticism of
structure in <u>Hamlet</u> a bias in favor of a certain
kind of form : a form in which each scene is
causally related to the next in a straight line; in
which everything that happens is a result of the
hero's will; and in which absolutely nothing is
left to chance or the irrational. Probably Aristotle would have concurred with Johnson about <u>Ham-
let</u>, treating it no more indulgently than <u>Medea</u>.

In our own century T.S. Eliot (who described himself as a classicist in literature) once declared: "So far from being Shakespeare's master-piece, [Hamlet] is most certainly an artistic failure." Eliot arrives at this perspicacious judgment by arguing that the play "is full of some stuff that the writer could not drag to light, con-template, or manipulate into art"; that is, the playwright was unable to fashion an "objective cor-relative" for the emotion he wanted to express through the structure of his play. According to Eliot, Hamlet basically involves the "feeling of a son towards a guilty mother." Having thus simplified the drama, Eliot discovers--like Johnson before him--that there is much irrelevant matter encumbering the structure.[22]

Many contemporary critics, however, have defended the structure of Hamlet. "The effort to postpone the catastrophe," says Elmer Edgar Stoll, "is apparent in some of the greatest tragedies, like Oedipus, apart from those which deal with revenge." Stoll continues with the argument from tradition: "Such a Hamlet ... is in keeping with the whole play, of which he is only an inseparable component, and with the nature of drama. He is part of the structure, upholding and upheld by the other parts; and some of the mystery in him is only that of plot, some of it, a matter of emotional ef-fect, as his reticence and dignity. He is a dramatic figure, not a psychological study."[23]

If Stoll appears to err by excluding character in favor of structure, Ernest Jones simplifies the form of the play in another way by reducing the ac-tion to the transformations of the Oedipus complex. Hamlet hesitates, says Jones, because he has uncon-sciously identified with Claudius in his incestuous marriage to the hero's mother. Moreover, Hamlet feels that if he were to kill Claudius he would be committing symbolic parricide. "So of the two im-possible alternatives," concludes Jones, "Hamlet adopts the passive solution of letting the incest continue vicariously, but at the same time provok-ing destruction at the king's hand."[24]

Like Stoll, Jones sees that the play is larger than the central character. But where Stoll is content to make Hamlet serve the demands of the Revenge Play pattern, Jones stresses the father-son relationships in the structure. Although Jones's interpretation has the advantage of focusing our attention on what Fergusson calls the "analogical relationships"--and by doing so, pointing up the structural complexity of <u>Hamlet</u>--too much is claimed for the Oedipus complex.

In his landmark study, <u>Shakespearean Tragedy</u>, A.C. Bradley divides structure into three parts : the "exposition" (which "sets forth or expounds the situation, or state of affairs, out of which the conflict arises"); the "conflict" itself (which involves "the bulk of the play, comprising the second, third and fourth acts, and usually a part of the first and a part of the fifth"); and the "catastrophe" (which "shows the issue of the conflict"). Bradley declares that he has no wish to reduce all of Shakespeare's plays to one standard : "we must be prepared to find that, as the plays vary so much, no single way of regarding the conflict will answer precisely to the construction of all."[25]

Yet several pages later Bradley states that as a rule the turning point (Freytag's climax) occurs around the middle of a Shakespearean play, "and where it is well marked it has the effect of dividing the play into five parts instead of three."[26] The five parts which Bradley then describes retrace the dimensions of Freytag's pyramid. Consequently, a strain is felt throughout <u>Shakespearean Tragedy</u>. On the one hand, Bradley is sensitive to the different structural configurations, and he makes an effort to understand them in their individuality. On the other hand, Bradley conveys the impression that he would be much happier if Shakespeare remained consistent in construction.

For the most part, says Bradley, <u>Hamlet</u> conforms to the "general plan"; but <u>King Lear</u> and <u>Othello</u> reveal a "certain difficulty," the latter play being the "more peculiar" of the two. Bradley succeeds--at least to his own satisfaction--in hammering <u>King Lear</u> into the required shape; <u>Othello</u>, however, proves intractable (although the critic consoles himself that it does conform <u>in</u> <u>part</u>), for no amount of hammering will suffice to remove <u>all</u> its "striking peculiarity." With his Aristotelian-<u>cum</u>-Freytagian notions of structure, Bradley finds a number of "real defects" in the plays. Not only does Shakespeare indulge in structural "inconsistencies and contradictions," but he also errs in dwelling on matters which, in Bradley's view, have no bearing on plot development. Bradley concedes that "most of it we should be very sorry to miss . . . but who can defend it from the point of view of constructive art?" Finally, says Bradley, Shakespeare presents too many short, rapidly displaced scenes by switching back and forth from one line of action to another, thus betraying "the merely narrative arrangement common in plays before his time." Bradley is quite emphatic about Shakespeare's structural approach here : "it is a defective method."[27]

In his essay on form in Shakespearean drama, Maynard Mack points out that surely "Bradley missed something--that there is another kind of construction in Shakespeare's tragedies...." This other kind of construction, says Mack, is more "inward"; it is not wholly a matter of plot or a specific configuration of language. "Some of its elements arise from the playwright's visualizing imagination, the consciousness of groupings, gestures, entrances, exits." Mack thinks that other elements may belong to some model Shakespeare had in mind which was handed down to him from the past.[28]

Mack's analysis of Shakespeare's "inward structure" reveals a number of patterns in the major tragedies. In <u>Hamlet</u>, for example, Mack sees a pattern in which the overstater--namely, Hamlet--is juxtaposed to his foil, the understater, Horatio. Mack suggests a philosophical basis for this dual-character structure by reminding us of Greek tragedy, in which the first actor largely asserts the values of individualism as opposed to the community values represented by the chorus. And he goes on to assert that, because most of us hold that tragic drama is a study of man's relationship to transcendence (an arguable assumption today), there has to be a confrontation between the free, individualistic overstater and the secure, well-adjusted understater.[29] Unfortunately, these ideas are not worked out in relation to Hamlet, and with good reason Mack admits of their speculative nature. Although the overstater versus the understater pattern is not without its importance in Hamlet, Horatio remains too much of a minor figure to support all the meaning Mack assigns to him.

A more helpful insight into Shakespearean structure appears in Mack's analysis of mirror situations in the plays. Like Jones, Mack observes that there are three sons in Hamlet; unlike Jones, Mack has no psychoanalytical ax to grind. The three sons are, in one form or another, avengers of a dead father; and all three are temporarily blocked in their designs by an older man. At the end, however, the sons are victorious in unforeseen ways:

> The return of Fortinbras, having achieved his objective in Poland, to find his "rights" in Denmark achieved without a blow, is timed to coincide with Hamlet's achieving his objective in exposing and killing the king and Laertes's achieving his objective of avenging his father's death on Hamlet. When this episode is played before us in the theater there is little question . . . but that something of the glow and martial upsurge dramatized in Fortinbras's entrance associates itself to Hamlet, even as Fortinbras's words associate Hamlet to a soldier's death. Meantime, Laertes, who has been trapped by the king and has paid with his life for it, gives us an alternative reflection of the prince, which is equally a part of the truth.[30]

Now, Lily B. Campbell has argued that Hamlet is a tragedy of grief, and that the three sons represent the ways men accept grief when it comes to them. Each of the three young men mourns the loss of a father; but because each has a different tem-

perament, their responses differ. Fortinbras's
sorrow is dominated by reason; the grief of Hamlet
and Laertes, however, remains excessive and leads
to death.[31] Obviously, Mack and Campbell--in spite
of their different approaches--are both concerned
with the same kind of structure : one in which Hamlet remains a single element in a complex design.

Lastly, Mack calls attention to another kind of
structure in Hamlet. He notes that "a story of
poisoning forms the climax of the first act, a mime
and 'play' of poisoning the climax of the third,
and actual poisoning, on a wide scale, the climax
of the fifth."[32] Mack seems to be using the word
"climax" to designate not just the turning point as
understood by Aristotle and Freytag, but any
decisive turning point. His second example is, of
course, open to criticism.

Mack may have taken his lead on the poisoning
motif from the long chapter on Hamlet in
Fergusson's book. No one has studied in greater
detail than the author of The Idea of a Theater the
multiple levels of structure in Shakespeare's most
famous play. Fergusson also believes that a distinction must be made "between the story of Hamlet
the individual and the story of the play as a
whole."[33] The various lines of action in Hamlet
are both logically related and ironically parallel;
there is one general action--but no one causally
related plot development. According to Fergusson:
"The main action of Hamlet may be described as the
attempt to find and destroy the hidden 'imposthume'
which is poisoning the life of Claudius's Denmark."
He then attempts to show how this central action is
expressed in terms of the "traditional scheme." By
the latter term Fergusson intends : the prologue;
the agons; the climax, reversal, and recognition;
the pathos; and the epiphany. It is not clear what
"traditional scheme" Fergusson is using, although
some of what he has to say squares with Aristotle
and Freytag on structure. As noted earlier, Fergusson moves the logical place for the climax or
turning point from Act III, Scene 3 back to the
previous scene in order to make the play accord
better with his conception of Hamlet as ritual.[34]

This is an important point. For Fergusson the Elizabethan theater is heir to the Greek tragic theater with its ritual foundation; Shakespeare's theater thus resembles the theater of Sophocles. No doubt, both plays deal with the subject of pollution. But since the thesis of the Cambridge School of Classical Anthropologists, as was noted in the previous chapter, is questionable, it would seem wise to refrain from emphasizing the ritual basis underlying Shakespearean tragic structure. Furthermore, in order to bring _Hamlet_ into line with his thesis, Fergusson is forced to give more importance, both quantitatively and qualitatively, to Fortinbras ("Fortinbras . . . appear[s] with his new faith and hope")[35] than would seem warranted by the text. Fergusson's attempt to mediate between the various critical approaches, so that the structure of _Hamlet_ is seen to be unified by one theme, also leads to oversimplification. Hence Fergusson is obliged to suggest that the ritual pattern may not be too distinct because of "too bewildering a richness and complexity" in the play![36]

Freytag's pyramid--which is fundamentally Aristotelian--accounts satisfactorily for one line of progression in _Hamlet_; however, the Freytagian approach leaves out of consideration the multiple patterns which make Shakespeare's great tragedy so much more than a single-action drama. (And by "so much more," I do _not_ mean "so much better." After all, _Oedipus_ is a single-action drama.) The same point can also be made against the historical approach, or genre criticism, which views _Hamlet_ as conforming to the narrow specifications of the Revenge Play. What earlier critics like Johnson took to be defects in _Hamlet_ ("The action is indeed for the most part in continual progression," says Johnson, "but there are some scenes which neither forward nor retard it")[37] are in reality largely evidence of that multiformity characteristic of Elizabethan dramaturgy.

Since this multiformity varies--particularly in Shakespeare--rigid preconceptions about structure cannot be made to adjust harmoniously with specific works. Each play by Shakespeare must be viewed in its uniqueness and totality. This means that most of the ways in which the critics discussed in this section have analyzed <u>Hamlet</u> are valid up to a point, but that no one reading tells all that is going on structurally. This unspectacular conclusion is, unfortunately, too often forgotten.

5. <u>Othello</u>

If we turn immediately from <u>Hamlet</u> to <u>Othello</u>, the difficulty of speaking about a "typical" Shakespearean structure becomes manifest. Although there are some similarities between the two plays, their fundamental differences are more important.

A number of critics (among them Bradley) have called <u>Othello</u> the best constructed of all Shakespeare's plays; some have even described its form as "classical." Now it is true that the action of <u>Othello</u> seems more concentrated than that of most other Shakespearean plays; yet if we compare <u>Hamlet</u> and <u>Othello</u> in terms of structure, we will find that the earlier play is actually more "classical" in some respects than the later one. In <u>Hamlet</u>, for example, the title character takes the initiative; he may hesitate for a time, but throughout the play he remains the primary driving force in the action; he is, in short, a true protagonist. <u>Hamlet</u> may be more loosely organized than <u>Oedipus</u> or <u>Othello</u>; but <u>Hamlet</u>, like <u>Oedipus</u>, conforms in its main line of progression to Aristotle's and Freytag's ideas on structure (although Aristotle, as noted, would probably not have been happy with Shakespeare's overall strategy).

The reader will recall that Freytag does not present a complete analysis of <u>Othello</u> in terms of his famous pyramid, and that Bradley has great difficulty trying to make the play agree with Shakespeare's "usual method." For it is clear that, although Othello is the hero of the piece, Iago remains the protagonist. It is Iago who arouses Brabantio; Iago who stirs up Roderigo; Iago who gets Cassio into trouble; Iago who contrives to get Desdemona to help Cassio; Iago who then casts

suspicion on Desdemona's motives in helping Cassio;
Iago who instructs Emilia to steal Desdemona's
handkerchief, and who then deceives Othello into
thinking his wife gave it to Cassio; Iago who sets
another trap for Cassio, and who gets Roderigo
killed; and Iago who brings on the catastrophe
which results in the death of both Desdemona and
Othello.[38]

Bradley observes: "But then, if Iago is taken
as the leading figure, the usual mode of construction is plainly abandoned, for there will nowhere
be a crisis followed by a descending movement.
Iago's cause advances, at first slowly and quietly,
then rapidly, but it does nothing but advance until
the catastrophe swallows his dupe and him
together." It is apparent that Bradley misses what
Freytag calls the counterplay. Consequently, he
shrinks back from the implications of his own
analysis: "this way of regarding the action does
positive violence, I think, to our natural impressions of the earlier part of the play"; and he
adds: "I think, therefore, that the usual scheme is
so far followed that the drama represents first the
rise of the hero, and then his fall."[39] It would
seem more correct to say that the first half of the
play shows Othello secure in his love, and the
second half presents his jealousy and destruction.
There is, properly speaking, no rising and falling
action in Othello. Therefore, it would be misleading to speak of a turning point in Act III, Scene 3
(the same place as in Hamlet), when Iago first
begins to arouse Othello's jealousy (both Freytag
and Richard G. Moulton opt for this reading),[40] because to identify it as such would give the impression that the rest of the structure is in conformity with the Aristotelian-Freytagian model, which
is clearly not the case.

"Conflict," says Lajos Egri, "is the heartbeat
of all dramatic writing."[41] The trouble with this
generalization--which appears in many books on
playwriting--is that it does not apply to every
great play. It certainly does not apply to
Othello. In Hamlet there is a battle of wills between the hero and the king. Othello, however, is
not pitted against Iago; nor is there any overall

network of conflict in the play. Contrast, not conflict, is the chief structural method used by Shakespeare in Othello.

The first part of the play is relatively calm; the second part is unrivaled in Shakespeare's work for sustained turbulence. The early Othello is contrasted with the later Othello; the "romantic" Othello is contrasted with the "realistic" Iago; Desdemona's love is contrasted with Iago's hate; and there is contrast between what Othello accuses Desdemona of being, and what she really is. Indeed, the number of contrasts could be extended almost indefinitely.

Hamlet gives the impression of being a mirror which reflects the world in several directions; Othello seems more Greek, more closely focused on a single subject. Bradley says that Oedipus and Othello have this in common : they both convey a strong feeling that the characters are hemmed in by fate.[42] Closer examination of form in Othello, however, reveals an intricate architectonics foreign to Greek tragedy. As a matter of fact, Hamlet and Othello both have a mirror structure, though the latter play is less elaborately developed in this respect.

If Hamlet depicts three sons responding diversely to the death of a father, Othello depicts four characters--Othello, Iago, Roderigo, and Bianca--suffering various degrees of jealousy. Richard G. Moulton has shown, perhaps better than anyone else, how Othello is at once economical and complex. "The leading personages in Othello," he says, "are, in character, variations of a single passion, suspicious jealousy, and their position in the play is exactly determined by their relation to this passion."[43] Moulton isolates three tragic actions: one, the true love of Othello and Desdemona--which concludes in jealousy, murder, and suicide; two, Bianca's relationship with Cassio-- which results in her arrest as his murderer; and three, Roderigo's desire for Desdemona--which ends in his murder. Added to these three tragic actions are four evil intrigues by Iago: one, the intrigue against Roderigo; two, the intrigue to supplant

Cassio; three, the intrigue to remove Cassio entirely; and four, the intrigue to destroy Othello
and Desdemona. The structure then is made up of
seven actions, which finally unite and result in an
eighth action, "or rather, reaction; the recoil of
this catastrophe upon Iago himself." Emilia sees
through her evil husband's intrigue, and finally
exposes him--too late, of course--to Othello and
the authorities. "The principle underlying this
nemesis," says Moulton, "is one of the profoundest
of Shakespeare's moral ideas--that evil not only
corrupts the heart, but equally undermines the
judgment."[44]

Moulton's analysis again makes clear that Iago,
not Othello, is the protagonist or active force in
the structure. But Othello is the main character
or hero. Nothing could be more illustrative of the
limitations inherent in a purely structural approach to drama, however, than an awareness of this
fact. For no one--after studying all the elements
(that is, after studying structure, character, language, thought, and enactment)--would dream of
relegating the hero, Othello, to second place in
one's total experience of the play.

6. King Lear

King Lear is the only major tragedy of
Shakespeare in which the mirror pattern is
developed to the dimensions of a subplot. There is
the story of Lear and his daughters; and then, running side by side with it, and interwoven with it,
is the story of Gloucester and his sons.

Bradley is forced to admit that Lear is not,
from the point of view of structure, the
protagonist (as Lear himself puts it: "I am a man
more sinned against than sinning"), that Goneril,
Regan, and Edmund propel the action forward.
Referring to the latter three characters, Bradley
remarks: "Their fortune mounts to the crisis, where
the old King is driven out into the storm and loses
his reason, and where Gloucester is blinded and ex-
pelled from his home. Then the counter-action

66

begins to gather force, and their cause to decline; and, although they win the battle, they are involved in the catastrophe which they bring on Cordelia and Lear. Thus we may still find in _King Lear_ the usual scheme of an ascending and a descending movement of one side in the conflict."[45]

By the "usual scheme," of course, Bradley intends an Aristotelian-Freytagian pyramid—a pattern which, by any means, he finds to some extent in _all_ of Shakespeare's tragedies.

If Lear _were_ the protagonist, Bradley argues, then the turning point would occur in the first act when the hero foolishly divides his kingdom between Goneril and Regan, and at the same time disinherits Cordelia against the protest of Kent, who is banished for his pains, because from this point on Lear's fortune steadily falls. Rightly, Bradley dismisses such an analysis as absurd.[46]

A vital element in any play structure—regardless of type—is an increase of tension; and _King Lear_ is no exception. But even a good critic like Moulton can apparently overlook this basic fact about dramatic form. (I am speaking of _artistically_ _successful_ dramatic form. Naturally one could write a play which lacks a building up of tension, but it seems doubtful whether that play would live through the ages.) Says Moulton: "The 'catastrophe,' or turning point of [_King Lear_] at which the ultimate issues are decided, appears in the present case, not close to the end of the play, nor (as in _Julius Caesar_) in the center, but close to the commencement: at the end of the opening scene. Lear's act of folly has in reality determined the issue of the whole action; the scenes which follow are only working out a determined issue to its full realization."[47] Ten pages later, however, Moulton (who, as can be seen from the above quote, confounds the turning point with the catastrophe), contradicts himself and designates Act III, Scene 4—when Lear encounters Edgar disguised as a madman—as the turning point. If we call the beginning of _King Lear_ a "catastrophe," what will we call the ending?

Moulton may seem to be closer to locating the turning point in King Lear in the second instance, when he sees it as occurring in the fourth scene of the third act. Harley Granville-Barker argues, however, that the turning point comes in Act Three, Scene 2: "This is the argument's absolute height; and from now on we may feel (as far as Lear is concerned) the tension relax, through the first grim passage of his madness, slackening still through the fantastic scene of the arraignment of the joint-stools before that queer bench of justices, to the moment of his falling asleep and his conveyance away--his conveyance, we find it to be, out of the main stream of the play's action."[48]

In reality, it is impossible to cite any one scene in King Lear as decisive, simply because the play has a double-story structure. Here Beckerman would appear correct in maintaining that analysis of Shakespeare's structure reveals, not a "climactic point," but a "climactic plateau." That is to say, Scenes II and IV, in which Lear is shown on the heath, and Scene VII, in which Gloucester is blinded, would together constitute, in Act III, the turning point.[49]

But can we properly speak of a turning point at all in King Lear? Is there any part--climactic point or climactic plateau--which starts what Aristotle calls the unraveling or what Freytag labels the falling action? We return to two pertinent observations made earlier: one, Lear (like Othello) is not the protagonist; and two, Bradley's attempt to find the "usual scheme" (in other words, the pyramid) seems even more questionable here than was the case with Othello.

In Oedipus the turning point occurs when the hero first reveals evidence of self-doubt; in Hamlet the turning point arrives when the hero spares the king at his prayers. There is a link between the turning points and catastrophes in both plays. It would seem impossible to locate either a climactic point or a climactic plateau in King Lear, however, which bears the same relation to the catastrophe that the turning points in Oedipus and

Hamlet bear to their endings. King Lear begins
with a decision by the hero, who afterwards merely
reacts to the decisions of others.

This is not to argue, of course, that the
catastrophe occurs at the beginning. In Act I,
Scene 2 we want to know what the result will be of
Lear's unwise division of his kingdom and his un-
just treatment of Cordelia; in Scene 2 we want to
know how the Lear story will relate to the
Gloucester story. Structurally and thematically,
Shakespeare alternates and fuses the two lines of
action in a masterly fashion. Both Lear and
Gloucester err in their judgment of their children;
both are guilty of pride and anger; and both are
victimized by scheming offspring. If the argument
(Granville-Barker) reaches its highest point in the
center of the play, or if the emotional effects
seem strongest there (Beckerman)--then couldn't it
be maintained that the last two acts remain anticlimactic? But such is not the case. King Lear
moves forward, gaining in intensity as it does so,
from start to finish, without any turning point
(however defined). The expectations aroused in us
during Act I are not satisfied until Act V when
Cordelia is hanged and both Lear and Gloucester die
of grief; however, the evil daughters of Lear--
Goneril and Regan--and Gloucester's bastard, Edmund, also perish. Clearly, the catastrophe appears where we normally expect it to appear: at the
end of the play.

Nevertheless King Lear does not--in its
totality--exemplify any typical Shakespearean pattern or "usual scheme" (pyramidal or otherwise).
Structurally, King Lear exemplifies King Lear.

7. Macbeth

Macbeth has frequently been referred to as
Shakespeare's most "classical" play. It is much
shorter than Hamlet, Othello, and King Lear, and it
has a single-action structure. Although Lady Macbeth is important, and although she is portrayed as
the title character's opposing voice (Mack) or an-

tithesis (Moulton), throughout most of the action Macbeth remains not only the hero but also the protagonist. As Bradley points out, simplicity distinguishes Shakespeare's dramaturgy in Macbeth,[50] and simplicity is generally thought of as a classical attribute. So far so good.

But by "classical" most critics also have in mind Oedipus, or a play in conformity with Aristotle's conception of tragic structure. Now is Macbeth "classical" according to such an assumption? Does Macbeth follow the lines of Sophocles's Oedipus or Aristotle's mini-pyramid?

In the first half of Macbeth, we watch the hero's rise to power through evil actions; in the second half, we observe his fall to destruction. Critics frequently speak of an Aristotelian turning point or Freytagian climax midway in the action. They have difficulty agreeing, however, as to where precisely it occurs. Moulton argues that the decisive event which brings forth the downturn appears in Act III, Scene 3: "Success . . . constituting the first half of the play and failure the second half of the play, the transition from the one to the other is the expedition against Banquo and Fleance, in which success and failure are mingled: and this expedition, the keystone to the arch, is found to occupy the exact middle of the middle act." Freytag designates the following scene at the banquet as the turning point, but offers no reason for his choice. Harbage calls Act III, Scene 6 a turning point because the dialogue between Lennox and another lord presents the prospect of "active opposition . . . and of gathering forces of resistance."[51] There is some merit in each of these selections.

In terms of Macbeth's physical destruction by his enemies, Fleance's escape promises a change in fortune for the hero--a change which is clearly articulated for the first time in Act III, Scene 6. The emphasis in the banquet scene is, of course, on Macbeth's inner state; it is here that the hero begins to markedly lose self-control ("markedly," because he shows evidence, even earlier, of instability). In Oedipus the turning point occurs when the hero shows the first signs of doubt in himself, when the initial crack appears in his protective armor. Thus the banquet scene is comparable to the climax in Sophocles's play: Oedipus's "restlessness of soul" and "tumult of the mind" find their equivalent in Macbeth's cheeks "blanch'd with fear." Perhaps Freytag chose this scene because the hero's inner condition makes him vulnerable to the forces which eventually destroy him.

It is impossible to pinpoint any <u>one</u> scene in <u>Macbeth</u>, however, as <u>the</u> turning point. Nor would the three scenes discussed above square with what Beckerman calls a climactic plateau; Scenes 3 and 6 are too brief to qualify as part of a "coordination of intense moments." Beckerman himself says that the climactic plateau is easily discerned in Scene 4 of Act III and Scene 1 of Act IV.[52] True, both scenes are intense. But isn't it arbitrary to choose these two scenes and ignore Scenes 3 and 6 in Act III, especially when no evidence is offered in defense of the climactic plateau? The scenes chosen by Moulton and Harbage prepare us for the catastrophe just as much as those selected by Freytag and Beckerman. Consequently, we are forced to conclude that <u>Macbeth</u> does not fit snugly into the Aristotelian-Freytagian scheme--or into any other known scheme--of dramatic structure.

Fergusson has written an essay, however, in which he has tried to show that <u>Macbeth</u> "may be understood as 'the imitation of an action,' in approximately Aristotle's sense of this phrase."[53] In order to give the seal of approval to <u>Macbeth</u>, Fergusson is obliged to restrict the thematic content of the play to the following statement: "to outrun the pauser, reason" ("which seems to me," says Fergusson, "to describe the action, or motive, of the play as a whole").[54] The key event is now seen to occur in Act IV, Scene 3, wherein a doctor informs Macduff of King Edward's miraculous power to cure sickness. Says Fergusson: "It marks the turning point, and it introduces the notion of the appeal by faith to Divine Grace which will reverse the evil course of the action when Malcolm and Macduff learn to outrun reason in that way, instead of

71

by responding to the witches's supernatural solicitations as Macbeth has done."[55] As the foregoing quotation might suggest, Fergusson also discovers in Act IV, Scene 3 an Aristotelian reversal and recognition (two developments which are difficult enough to locate in most Greek tragedies). Thus the structure of <u>Macbeth</u> is chiseled into shape in order to conform with still another critic's view of Shakespeare's "usual method."

<u>Macbeth</u> can be said to have at least five turning points--surely an odd feature in a "classical" play. But then, as we have seen, most Greek tragedies also remain unclassical in the extreme. <u>Macbeth</u> lacks the tight plotting of <u>Oedipus</u>. In Sophocles's play each scene inevitably follows the preceding one in causal progression; in Shakespeare's play--although the scenic arrangement is more closely joined than in <u>King Lear</u>--the form is still episodic by Aristotelian standards (although not, in some instances, by either Aeschylean or Euripidean standards). Even if we compare <u>Macbeth</u> to Greek tragedy as a whole, we find a significant difference. The plays of Aeschylus, Sophocles, and Euripides characteristically begin in the middle of things, or close to the catastrophe; <u>Macbeth</u>, like other plays by Shakespeare and his contemporaries, begins at the beginning, or at some distance from the ending. Almost all Greek plays take place in twenty-four hours; Macbeth's tragedy spans about ten weeks.

8. <u>Antony and Cleopatra</u> and <u>All for Love</u>: A Neo-Classical Alteration of Structure in Shakespearean Tragedy

The neo-classical critics recognized Shakespeare's genius, but they found the forms through which he expressed that genius barbaric compared to Greek and Roman models. The analogical manner of thought characteristic of the Middle Ages and the Renaissance gave way to an age stamped by Cartesian rationalism. Decorum, propriety, regularity--these were the qualities extolled by neo-classical theorists. Mathematics became the ideal discipline; so much so, that it was thought dramaturgy could be reduced to the exactness of geometry. (And in that naive and dogmatic era, men still believed that Euclidean geometry was the sole possible geometry.) Renaissance critics, who had derived their ideas from readings and misreadings of Aristotle, Horace, and other venerable ancients, seemed to have exercised scant influence on the practice of dramatists in the public playhouse. Neo-classical thinkers carried more weight than their predecessors, however, and succeeded in imposing the "rules."

Most discussions of the time raged around the three unities and the liaison des scenes. Dramatic structure equalled observance of what the neo-classical age took to be Aristotle's strictures on unity of time, place, and action. No play should be stretched out longer than twenty-four hours; better still, a play should correspond exactly to the actual time of performance in order to guarantee credibility. Nor should the place of the action change during the course of performance, since the critics felt that the audience could not imagine itself present in two different places at once--or, in fact, even successively. Out went subplots--indeed, out went all types of mirroring--and anything else which was not strictly necessary to the action. As for the liaison des scenes, it was the requirement that each scene be inevitably linked to the following scene for the purpose of optimum structural unity. Clearly, it was a mechanical approach to dramatic structure.

The difference between Shakespearean and neo-classical structure can be brought out by a comparison of Antony and Cleopatra with Dryden's All for Love. Episodic and diffuse, Antony and Cleopatra covers ten years; it has over thirty-four speaking parts (plus sundry walk-on characters); and it takes place in Alexandria, Messina, Rome, Misenum, Syria, Athens, Actium, and elsewhere in the Roman Empire. The Globe text of the play indicates forty-two scenes. Closely based on Plutarch's Life of Antony, Shakespeare's dramatization resembles the form of a chronicle play; consequently, the piece has even less plot in the Aristotelian sense than the other great tragedies. "Shakespeare's noteworthy achievement of coherence in _Antony and Cleopatra_ was made not by the exclusion or even reshaping of much of his source material," observes Madeleine Doran, "but by the exploitation of character and of setting to emphasize dramatic conflict and by the use of various poetic devices to secure the harmonious repetition and contrast of emotional tones."[56]

All the same, G.B. Tennyson has attempted to force _Antony and Cleopatra_ into the "usual scheme"--that is, into the Aristotelian-Freytagian pyramid--although he admits that the play is "far from the perfect illustration."[57] According to Tennyson, the introduction occurs in the opening speech between Philo and Demetrius; the rising action occupies the following act and part of III, wherein we learn "of the news that comes to Antony in Alexandria, of domestic strife in Rome, and of the death of his wife. This sets in motion a sequence of events that shatters the Egyptian luxuriance of Antony's life"; the turning point involves two scenes, 10 and 11, in Act III, as Antony is defeated at sea and suffers the loss of both honor and power (Beckerman finds a climactic plateau in scenes 11, 12, and 13; but, as is often the case, he fails to explain his selection); the falling action takes up most of Act IV; the catastrophe appears at the conclusion of Act IV, and is continued in the last scene of Act V with Cleopatra's death.[58]

It is not hard to see what is wrong with the Aristotelian-Freytagian approach here. Until Act IV the structure of _Antony and Cleopatra_ is analyzed as though the hero was the only important character; then, when Antony disappears from the play, the critic is forced to account for the final movement, and so Cleopatra is made to share the catastrophe with Antony. Freytag boldly declares: "In _Antony and Cleopatra_, Antony is the leading character up to his death"; elsewhere he remarks: "the piece lacks climax."[59] What Freytag and Tennyson overlook is that, right from the beginning of the play, _Antony and Cleopatra_ features Antony _and_

Cleopatra. If there are two catastrophes, then there might be two turning points, or one turning point involving two characters. But Freytag's pyramid is not really suitable to a structure with two leading figures; no wonder he fails to locate a climax in Antony and Cleopatra. (Although Freytag states that Romeo and Juliet has two heroes, and although he draws upon this play for his examples of introduction and rising action, he drops it--not surprisingly--as an illustrative source for his discussion of climax, falling action, and catastrophe.)

Unlike Hamlet and Othello, Antony and Cleopatra has no mirror patterning, except for a slight parallel established between the comical pair Alexas and Charmian and the leading figures. Unlike King Lear it has no subplot. But unlike Macbeth, it is not really a single-action play, either. There is too much switching back and forth between Cleopatra in her Egyptian world and Antony in his Roman world for that to be possible. Given the sprawling nature of the action, and a structure with two main characters who die in separate acts, it might prove best not to subject the play to an analysis inspired by Aristotle and elaborated on by Freytag. Perhaps the critic should follow Doran's lead and search for the structure that is present.

In 1668--about nine years before All for Love was first acted--Dryden wrote An Essay of Dramatic Poesy. Through the person of Neander, Dryden attacks the French as being too slavish in respect to the unities of time and place and the integrity of scenes; and he praises English plays--especially those of Shakespeare (who "had the largest and most comprehensive soul")[60]--as being more various and lively than French models. Unlike some of the narrower minds of his time, then, Dryden had great critical respect for Shakespeare's dramaturgy.

Nonetheless, when Dryden wrote his version of Antony and Cleopatra, he produced a work closer in form to French neo-classical models than to Shakespeare's play. In his preface to All for Love, Dryden says: "The fabric of the play is regular enough as to the inferior parts of it, and

75

the unities of time, place, and action more exactly observed than, perhaps, the English theater requires. Particularly, the action is so much one that it is . . . without episode or underplot, every scene in the tragedy conducing to the main design, and every act concluding with a turn of it."[61]

The action of All for Love is confined to a single location--Alexandria--and unfolds in one day. Dryden also reduces the cast to about one-third the number used in Antony and Cleopatra. Shakespeare uses a technique similar to parallel editing in film--wherein a juxtaposition of shots, scenes, or even whole sequences allows the audience to be in two or more places at once (a technique which must have been very disturbing for neo-classical critics)--whereas Dryden substitutes a single rising line of action in which there are as few interruptions in progression as possible.

The neo-classical theater--so different in form from the Elizabethan playhouse--was a long, rectangular construction with a proscenium arch stage; the audience sat in front, separated from the stage by the frame. In short, it was a theater which helped to shape the closed or focused development of action in All for Love.

Structurally, Dryden's treatment of the main characters in his tragedy also differs from that of Shakespeare. In the earlier work, Antony and Cleopatra appear together in the opening scene. Dryden, however, gives Act I wholly to Antony; Cleopatra is not introduced until Act II; and it is not until the mid-point of the same act that the lovers actually confront each other. Antony disappears at the end of Act IV in Shakespeare's play, whereas he continues on throughout most of Act V in All for Love, dying only a hundred lines or so before Cleopatra's own death.

Dryden's strategy seems clear: it is to rivet attention more closely on Antony than is the case in Shakespeare's play. Evidently Dryden felt that this design would make All for Love more classical. (One wonders what Dryden thought of Antigone, which has two characters of equal importance in the action--one of whom vanishes with about one-third of the play remaining.)

What Dryden gains in unity (if unity be judged superficially), he loses in complexity. Take, for instance, the matter of time. By limiting the action to a single day, Dryden is able to subject his characters to a steady tension--a tension which continues to build until the end. Time in All for Love appears objective, unvarying for each character in the play, and for each member of the audience. Such is not the case in Antony and Cleopatra. In Act II, Scene 5 of Shakespeare's play, Cleopatra sends an attendant to fetch a messenger who can describe Antony's bride, Octavia, for her. It is not until Act III, Scene 3--five scenes later--that the messenger actually enters. Apparently, only several moments have elapsed between the two scenes in objective time; yet the intervening action reveals important alterations in the organization of the Roman Empire.

As David Kaula notes: "Through his abrupt shifts of locale Shakespeare . . . creates the impression that time moves at different velocities in different places . . . Thus if time in the world of political affairs moves with relentless speed, in Alexandria, while Cleopatra has nothing to do but wait for Antony, it is almost static."[62]

To put the matter differently: Shakespeare allows to coexist, through the structure of his play, what Henri Bergson calls "time" and "duration"--a feat he would not have been able to accomplish had he adhered to Dryden's plan. If Shakespeare was the most comprehensive playwright who ever lived, then the variety of structures he used helped make him so.[63]

VARIETIES OF DRAMATIC STRUCTURE

Notes

[1]John Gassner, ed. _Medieval and Tudor Drama_ (New York: Bantam, 1963), p. xv.

[2]Alan S. Downer, _The Art of the Play_ (New York: Henry Holt and Co., 1955), p. 88.

[3]I say "probably" because, though most scholars favor a theory of evolutionary development from liturgy through medieval drama to secular Renaissance drama, some writers have rejected the so-called liturgical argument. Oscar Cargill, for example, believes that drama did not evolve from liturgy because the extra-liturgical devices introduced into the liturgy were not essentially dramatic; it was the lay people who later took over the rites who injected the dramatic techniques. Therefore, according to Cargill, the drama did not stem from the liturgy but was, on the contrary, a corruption of the liturgy. Similarly, F. M. Salter maintains that the religious plays were never secularized because the Catholic Church controlled the plays until the Church of Rome in England itself disappeared; afterwards the new Church stamped out the bad old plays associated with "popery." Finally, H. C. Gardiner argues that the religious drama could not have evolved into secular drama because the religious plays never died--in fact, they were very much alive when secular drama first appeared. See the books on my bibliography by Cargill, Gardiner, and Salter, where each argues his thesis at length.

[4]Madeleine Doran, _Endeavors of Art: A Study of Form in Elizabethan Drama_ (Madison, Wisconsin: University of Wisconsin Press, 1964), p. 18.

[5]See my bibliography for Downer, Rosenberg, and Beckerman where these terms are used throughout their studies.

[6]John Dryden, "An Essay of Dramatic Poesy," in _The Works of John Dryden_, vol. XVII, ed. Samuel Holt Monk (Berkeley: University of California Press, 1971), pp. 55-56.

[7]Jackson G. Barry, _Dramatic Structure: The Shaping of Experience_ (Berkeley: University of California Press, 1970), p. 12.

[8]Gustav Freytag, _Technique of the Drama_, trans. Elias J. MacEwan (Chicago: Scott, Foresman, 1904), pp. 104-140.

[9]Horace, "The Art of Poetry," trans. C. Smart, in _European Theories of the Drama_, ed. Barrett H. Clark (New York: Crown, 1947), p. 32.

[10]_Johnson on Shakespeare_, in _The Yale Edition of the Works of Samuel Johnson_, vol. VII, ed. Arthur Sherbo (New Haven: Yale University Press, 1968), p. 107.

[11]James E. Hirsh, _The Structure of Shakespearean Scenes_ (New Haven: Yale University Press, 1981), pp. 14-15.

[12]Ibid, pp. 29-31.

[13]Wilfred T. Jewkes, _Act Division in Elizabethan and Jacobean Plays, 1583-1616_ (Hamden, Conn.: Shoe String Press, 1958), p. 101.

[14]Alfred Harbage, _William Shakespeare: A Reader's Guide_ (New York: Farrar, Straus & Giroux, 1963), p. 74.

[15]For Freytag's analysis of _Hamlet_, see pp. 190-192.

[16]Fergusson, _The Idea of a Theater_, p. 133.

[17]Charles Forker, "Shakespeare's Theatrical Symbolism and Its Function in _Hamlet_," in _Essays in Shakespearean Criticism_, ed. James L. Calderwood and Harold E. Toliver (Englewood Cliffs, N.J.: Prentice-Hall, 1970), p. 443.

[18]G. Wilson Knight, _The Wheel of Fire_ (Cleveland: Meridian, 1957), p. 42.

[19]See my bibliography for the Howard Baker book, where he develops this argument in detail.

[20]T. S. Eliot, "Hamlet and His Problems," in _Selected Essays_ (New York: Harcourt, Brace and World, 1932), p. 123.

[21]_Johnson on Shakespeare_, vol. VIII, p. 1011.

[22]Eliot, pp. 123-124.

[23]Elmer Edgar Stoll, _Art and Artifice in Shakespeare_ (New York: Barnes & Noble, 1962), pp. 101 and 121.

[24]Ernest Jones, _Hamlet and Oedipus_ (New York: Anchor, n.d.), p. 103.

[25]A. C. Bradley, _Shakespearean Tragedy_ (Cleveland: Meridian, 1963), pp. 41 and 46.

[26]Ibid, p. 50.

[27]Ibid, pp. 46-66.

[28]Maynard Mack, "The Jacobean Shakespeare: Some Observations on the Construction of the Tragedies," in _Essays in Shakespearean Criticism_, p. 23.

[29]Ibid, pp. 26-30.

[30]Ibid, pp. 36-37.

[31]Lily B. Campbell, _Shakespeare's Tragic Heroes_ (New York: Barnes & Noble, 1963), pp. 109-147.

[32]Maynard Mack, p. 38.

[33]Fergusson, _The Idea of a Theater_, p. 113.

[34]Ibid, pp. 117-124.

[35]Ibid, p. 127.

[36]Ibid, p. 153.

[37]_Johnson on Shakespeare_, vol. VIII, p. 1011.

[38]Just as it is Hamlet who undertakes to avenge his father's death; Hamlet who feigns madness; Hamlet who arranges the Players's Scene as a plot to "catch the conscience of the king"; Hamlet who kills Polonius; Hamlet who sends Rosencrantz and Guildenstern to their deaths; and Hamlet who also kills Laertes and Claudius.

[39]Bradley, pp. 52-53.

[40]Bradley calls Act II, Scene 1--Othello's reunion with Desdemona in Cyprus--the turning point because it represents the apogee in the hero's rise. But at the same time he admits that this moment is "but faintly marked: indeed, it is scarcely felt as a crisis at all." Nevertheless Bradley makes a determined effort to mold the structure, as much as he can, into the "usual scheme." See Bradley, p. 52.

[41]Lajos Egri, The Art of Dramatic Writing (New York: Simon and Schuster, 1946), p. 178.

[42]Bradley, p. 149.

[43]Richard G. Moulton, Shakespeare as a Dramatic Artist (New York: Dover, 1966), pp. 225-226.

[44]Ibid, p. 238.

[45]Bradley, pp. 51-52.

[46]Ibid, p. 51.

[47]Moulton, p. 205.

[48]Harley Granville-Barker, "Prefaces to Shakespeare," in King Lear: Text, Sources, Criticism, ed. G. B. Harrison and Robert F. McDonnell (New York: Harcourt, Brace, & World, 1962), p. 126.

[49]Bernard Beckerman, Shakespeare at the Globe (New York: Collier Books, 1965), pp. 41-42.

[50]Bradley, p. 309.

[51]See Moulton, p. 127; Freytag, pp. 129-130; and Harbage, p. 390.

[52]Beckerman, p. 42.

[53]Fergusson, "Macbeth as the Imitation of an Action," in Essays in Shakespearean Criticism, p. 513.

[54]Ibid, p. 515.

[55]Ibid, p. 518.

[56]Doran, p. 297.

[57]G. B. Tennyson, An Introduction to Drama (New York: Holt, Rinehart and Winston, 1967), p. 23. Why Tennyson should use Antony and Cleopatra as an "illustration" is baffling, until one realizes that many writers--in spite of evidence to the contrary and of every rule of logic--remain determined upon forcing all plays into some kind of structural uniformity. Apparently, that way lies security.

[58]Ibid, pp. 20-23. For Beckerman's view, see p. 42.

[59]Freytag, pp. 306 and 61.

[60]Dryden, "An Essay of Dramatic Poesy," p. 55.

[61]Dryden, "Preface," All for Love (New York: Appleton-Century-Crofts, 1966), pp. xxvi-xxvii.

[62]David Kaula, "The Time Sense of Antony and Cleopatra," in Essays in Shakespearean Criticism, pp. 577-578.

[63]Two "classical" tragedies--Euripides's Hippolytus and Racine's Phaedra--differ from each other in significant ways; yet they seem more nearly alike in structure when they are compared to Shakespeare's major tragedies. "You can summarize the whole plot of a Racinian tragedy in a short paragraph," observes Elder Olson; "a summary of the main plot alone in a Shakespearean one will run into pages and still not be adequate. Indeed, some

of Shakespeare's subplots, even, are in this sense more extensive than Racine's plots; the Gloucester subplot in King Lear, for instance, contains more incidents than the plot of Phaedra" (Olson, p. 222, italics in original).

Hippolytus involves a prologue, four episodes, four choral odes, and an exodus (the quantitative parts), whereas Phaedra is simply divided into five acts and opens immediately on the action. Racine not only eliminates the chorus, but he also does away with the two goddesses, Aphrodite and Artemis. Aristotle was unhappy with the deus ex machina in Euripides's play; hence the philosopher would have applauded Racine's elimination of this feature in his own version, wherein the title character--not Artemis--reveals the innocence of Hippolytus to Theseus. If such changes tend to simplify the structure, other alterations make the action more complicated. For example, Racine adds the circumstance of Hippolytus's love for Aricie, the supposed death of Theseus and his unexpected return, and some political motivation. Whether these various changes make Phaedra a better play than Hippolytus--or simply an equally good version of the myth--remains a moot question.

The most important difference between Hippolytus and Phaedra is apparent in the change of title. Although some critics have claimed that Euripides's play has a bipartite structure--that Phaedra is more interesting than Hippolytus, and that her early disappearance from the action represents an artistic failure on Euripides's part--close analysis of the piece reveals that the focus is on the hero. Racine, however, takes no chance on being accused of bipartitioning the action: he makes Phaedra the protagonist, and he keeps her on stage until the end. Note the similarity here to Dryden's strategy in All for Love, in which Antony and Cleopatra--unlike in Shakespeare's play--are both kept alive through most of the last act. Once again, whether Racine's decision to re-structure the action and shift the emphasis from Hippolytus to Phaedra results in a superior technique is arguable. The main point to bear in mind is that Hippolytus and Phaedra are basically similar in structure, whereas Shakespeare's plays remain much different from them and reveal greater multiformity when viewed as a whole.

III

Structure in Modern Drama

1. Ibsen and Shakespeare

Although a tight play structure is rightly associated with Ibsen's name, the great Norwegian's early efforts were inspired by the dramaturgy of Shakespeare. His first play, <u>Catiline</u>, is comparable in its number of scene changes to <u>Julius Caesar</u>; his fairy comedy, <u>St. John's Night</u>, resembles <u>A Midsummer Night's Dream</u>; and his <u>Lady Inger</u> has more than a few points in common with <u>Hamlet</u>.

In 1855, about five years after <u>Catiline</u> was written, Ibsen delivered a public lecture entitled "Shakespeare and His Influence on Scandinavian Literature." It is unfortunate that the lecture has been lost. As Halvdan Koht points out, however, the title of the talk alone "gives sufficient evidence that Ibsen at this time studied Shakespeare and was influenced by him."[1]

The plays in the open form which Ibsen wrote in imitation of Shakespeare remain among his least important efforts. Although he claimed to be not much impressed by antique drama or its seventeenth and eighteenth century offspring, and although he stated a preference for the Gothic and baroque, his mature technique obliges us to place him squarely in the tradition of plays with a single-action structure. This is a tradition which leads from Attic tragedy through neo-classical tragedy to the well-made play.

VARIETIES OF DRAMATIC STRUCTURE

During the years Ibsen labored at the theater in Bergen, he directed no less than twenty-one works by Scribe. Much--too much--has been made of this fact. That Greek tragedy, neo-classical tragedy, the Scribean well-made play, and Ibsenian tragedy can all be called closed in structure is true; that Scribe influenced Ibsen to some extent is also true; but that Ibsenian structure is basically Scribean is false. This can be shown by a comparison of Scribean form with Ibsenian form.

2. Scribe: The Structure of the Well-Made Play

The neo-classical approach to form was already mechanical (it took a genius like Racine to create great drama in the stifling atmosphere of the time), but Scribe carried the slide rule method of construction even farther. <u>Oedipus</u> is "well-made" in the sense that each part is carefully balanced in terms of an overall design of large thematic scope. Scribe's plays are not well-made in this sense at all. Alone, logical progression on the stage is of little intrinsic value; such development becomes significant to the degree that it presents a vision of truth. Scribe did not care a rap for truth. His one aim was to keep the customers on the edge of their seats until the final curtain, and to accomplish that aim he would use any trick at hand. As William Archer succinctly puts it: "The trouble with the well-made play is that it is almost always, and of necessity, ill-made."[2]

According to Stephen S. Stanton, the well-made play manifests seven formal qualities:

[1] a plot based on a secret known to the audience but withheld from certain characters (who have long been engaged in a battle of wits) until its revelation (or the direct consequence thereof) in the climactic scene serves to unmask a fraudulent character and restore to good fortune the suffering hero, with whom the audience has been made to sympathize; [2] a pattern of increasingly intense action and

86

suspense, prepared by exposition (this pattern assisted by continued entrances and exits, letters, and other devices); [3] a series of ups and downs in the hero's fortunes, caused by his conflict with an adversary; [4] the counterpunch of peripeteia [by "peripeteia" Stanton intends "the greatest in a series of mishaps suffered by the hero"] and scene a faire [or the "obligatory" scene], marking, respectively, the lowest and the highest point in the hero's adventures, and brought about by the disclosure of secrets to the opposing side; [5] a central misunderstanding or quiproquo, made obvious to the spectator but withheld from the participants; [6] a logical and credible denouement; and [7] the reproduction of the overall action pattern in the individual acts.[3]

Stanton argues that no work can be rightly described as belonging to the genre of the well-made play unless it exhibits these seven structural features in the exact pattern given above. Now in those plays by Scribe which I have read the well-made play formula is followed without deviation. Since Scribe is said to have written, alone or in collaboration, about five hundred pieces for the theater, I am willing to take Stanton's word for it that the French dramatist adhered to the seven-step construction in the rest of his plays.

Emile Augier and Alexander Dumas (fils) both harnessed the Scribean piece bien faite to a "message" and produced the piece a these or thesis play. The results are not memorable. Scribe's machinelike technique is at odds with plausible characterization, and with whatever faint air of reality is possible in a work undertaken to prove a point. And if the Scribean structure is ill-suited to the problem play, it remains even more detrimental to the tragic mode.

This is not to deny, as noted earlier, that Ibsen's plays occasionally reveal contrivances reminiscent of Scribe at his most Scribean. Krogstad's letter in A Doll's House; the fire which brings down the curtain of the second act in Ghosts; the knock at the door just as Solness says

87

"presently the younger generation will come knocking at my door"--and in walks Hilda Wangel!--in The Master Builder; these moments call to mind the author of Bataille de Dames.

Nevertheless the structure of Ibsenian drama does not conform to the pattern of the well-made play. Hence it is incorrect to say, as many critics do, that Ibsen wrote problem plays--as though we had another Dumas or Augier on our hands. The "woman problem" which Ibsen deals with in A Doll's House and Ghosts is also treated by Scribe's disciples in the piece a these. But for that matter, the same problem is treated by Euripides in Medea--and no one would accuse the Greek dramatist of being Scribean.

3. Ibsenian Structure

Ibsen wrote for a playhouse in which the audience sat facing a platform stage with a proscenium arch; inside the picture frame the actors moved within a realistic setting. If the structure of the theater was congenial to a closed form, the mechanistic assumptions of late nineteenth century science also favored causal progression within that form. Ibsen was far more consistent in the basic structuring of his plays than the three Greek masters and Shakespeare. Having developed a medium which served his purpose, Ibsen closely adhered to it even when he moved away from realism into symbolism.

William Archer, Kenneth Thorpe Rowe, and Lajos Egri have made valuable contributions to our understanding of Ibsenian play construction.[4] If we borrow some ideas from each writer, we will be able to construct a system of analysis which will designate the major structural elements in Ibsen's plays. Briefly, the Ibsenian structure is composed of three basic parts: 1) a point of attack; 2) a turning point; and 3) a resolution made up of a crisis, climax, and conclusion. Let us consider each of these parts before turning to an analysis of specific Ibsen plays.

Like the Greek and neo-classical playwrights, Ibsen begins the action close in time to the ending. This approach is called a late point of attack. The point of attack is that part of a play in which the dramatic question is raised. Generally it involves a decision by the protagonist, or a change in the protagonist's environment, either one of which will precipitate conflict. Ibsen was partial to the late point of attack because he was concerned with the influence of the past on the present. By beginning the play close to the resolution, he could bring in the necessary background through steady exposition as the action progresses in the present towards the climax. Through this method the causal interaction of past and present is rendered in a striking way.

Ordinarily, Shakespeare begins at the beginning of his story, so that the entire action unfolds before the spectator's eyes, with little or no retrospective discussion. This contrast between Ibsenian and Shakespearean structure represents, as we saw in the previous chapter, one of the chief differences between closed and open structure. But there is also a difference within the closed form between Ibsen's practice and that of the Greeks. Probably Aeschylus, Sophocles, and Euripides could assume that the spectators knew the legend which the play would imaginatively recreate. Like other modern artists with an international audience, Ibsen had no universal legends upon which to draw, no common tradition which the playwright and his audience shared. As a result, Ibsen had to present long and involved expositions. The dramatic question, then, is generally projected much earlier in the action of a Greek play than in one by Ibsen. Exposition--especially in a realistic play--remains one of the most difficult structural problems with which a dramatist must cope, but Ibsen was expert at it.

The turning point in an Ibsenian play is causally related to the point of attack. At the beginning of the action a question is posed which must be answered at the ending; hence the turning point is that event--represented by another decision on the part of the protagonist, or by another

change in circumstances--which makes the resolution
inevitable. In a four-act play in the Ibsenian
form, the turning point occurs near or at the end
of the third act; in a three-act play, the turning
point occurs near or at the end of the second act.

The crisis is reached in the last act when the
answer to the dramatic question is impending.
Every scene in the structure has been devised to
lead up to this point. The climax is the key scene
in the action: it is the answer to the dramatic
question, the fullest revelation of theme. Afterwards comes the conclusion, or the rounding off of
the action. In A Doll's House the conclusion is
protracted; but in Ghosts and Ibsen's later plays
the conclusion follows immediately upon the climax.
And rightly so; for an Ibsenian play ends, logically speaking, with the climax.

As can be seen, structure in Ibsenian drama is
somewhat more complex than in Greek variations of
closed structure. It is also more intricate than
the Aristotelian model involving complication,
turning point, and unraveling. Likewise, the Ibsenian structure does not fit Freytag's equal-sided
pyramid. There is no extended falling action in
Ibsen's plays, nor are the terms climax and turning
point interchangeable.

4. A Doll's House

In his preliminary notes for A Doll's House,
Ibsen says: "There are two kinds of spiritual law,
two kinds of conscience, one in man and another,
altogether different, in woman. They do not understand each other; but in practical life the woman
is judged by man's law, as though she were not a
woman but a man."[5] This idea became the spine of
the play.

About three-fourths of Act I in A Doll's House
is devoted to the introduction and preparation.
Helmer, the husband, is shown as a pompous, overbearing, tyrannical bore; Nora, the wife, is
presented as a gay, flighty, submissive "little

squirrel" (but with just enough iron in her blood to make her transformation at the end credible). Unlike the characters in a well-made play, Helmer and Nora are fully developed. Through exposition we learn that when Helmer was ill, Nora secretly borrowed money from Krogstad in order to finance a vacation for the sake of her husband's health. In doing so, however, she not only committed an act which Helmer disapproves of on principle, but she also forged her late father's signature on the note. For seven years Nora has been paying off the loan without her husband's knowledge. Now Helmer has become the manager of a bank, and one of his first acts will be to fire Krogstad, whom he hates for being an ex-forger himself.

The point of attack is reached when Krogstad informs Nora that unless she persuades Helmer to retain him at the bank, he will expose her transaction with him to her husband. Hence we might formulate the dramatic question as follows: "If Nora fails to swerve the stubborn Helmer from his course, and if Krogstad exposes her, what will happen to the relationship between Helmer and Nora?" A marriage (though admittedly a far from ideal one) is at stake.

Tension rises throughout the following act as Nora tries unsuccessfully to make Helmer reconsider his intention of dismissing Krogstad. The turning point occurs at the conclusion of Act II when Krogstad deposits a letter in Helmer's mailbox which reveals Nora's secret. Just before the curtain falls, Nora makes Helmer promise not to read the letter until the following evening. Thus the audience is left with a number of questions: "What will be Helmer's reaction to the letter?"' "What will be Nora's response to Helmer's behavior?"; "Will Nora--as she now appears to suggest--commit suicide?"; "Is this marriage fated to be destroyed?"; "Should it be destroyed?"

The crisis occurs about midway in the last act. Helmer reads the letter--and remains in character. He fails to appreciate the fact that Nora borrowed the money and forged her father's signature purely out of love for him; he thinks only of himself, of

91

his principles and his reputation. Now that Nora sees Helmer as he really is, now that she clearly understands that he does not love her the way she had thought he loved her, or the way that she loves him--what will she do?

The questions raised at the point of attack and at the crisis are answered when Nora informs Helmer that she is going to leave him. This is the climax of the play. Nora realizes that--thanks to the men in her past--she has been poorly educated for life in a complex world. Therefore, she must now educate herself.

Ibsen then follows with a long conclusion (five pages in the published text) in which Nora expands upon the reasons for her decision. As Robert Brustein rightly points out, this discussion suggests "a structural incompatibility between the drama of ideas and the drama of action."[6] In The Quintessence of Ibsenism, Shaw observes: "The disadvantage of putting the discussion at the end was not only that it came when the audience was fatigued, but that it was necessary to see the play over again, so as to follow the earlier acts in the light of the final discussion, before it became fully intelligible . . . Accordingly, we now have plays, including some of my own, which begin with discussion and end with action, and others in which the discussion interpenetrates the action from beginning to end."[7] Actually, Ibsen used both methods indicated by Shaw in each of his plays subsequent to A Doll's House.

Analysis of the basic structure in A Doll's House shows to what extent Ibsen aimed for unity of action; there are no subplots or parallel developments in the play. Originally, the time-sequence was to have been eight days, but Ibsen decided to concentrate the story by reducing the time to three days. All the action takes place in a single room of Helmer's house.

Aeschylus, Sophocles, and Euripides had the unities more or less thrust upon them by the physical conditions of their theater and by the convention of the chorus. Ibsen, however, chose to adhere to the unities because a tightly restricted form suited his overall dramatic strategy. This point is nowhere better illustrated than in Ibsen's next play, Ghosts.

5. Ghosts

In Ghosts Ibsen carries the retrospective method much farther then in A Doll's House. The action--all of which takes place in a single room of Mrs. Alving's house--begins some twelve to fifteen hours before the resolution, but the plot covers about thirty years in exposition. Ibsen's interweaving of past and present remains an extraordinary technical achievement. Even more extraordinary, however, is the way in which the structure of action expresses the theme of Ghosts.

At the start we learn that Engstrand plans to open an "inn" for sailors, and that he wants his "daughter," Regina, to work in it. Regina, a servant in the Alving home, refuses; she has hopes of marrying Oswald, Mrs. Alving's son. Oswald, who has lived away from his parents since he was seven, has just returned from abroad. Mrs. Alving has had an orphanage built which is to be a memorial to her late husband. The pastor of the local parish, Manders, visits her to discuss the problem of whether they should insure the orphanage. Finally they decide against insurance. This relieves the pastor who fears that the faithful might suspect they lack trust in God's providence. Mrs. Alving informs Manders, however, that she would not make good the damages should the orphanage burn.

Throughout Act I Ibsen builds slowly towards the point of attack. Manders tells Mrs. Alving that he disapproves of Oswald's free love and of his disdain for the sanctity of the marriage bond. The pastor reminds Mrs. Alving that, shortly after her marriage, she had left Alving and come to him for love and protection. At that time, Manders had urged Mrs. Alving to do her duty--which was, as the pastor saw it, and as convention decreed, to return to her drunken, profligate husband. And she had done so, the pastor observes with satisfaction, thus saving both her husband and her marriage. Now Manders is disturbed because Mrs. Alving approves of her son's wicked ideas.

The point of attack begins when Mrs. Alving informs Manders that her return to Alving did <u>not</u> change him. Indeed, Alving went so far as to seduce their own housemaid (Regina's mother, we discover later--so that Alving, not Engstrand, is the girl's father). Nevertheless Mrs. Alving did her best to conceal her husband's debaucheries. She was motivated partly by what Manders called her "duty," and partly by her love for Oswald--who was born after her return to Alving--because she wished her son to admire his father. To make the task of concealing Alving's true character from Oswald easier, Mrs. Alving sent her son abroad even though the pain of separation from him was almost unbearable. Clearly, Mrs. Alving had relinquished her normal desire for the joy of life in favor of self-sacrificing duty. Hence the major question posed by the play is: "Did Mrs. Alving act correctly in returning to her husband, in giving birth to Oswald, and in keeping her son ignorant of his father's true character?"

In Act Two Oswald tells his mother that he has a serious disease, and that the doctors who examined him abroad remarked: "The sins of the fathers are visited upon the children." Since Oswald had been given only an idealized picture of his father, he believes that his own joyous happy life is to blame. The turning point comes just before the end of the act. When Oswald announces his intentions of marrying Regina, Mrs. Alving decides to inform the couple that they have the same father. Mrs. Alving's decision will force the resolution, and thus answer the dramatic question. But the act ends with a report that the orphanage is on fire.

Because of its Scribe-like neatness and showiness, the report of the fire seems a crude prolongation of suspense (reminiscent of Nora's insistence at the turning point in <u>A Doll's House</u> that

Helmer not read Krogstad's letter until Act III), and tends to distract attention from the turning point.

The crisis arrives in Act III when Mrs. Alving finally discloses the truth to Oswald and Regina. The latter is angry because she was not educated as Alving's daughter; and when she learns that Oswald is sick, she decides to work in Engstrand's "inn"--in reality, a whorehouse. But Mrs. Alving is more shocked by her son's reaction. Oswald confesses that, as a result of his separation from his mother and father over the years, he has very little love for either of them. Furthermore, he informs his mother that he is going insane from the venereal disease he inherited from his father, and that he expects her to kill him with an overdose of morphia pills when the next attack begins. Grudgingly, Mrs. Alving agrees.

As the dawn ironically brightens the gloomy, ghost-ridden Alving livingroom, Oswald suffers an attack and begins asking his mother to give him the sun. This is the climax of the play. People were outraged when Nora left Helmer; they thought it was her "duty" to remain with her husband. Very well, Ibsen decided, I will show you what happens when a wife stays with an unworthy mate. The result was Ghosts. If Mrs. Alving had not gone back to her husband, Oswald would not have been born. She sacrificed herself in vain. Now she must decide whether or not to kill her own son--a syphilitic, psychotic wreck of a man. This is the upshot for Mrs. Alving, then, of doing her "duty."

The conclusion--Oswald again asking his mother for the sun--is simply the last line of the play. Here there is no question of a "structural incompatibility between the drama of ideas and the drama of action." Ghosts, unlike A Doll's House, fuses discussion and action right up to the final curtain.

Ghosts is far from being a piece a these on the subject of venereal disease. Ibsen's main theme involves the dead weight of all that we have inherited, not only from our parents, but also from

95

our whole cultural tradition--religious beliefs, educational approaches, prejudices, political ideologies, everything--and how these dead ideas prevent us from living now in the present. Because she is at the center of the structure of action-- because the theme is mainly revealed through her-- Mrs. Alving is the protagonist. Clearly, <u>Ghosts</u> is no more a thesis play than <u>Oedipus</u>.

Not surprisingly, <u>Ghosts</u> has frequently been compared to Sophocles's masterpiece. Both plays are closely-knit and highly concentrated; both use the retrospective method; and both begin near the resolution at a point where a Nemesis is about to fall on the protagonist. There are roughly twenty scenes in <u>Ghosts</u> (that is, scene units or portions of the play wherein the number of characters on stage remains constant): one scene takes place with five characters; one with four; six with three; and twelve with two. The majority of scenes in <u>Oedipus</u> also involve two characters.

Nevertheless, <u>Oedipus</u> and <u>Ghosts</u> differ sig- nificantly in structure. For example, the absence of a chorus in the modern play is much more impor- tant to the action than at first might seem the case. Sophocles achieves thematic extension through the chorus; Shakespeare accomplishes the same end through mirror patterns. In <u>Ghosts</u> Ibsen uses the relationship between Engstrand and Manders, and the relationship of both of them to Regina, instead of a chorus. Regina's decision to work in Engstrand's whorehouse makes a thematic statement about ghosts. At the same time, however, Regina's behavior relates to Mrs. Alving's position as a dutiful wife. By sleeping with a man she did not love, Ibsen suggests, Mrs. Alving acted like a whore. When Manders attempts to get Regina to live with Engstrand (at this point the pastor thinks Engstrand is the girl's father), and to work at the "inn," the past is repeated. The action involving Manders, Engstrand, and Regina is not developed fully enough to warrant being called a comic underplot.[8] Still, the use of these three characters--even though they are integrated into the single-action structure--does call to mind the mirror constructs of multi-action plays like _Hamlet_ and _Othello_.

Analysis of _Ghosts_ suggests that Ibsen tried to find a way to combine the open form of Shakespeare--the first influence on his dramaturgy--with the closed form of his mature years. Ibsen's control over the various elements of structure in _Ghosts_ represents a supreme technical achievement.

6. Chekhovian Structure

Chekhov's recorded view of Ibsen is not a consistent one. According to Ernest J. Simmons, Chekhov once remarked: "Ibsen is really not a dramatist"; and he specifically described _Ghosts_ as "a rotten play."[9] Yet in a letter written a year before his death, Chekhov expressed a keen desire to see _The Pillars of Society_--adding: "you know Ibsen is my favorite writer."[10] Did Chekhov change his mind about Ibsen, or was he being facetious?

Whatever his personal opinion of the Norwegian might have been, Chekhov was constitutionally incapable of writing effective plays in the Ibsenian manner. His first full length works for the stage--_Platonov_ and _Ivanov_--show him attempting to copy the methods of popular Russian dramatists; however, both plays remain plotty, theatrical, and deserving of neglect. _The Sea Gull_, _Uncle Vanya_, _The Three Sisters_, and _The Cherry Orchard_ are, of course, another matter. These last four plays represent a new departure in dramatic structure.

It is not easy to analyze the structure of a mature Chekhov play, although numerous critics have attempted to do so. Perhaps the best known and most influential study is David Magarshack's _Chekhov the Dramatist_. Magarshack divides the plays into two categories: plays of "direct action" and plays of "indirect action." In the first category belong plays "in which the main dramatic action takes place on the stage in full view of the audience"; in the second category belong plays "in which the main dramatic action takes place off the stage and in which the action that does take place on the stage is mainly 'inner action'." Chekhov, says Magarshack, found the direct action plays too contrived; hence the last four indirect action plays can be seen as a movement towards greater realism. Magarshack further argues that Chekhov, before writing his great plays, made a "thorough study of Greek drama, a fact of some consequence to the understanding of the structure of his last four plays."[11]

For example, Greek and Chekhovian plays are both essentially drama of indirect action, says Magarshack. In Greek tragedy the gods--who remain invisible--determine the fate of the characters; in Chekhovian drama there are also invisible characters--that is, characters who never appear on stage--who also determine the denouement. Both Greek and Chekhovian drama, therefore, rely on messengers to report off-stage action. Similarly, both forms of drama are distinguished by what Aristotle calls reversal, and both have a chorus. As for the latter, Chekhov divides the Greek chorus among several characters; these characters, who are integrated into the action of the play, "assume the mantle of the chorus whenever their inner life bursts through the outer shell of their everyday appearance, and overflows into a torrent of words." Chekhov's chorus scenes--again according to Magarshack--are "conducted in a sort of strophe and antistrophe manner."[12]

Magarshack's division of Chekhov's plays into direct action and indirect action forms is questionable. Frequently, Ibsen has some of the main dramatic action occur off stage--Hedda Gabler's suicide, for instance, and Solness's fall from the tower to his death. Such being the case, it would seem a matter of degree alone which separates the indirect action plays of Chekhov from the presumably direct action plays of Ibsen. There is a radical difference between Ibsenian and Chekhovian form, however, and that difference is qualitative, not merely quantitative.

By "action," Magarshack appears to mean that the characters are doing something. It is hard to know, then, what constitutes "inner action." On the stage thought must be externalized in some way. By inner action, Magarshack perhaps intends self-revelation in the form of dialogue, gesture, and movement. If so--how does the art of Ibsen, who uses the same technique of inner action, differ from that of Chekhov? Does the main action of a Chekhov play occur off stage or between the acts? This would make the enactment itself secondary in importance to some unseen, allegedly primary development going on elsewhere.

One can agree with Magarshack that Chekhov's last four plays represent a quest for greater realism (at least as the playwright saw it) without necessarily accepting his attempt to turn the Russian into a Greek. For that matter is it true that the main action of Greek plays takes place off-stage? Scenes of violence normally occur out of sight, but all other key scenes unfold in front of the audience. Are the gods always invisible? One thinks of Apollo and Athena in the Oresteia, of Aphrodite and Artemis in Hippolytus, and of Poseidon and Athena in The Trojan Women. And do the gods determine the fate of the characters? What has happened to the dual plane of action in Greek tragedy? Is it even true that Nina's parents in The Sea Gull, Protopopov in The Three Sisters, and Mrs. Ranevsky's aunt and her Paris lover in The Cherry Orchard resemble Greek gods, and that they are so important to Chekhov's design, that without them the denouement would not come to pass? Is anything really gained by calling scenes in which exposition is given "messenger scenes" and scenes in which characters reveal their deepest feelings "chorus scenes"? Isn't it possible to find both kinds of scenes in play structures of every conceivable description?

Now, Chekhov might have studied Greek drama before writing his major plays. But he would not have learned much about reversal from either Aeschylus or Euripides, two dramatists whose structural practices are normally ignored in most general discussions of Greek tragedy. Furthermore,

the strophe and antistrophe division of the choral
passages in Greek tragedy do not represent ironic
contrasts in viewpoint; generally, not even the
choral passages taken as a whole operate ironically
in contrast to the enactment. To apply terms like
strophe and antistrophe, then, to the opening scene
of The Three Sisters, in which the pathetic
dialogue of Olga and Irene is sharply undercut by
the laughter and crude remarks of Chebutykin and
Tusenbach, seems wide of the mark. By equating
Greek tragedy and Chekhovian drama, we obscure important differences between Chekhovian structure
and other kinds of structure, and thereby ignore
what is original in Chekhov.

Chekhov's later plays are not plotted. His
structures do not conform to Aristotle's complication, turning point, and unraveling; or to
Freytag's pyramid; or to Scribe's well-made play
formula; or to Ibsen's point of attack, turning
point, and resolution made up of a crisis, climax,
and conclusion. There is no real turning point or
climax in Chekhov's plays because there is no
decisive change in the character's lives.

In length, Chekhov's plays do not exceed
Ibsen's and in terms of place the Russian is nearly
as sensitive to unity as the Norwegian. But in his
handling of time and action, Chekhov inclines
toward the open form. Over two years elapse in The
Sea Gull; The Three Sisters has a time sequence of
three and a half years; and The Cherry Orchard
begins in May and ends in October. It is not clear
how much time is supposed to pass in Uncle Vanya.
Chekhov's plays, like most of Shakespeare's, are
polylinear; however, Shakespeare alternates his
stories in rounded scenes, whereas Chekhov presents
what might be described as bits of each story, often juxtaposing and contrasting them simultaneously.

By playing off one action against another,
Chekhov relates them both spatially and thematically. And because such a technique resembles
counterpoint, his form has been called musical,
contrapuntal, symphonic. The reader might recall
that some of Aeschylus's plays are also structured

along musical lines, inasmuch as they are not logically ordered and work lyrically through intensification of mood and repetition of idea. Need it be pointed out that there is nothing essentially Greek about this technique? After all, Oedipus is not musical in form. George R. Kernodle has suggested that the structure of King Lear is symphonic because of the way Shakespeare orchestrates the various lines of action thematically in the play.[13] But neither Aeschylus nor Shakespeare aim for that appearance of simultaneity which remains perhaps the most notable feature of Chekhovian structure.

Chekhov's plays are difficult to interpret because no single character speaks for the author, because there are no heroes or protagonists in his world. Other dramatists have written plays in which the structure does not revolve around one or even two central characters, but they have generally found a way--through a chorus, raisonneur, or clear single action--to underline the theme. Chekhov obliges us to piece together the various strands of juxtaposed action, and in the process to discover the meaning of the play for ourselves.

7. The Sea Gull

The Sea Gull is subtitled A Comedy in Four Acts. Perhaps Chekhov also considered Uncle Vanya and The Three Sisters comedies, although The Cherry Orchard is the only other play specifically identified by him as a comedy. It is well-known that Stanislavsky insisted on presenting Chekhov's plays as tragedies, an interpretation which angered the playwright. Perhaps the most sensible approach to Chekhovian drama is to view the four plays as tragicomedies. In some tragedies--Hamlet, for example, or Macbeth, or Antony and Cleopatra--there is comic relief; but in Chekhov's plays the comic and tragic views of life are balanced and contrasted. Thus the question of genre has a bearing on the principle of selection which underlies Chekhovian form as a whole. In short, the tragicomic nature of <u>The Sea Gull</u> merely represents one of a number of juxtapositions which determine its structure.

In place of a series of actions moving from a beginning to a logically related middle to a logical end--that is, in place of a plot--Chekhov presents a number of characters involved with each other in various ways, the sum total of their involvements not reducible to a single statement but rather comprising multiple viewpoints on the universal themes dealt with in the play. Such being the case, it is an error to allow, as some productions do, Madame Arkadin, or Treplev, or Nina, to assume a central place. All the characters in the play are important. They may not all be equally important--some have more lines than others--but no one character stands out. Because Chekhov refuses to identify wholly with any single character, he also makes it difficult for us to do so. Dorn, the local doctor, remains perhaps somewhat more perceptive than the other twelve characters; but, as Cleanth Brooks and Robert B. Heilman have suggested, he does not fully comprehend events either.[14]

The structure of <u>The Sea Gull</u> is thematic. In the course of the action, Chekhov contrasts young love and middle-aged love, new forms of writing and old forms, beginning actresses and established ones, optimism and pessimism, comedy and tragedy--the aim being to project a complex picture of reality. The themes are stitched together, in part, by a number of triangles and near triangles which could be described in various ways: Treplev-Nina-Trigorin; Treplev-Madame Arkadin-Nina; Madame Arkadin-Trigorin-Nina; Masha-Trigorin- Medvendenko; and Polina-Dorn-Shamraev.

Chekhov has been criticized because the theme of love in <u>The Sea Gull</u> gets in the way of the play's main line of development, makes for a messy effect, goes nowhere, and settles nothing.[15] But surely the love relationships are not intended to lead anywhere or resolve anything: that is the whole point of the action. Chekhov was not interested in being graded for neatness; he wished to present what he conceived to be a true image of human experience; and in his view the A loves B loves C relationships underlie life's tragicomic nature. Far from being subordinate in function, or concealing some non-existent main line of plot development, the triangles are a means through which Chekhov presents not only his love theme but also his other themes.

What really gives form to The Sea Gull, as well as to Chekhov's other mature plays, however, is the way the themes are presented. The individual scene units in an Ibsenian structure largely focus on a single main character and move the plot forward to a climax which answers the dramatic question posed at the start. The scene units in a Chekhovian structure, on the other hand, shift the focus continually from one character to another, from one mood to another, from one theme to another--the juxtapositions raising a host of questions, but answering few, if any, of them. We may not be able to state the theme of The Sea Gull succinctly. No matter. We remain convinced that Chekhov has rendered a complex view of life. Dramaturgically, the marvel is that The Sea Gull is not only extremely dense but also formally coherent. Chekhov accomplishes this difficult feat by his strict adherence to the basic pattern of alternation and contrast, or by his consistent tragicomic bipolarization of elements. And he does this without emphasizing any one character or any one line of development to the extent that we can speak of a main character or a main action.

An analysis of the opening scenes of The Sea Gull shows clearly the nature of Chekhovian structure. The first scene involves Medvendenko and Masha, and it introduces the love theme and the art theme. It is followed by a scene in which Treplev and Sorin join Medvendenko and Masha; this scene contrasts the frustrations of youth and the miseries and regrets of old age. Medvendenko and Masha then exit--followed by a brief appearance of Yakov, a worker. Alone, finally, Treplev and Sorin discourse on subjects relating to the ideas developed in the previous scenes. Presently the two men are joined by Nina; Sorin exits--and the

love theme is played again. Nina and Treplev
vanish; Polina and Dorn appear, and speak of love
and old age. Enter Madame Arkadin, Sorin,
Trigorin, Treplev, Shamraev, Masha, and Medvendenko.

The occasion for this scene is the presentation
of a play by Treplev in which Nina performs. Here
Chekhov achieves a striking effect of counterpoint,
or simultaneity. The play-within-a-play (among
other purposes) raises questions about "the meaning
of it all." But the device also permits Chekhov to
move back and forth between Nina as performer and
the other characters as spectators, between the
sentiments Treplev has embodied in his play and his
mother's reaction, thus creating an ironic juxtaposition. In Hamlet (and Chekhov reminds us of
Shakespeare's play by having Madame Arkadin and
Treplev quote from the closet scene before Nina
begins to perform), the play-within-a play grips
the onlookers and constitutes an important link in
the tragic course of action. In The Sea Gull the
play-within-a-play is ended prematurely by Treplev
because of his mother's levity and the inattention
of the others. Hamlet is a tragic figure; Treplev
is a tragicomic one--a fact which, as noted, has a
bearing on the structure of the play.

Examples of tragi-comedy are not hard to find.
In Act II, Masha asks Nina to read some lines again
from Treplev's play. Nina feels the play is
boring, but Masha praises the poetic intensity of
Treplev. While she is thus expressing admiration
for Treplev, we hear Sorin loudly snoring. Immediately after an emotional scene in Act III between Madame Arkadin and Trigorin--a scene in which
the woman tries unashamedly to hold on to her lover
who is attracted to Nina--Chekhov has Shamraev
puncture the mood with a funny story about two
tragedian actors, Suzdaltsen and Izmalov. Once
while acting in a play, relates Shamraev, Izmalov
had to report that the two were caught in a trap.
Instead the actor mistakenly shouted that they were
caught in a "tap." Remembering it, Shamraev laughs
heartily. And in the last act, Chekhov plays off
the sad reunion of Treplev and Nina in the garden
against the other characters who are seated at a

card table in the dining room, enjoying themselves. After Nina exits, Treplev decides to commit suicide--one reason being that Nina still loves Trigorin. He too exits. In the dining room Shamraev approaches Trigorin and shows him a stuffed sea gull (which is a symbol, on one level, of Nina) which Trigorin had ordered. Not surprisingly, however, Trigorin does not remember anything about it. From stage right comes the sound of a pistol shot. Everyone suddenly gets excited. And Dorn-- who has exited to investigate but quickly returns --whispers to Trigorin that Treplev has shot himself.

The style is the man. Gorky tells us that once Chekhov began to speak with animation to him about the poor state of the Russian teacher. "It is ridiculous to pay in farthings the man who has to educate the people," Chekhov said. "All this is disgusting; it is the mockery of a man who is doing a great and tremendously important work . . . Do you know, whenever I see a teacher, I feel ashamed for him, for his timidity, and because he is badly dressed . . . [I]t seems to me that for the teacher's wretchedness I am myself to blame--I mean it." Gorky, however, adds: "A shadow of sadness crossed his beautiful eyes; little rays of wrinkles surrounded them and made them look still more meditative. Then, looking round, he said jestingly: 'You see, I have fired off at you a complete leading article from a radical paper. Come, I'll give you tea to reward your patience.'--That was characteristic of him, to speak so earnestly, with such warmth and sincerity, and then suddenly to laugh at himself and his speech."[16]

Clearly, the various juxtapositions in The Sea Gull remain formal equivalents of the dramatist's bipolar view of life; hence structure and meaning in a Chekhov play are one.

8. Brecht: Expressionism and Epic Theater

Like Chekhov, the German Expressionists of the Twenties broke with the traditions of both Scribe and Ibsen. They patterned their plays on musical structure, which, as we have seen, was also true, to one degree or another, of Aeschylus, Shakespeare, and Chekhov. In the work of Goll, Kokoschita, Hasenclever, Toller, and Sorge syllogistic progression is replaced by alternation, contrast, and narrative; plot structure gives way to thematic structure. The form is open rather than closed, panoramic rather than focused. Expressionist theater resembles the episodic religious plays of the Middle Ages and the loosely constructed chronicle plays or history plays of the Elizabethan period.[17] The alogical structure, schematic characterization, and emphasis on theater which marks Expressionism had a strong influence on both Brecht's Epic Theater (Baal, an early play by Brecht, is of course an Expressionist play) and the Theater of the Absurd.

In his theoretical writings, Brecht distinguishes the structure of his own non-Aristotelian drama from the structure idealized by the Greek philosopher. Because the material conditions of life have changed since the fifth century B.C., argues Brecht, the form of drama must also change. The five-act structure cannot be imposed on the subject matter of contemporary experience. Although the tragedies of yesterday might have moved in a linear way, the catastrophes of today assume a cyclical form. Brecht took the term "epic" from Aristotle to point up the difference, as he saw it, between dramatic theater and epic theater. In dramatic theater, according to Brecht, there is action, the spectator is involved in the action, one scene exists for another, and there is linear progression with suspense over the outcome. In epic theater there is narrative, the spectator is an observer, each scene exists for itself, and there is a curved course of events with suspense over the process, or over what happens in each segment. Brecht could not accept Aristotle's idea of catharsis; he wanted, not purgation, but alienation--that is, he wanted a theater which would require decisions from spectators instead of merely subjecting them to an affective experience.

Brecht's emphasis on making the audience think accounts for his rejection of progressive structure and explains the form of his own plays. In A Short Organum for the Theater, Brecht argues that--since he does not want playgoers to lose themselves in their experience of a play--the episodes have to be joined together in such a way that the joinings are obvious rather than concealed, as is normally the case. If spectators discern the links which separate each part of the play, they will be in a better position to think about what the playwright is saying. Each scene will have its own independent structure as a play within the play. Titles would help to focus the social or thematic point. Brecht draws a comparison between his own form of structure and that of a chronicle or morality play.[18]

In his notes to The Threepenny Opera, Brecht justifies what he calls "the literarization of the theater." According to the traditional playwright, the theme of a play should be embodied within the action. Titles remain inartistic--a form of editorializing. Nonsense, replies Brecht. Plays must become more complex, more like novels and scholarly works. "Footnotes, and the habit of turning back in order to check a point," Brecht writes, "need to be introduced into playwriting, too."[19]

If Chekhov's dramaturgy can be called spatial and contrapuntal, so can Brecht's. His plays move not only horizontally, but also vertically, as progression is repeatedly and deliberately broken. According to Aristotle, epic progresses by employing only words and a single meter, whereas tragedy makes use of words, harmony, rhythm, and--in the choral episodes--a mixture of meters.[20] In epic theater, narration and debate often alternate with drama; for, contrary to Brecht's theory, Brecht's plays do not entirely dispense with drama, that is, with action, spectator-involvement, and suspense over the outcome. Often there are songs, recitations, dance sequences, and the use of signs, slides, and motion pictures.

Now, the previously mentioned concept of alienation--the so-called "A-Effect"--remains crucial to an understanding of Brecht's theory of play structure. The German word "Verfremdung" and the resultant translation into "alienation" has prompted much discussion. Martin Esslin, for example, feels that "alienation" or "estrangement" (the latter a term which some critics favor) have unhappy philosophical and psychological "overtones," and thus remain inadequate equivalents for what Brecht intended.[21] Esslin favors the French word "distantiation." Still, even though "Verfremdung" is hard to translate, argues Ronald Gray, it basically means "to make strange." And this is, of course, what many philosophers and psychologists are getting at when they use the words "alienation" or "estrangement." For Brecht, the Marxist playwright, to make society look "strange," is to persuade the viewer to want changes brought about in conformity with Communist ideology. Drama can be seen, then, as a weapon in the class struggle. All the same, as Gray observes, Brecht's theory has never become popular in the Soviet Union, or in any other Communist country.[22] True, Brecht was given the Stalin Peace Prize in 1955. Yet, as Esslin reminds us, only two of his plays--The Measures Taken ("which in its frankness about the use of force within the party was a propaganda catastrophe") and The Mother ("a play so starkly didactic that the audience could not associate it with any real happenings in pre-revolutionary Russia")--have overt Communist thematic structures.[23]

What is interesting about even some of Brecht's unsuccessful plays, at least from the perspective of the present study, is how he introduces filmic techniques into his play structures. Historically, Vsevolod Meyerhold may have been the first to use mixed-media in the theater. As early as 1920 the Russian director was projecting sequences of film on stage and fragmenting play structures into thirty-five or more scenes--each scene moving quickly by with cinematic fluidity. During the 1920's Erwin Piscator also used film on stage. For Ernst Toller's Hurrah We Live, Piscator worked with the film-maker Walter Ruttmann, who shot over ten thousand feet of film. To achieve a sense of simultaneity, Piscator used four film projectors. Brecht--who owed much to his relationship with Piscator, including the term "epic theater" itself-- felt that drama had to be as scientific as the twentieth century. (Naturally, Brecht saw Marxism as scientific in its analysis of history.)

Since film remains the most representative art of our technological age, as Arnold Hauser has indicated,[24] it seemed ideal to Brecht for his purposes. In "The German Drama: pre-Hitler," Brecht speaks glowingly of Piscator and his use of mixed-media. And in "The Film, the Novel, and Epic Theater," he maintains that the movie audience now looks at all art forms differently because that audience has been conditioned by the screen. The playwright, according to Brecht, must take that new way of seeing into account.[25] It was not easy, however, for Brecht to introduce film into his epic play structures. Consider, for example, The Mother, which Brecht wrote about the same time he was composing "The Film, the Novel, and Epic Theater."

The structure of The Mother (based on Gorky's novel of the same name)--which has as its subject matter the revolutionary stirrings of the masses just before 1905--is divided into fifteen scenes. In Scene One when Vlassovna, the title character, bewails her fate, Brecht has "The Vlassovnas of All Nations!" flashed on a screen, thus shifting the thematic focus from the particular to the general. During Scene Four, as a counterpoint to the enactment, Marx's "Theory Turns Into a Material Force Once the Masses Have Understood It!" is projected, with the hortatory intention of awakening the slumbering proletariat. Pictures of the victorious hammer-and-sickle are juxtaposed to photographs of the Czar, the Kaiser, and Woodrow Wilson, in an effort to achieve the Brechtian A-Effect. Unfortunately, such crude devices are reminiscent of agit-prop plays and fail to show Brechtian structure at its finest.

From The Mother to Mother Courage is, however, a giant step in dramatic form.

9. The Structure of Mother Courage

Mother Courage is subtitled A Chronicle of the Thirty Years's War. Since alienation or estrangement was Brecht's aim in structuring the play, setting the action back in the seventeenth century would help him--or so he reasoned--in preventing the audience from getting emotionally involved in the action. As a "teaching play" ("Lehrstuck"), Mother Courage was intended to encourage thinking on the part of the viewer, instead of feeling or experiencing empathy with the characters on stage.

Although Brecht is writing about the Thirty Years's War, he is not really concerned with the war in itself; he makes no attempt to probe the origins of that distant conflict. Rather, Brecht is trying to throw light on the present. Or, more correctly, he is offering an indictment against the stupidity of all wars. If there is a contemporary parallel, it is only because it is in the present that something can be done to end war. Mother Courage is pacifist drama.

Robert Brustein has observed: "Mother Courage haggles while her children die--this is the spine of the play. For while Courage is pursuing commercial advantage, her family is sacrificed, one by one, to the war."[26] Indeed, the deaths of Eilif, Swiss Cheese, and Kattrin--each child symbolically fathered by a man of a different nationality-- segments the twelve scenes of the structure into three parts. The number three also has relevance to the form of Mother Courage in another way. Frederic Ewen points out that Brecht's structure is knitted together by three elements: the omnipresent, seemingly endless war; Mother Courage, who is in all but one scene; and the canteen wagon, which she pulls around the stage, and from which she haggles while her children die.[27]

Action in <u>Mother Courage</u> takes place in various parts of Europe between the years 1624 to 1636. The length of each episode varies greatly. In the published text, for example, Scene Three runs to twenty-three pages, whereas Scene Five is only three pages. Scene Ten (one page in the published text) merely calls for a song as a prelude to the most dramatic scene in the play--namely, Kattrin's self-sacrifice in an effort to save the besieged Protestant town of Halle from Catholic troops. Kattrin's death, however, is in vain. Even though her warning has alerted the townspeople, the war continues in the last scene--and will continue for another twelve years.

Ibsen compresses time; Brecht presents time with less distillation, with more "realism." In scene after scene, time moves slowly, as the war seems to go on and on and on. At the end of the play, the soldiers sing the song that Mother Courage sang in the opening scene--thus underlining that curved course of events which Brecht cited as characteristic of epic structure.

"The classical play is constructed so that the action, piling up suspense from scene to scene and compressing time, flies like an arrow to the target waiting in the future," observes Norbert Mennemeier. "The result is that the audience paradoxically does not notice how time goes by. Epic theater radically breaks through this dramatic structure." As Mennemeier indicates, time in <u>Mother Courage</u> seems especially difficult to endure since Brecht offers his audience no redeeming benefits for humanity to throw into the balance against the war. "Rather, one sees a crippling recurrence of the same thing, the hideous picture of a war constantly expanding...."[28]

In spite of his loose time sequence, however, Brecht orchestrates each scene with superb mastery. Like Chekhov, Brecht plays off comedy against tragedy. The history of the war is narrated on a

screen at the beginning of each episode. Within
the episodes, quite often, the action involving the
principle characters is shown in ironic contrast.
Unlike The Mother, the screen device here is not
used in a clumsy, propagandistic manner. For instance, in Scene Six the narration informs us that
Mother Courage is present at the funeral of the
fallen commander, Tilly. During the episode--and
this is where the comedy comes in--the Chaplain
tries to entice Mother Courage into bed and Kattrin
gets a pair of a whore's red boots. Such juxtapositions pervade the entire structure of Mother
Courage, thus contributing to that Verfremdung
which Brecht sought.

Although his structure was different from
Ibsen's, Brecht (working at the old Schiffbauerdamm
Theater in Berlin) accepted the proscenium arch
(which had served so well the closed form of
Ibsen's dramaturgy); for, in spite of his treatment
of time, he was not interested in creating the illusion of real life. Brecht's open form could accommodate itself to the picture-frame stage because
the spectator's awareness that the sprawling structure was being enacted in a theater furthered the
ends of alienation.

Yet, despite Brecht's intentions, his artful
construction, and the shape of his theater, the
audience at Mother Courage is never completely
alienated--far from it. As the structure unfolds,
as the time sequence expands, and as the title
character loses more and more, there is a growing
sympathy and identification on the part of the
spectator with her plight. Mother Courage has been
deprived of three children by the war, but she has
learned to endure. Stupid and greedy--endurance
is, unfortunately, all she has learned. There is
no insight, no recognition scene. At the end of
the play, she is still going around in circles with
her wagon on the stage, and she is still in business. If the audience sees what Brecht wants it to
see, and what Mother Courage cannot or will not
see, it also feels what Brecht--at least consciously and according to his theory--did not want
it to feel. Alone at the end, Mother Courage
remains a symbol for the audience of the human

being's ability to go on in the face of disaster. To see the wrongness of Mother Courage's values and way of life, and yet to identify with her and to feel for her and even to admire her--all this may not be logical or what Brecht aimed for. But in the complicated response Mother Courage calls forth in the viewer, Brecht's play certainly underlines what great art is all about.

Nevertheless, for all its laudable form, the structure of Mother Courage is frequently dismissed as static. The assumption behind such criticism is that action equals conflict, or action equals plot. But even within the overall curved form of epic theater, Brecht provides for development from scene to scene. The final test of any play, of course, is production. Herbert Blau, who co-founded the Actor's Workshop of San Francisco, tells us that after a first reading of Mother Courage his company was bored by Brecht. But once the cast began to get involved with the script, they made a discovery.

"What we soon realized about the play . . . was that its activity is manifold and unceasing," says Blau. "Where it seemed to stand still, there were countless implicit demands for business . . . [S]omehow the diffuse, omnibus, verbal, novelistic character of the play became more active, empathic, concentrated, and dramatic as it approached the end. There was meaning in the more obvious interruptions of structure."[29]

Nevertheless the myth continues that "nothing happens" in the structure of a Brecht play--a charge which is leveled just as often at the structure of Chekhov's plays, as well as at plays in the Theater of the Absurd.[30]

10. Ionesco and the Absurd

By now it is well-known that Ionesco's entrance into the history of the drama came about as a result of an apparently harmless activity. In 1948 he was studying an elementary textbook of conversa-

113

tional English and the sentences in the book--such as "This is London ... There are thirty days in September . . . Lemons are sour"--stunned him with both their obviousness and their oddity. Ionesco stopped memorizing from the French-English primer and straight away proceeded to write The Bald Soprano, the dialogue of which sounding much like the conversational sentences he had just read. After finishing The Bald Soprano (there is of course no bald soprano in the play), the author became aware that in it he had revealed the absurdity of life behind the commonplace discourse of daily existence. Thus did Ionesco link his name to those of Beckett, Genet, and Adamov in the Theater of the Absurd.

Scholars have traced the lineage of the Absurd back to the Latin mimus, the commedia dell'arte, Jarry's Ubu Roi, Apollinaire's Les Mamelles de Tiresias, surrealism, Antonin Artaud, and existentialism.[31] Like Brecht, Ionesco and his fellow Absurdists frankly accept the stage as a stage instead of trying to create on it the illusion of reality. For Ionesco, however, Brecht is an auteur du boulevard, a left-wing conformist who serves up knowledge already obtainable in other kinds of writing.[32]

Truth in the theater, Ionesco argues, has to do with the universal condition of mankind; it has nothing to do with "progress" or "social realism." He says: "No society has been able to abolish human sadness, no political system can deliver us from the pain of living, from our fear of death, our thirst for the absolute . . . A work of art is the expression of an incommunicable reality that one tries to communicate--and which sometimes can be communicated. That is its paradox, and its truth."[33] Still, Ionesco's expression of "truth"-- like Brecht's (and also like Chekhov's)--is squarely in the tradition of modern tragicomic play structure.

Of the synthesis of tragic and comic elements in his work, Ionesco says: "But it is not a true synthesis, for these two elements do not coalesce, they coexist: one constantly repels the other, they

show each other up, criticize and deny one another
and, thanks to their opposition, thus succeed
dynamically in maintaining a balance and creating
tension."[34] The tension which Ionesco refers to is
one source of movement in his plays. Real theater
develops, he believes, not through plot, but
through a sequence of intense emotional states.

Brecht calls on the chronicle-play tradition of
Expressionist theater to portray an objective
reality in an open narrative form, whereas Ionesco
works in the dream-play tradition of that same
movement to depict a subjective reality in a closed
poetic form. According to Ionesco, the shape of
his plays does not follow the logic of an order
dictated from without. Instead, structure can be
seen as a projection upon the stage of an inner
state of conflict, or being.[35]

Since Ionesco is concerned with dramatizing a
surreal world, one would not expect to find in his
work a rational kind of play structure. He hates
"the reasoning play, constructed like a syllogism,"
he says, "of which the last scenes constitute the
logical conclusion of the introductory scenes, considered as premises."[36] In place of plot, puzzles,
all forms of architectural construction, Ionesco
substitutes "the inscrutable ... a sequence of
events without sequence."[37] Ibsenian form, then,
is not one of this dramatist's passions.

Structure in Ionesco's plays is thematic or
musical. "The plays are not 'about' anything; they
refer only to themselves," Richard Schechner explains. "That is why I call their structure
musical."[38] But musical as applied to the form of
Ionesco's plays also means the way in which related
themes are orchestrated throughout the action. As
Ionesco sees it, to speak of "epic theater," as
Brecht does, is a contradiction in terms; for
theater, by definition, is ineluctably dramatic.[39]
Brecht emphasizes story or narrative; Ionesco
focuses on a rhythmic alternation of poetic and
symbolic imagery. In Ionesco horizontal progression by the clock largely gives way to vertical ex-
pansion of meaning, thus making time a wholly rela-
tive matter.

All the same, Ionesco tells us that in <u>The Chairs</u> he has given his play a classical form. What--one might ask--can the playwright intend here by the word "classical"?[40]

11. <u>The Chairs</u>

Published with the description "A Tragic Farce," <u>The Chairs</u> is a short play without act or scene divisions. All the action takes place in a single room. Only three characters appear in the flesh (as opposed to the twenty-five in the open form of Brecht's <u>Mother Courage</u>). But a great number of invisible guests arrive on the set and are seated in chairs arranged in the center of the stage. An old man and woman--both in their nineties--have invited everyone in the world to their room so that the husband can deliver a momentous communication to humanity, an account and a justification of the couple's existence. The most important of the invited guests is "His Majesty," who we never see either. When the old couple try to reach him (or Him?), they are prevented from doing so by the clutter of chairs on stage. In the course of the play we learn that the old man has hired an orator who will articulate the great message to the world for the couple. When all the guests have finally arrived, the couple--enraptured at the prospect of having their lives add up to something through the speech of the professional rhetorician--jump out their window to a joyous death into the water below. The appearance of the orator, however, reveals that he is mute and can only mumble gibberish. (In some productions a blackboard is used and the orator writes nonsense on it.)

The main point of <u>The Chairs</u>, Ionesco makes clear, is not really the old couple's philosophy which fails to get communicated, or the wreckage of their shallow lives together. No, the true subject of this "tragic farce" is precisely the empty chairs. In short, the theme of <u>The Chairs</u> is <u>neant</u>, nothingness, the metaphysical vacuum which human beings inhabit, and the alienation from themselves, each other, and God which they experience. That the orator is unable to speak tells us much about Ionesco's view of language. Life is devoid of significance, and there is nothing, really, to communicate. Life is a tale told by an idiot....

By "classical," as applied to the design of The Chairs, Ionesco intends "in their purest state, the permanent forms and forgotten ideals of the theater."[41] Tension arises not only from the opposition of tragic and comic elements, but also from the coexistence of the chaotic action--the seemingly endless multiplication of chairs--and the tight overall structure of the piece. In shaping The Chairs, Ionesco has actually fashioned a parody of the "classical" or logical play as exemplified by Oedipus. (With his empty chairs, Ionesco has also fashioned a parody of Ibsen, who is identified with the furniture of the realistic picture-frame stage.)

For example, preparation is an important element in the structure of the "classical" play. Expectation is aroused in the audience when, at the beginning of Sophocles's masterpiece, Oedipus declares that he will find the murderer of Laius. At the start of The Chairs the old woman tries to pull the old man away from the window, for she is afraid he may fall out into the water below. In the zany Theater of the Absurd, however, this hint of what is to occur at a later point in the action does not have the same effect as the grim foreshadowing in the Greek play. Although Aristotle's complication, turning point, and unraveling are discernible in The Chairs, the stages in the tragic structure of the "syllogistic" play appear negatively. Hence the farce results, in part, from the playwright's skillful frustrating, rather than satisfying, of our anticipations. From the decision of the old man to give a message to his fellow human beings, through the arrival of his invisible guests, to the conclusion in which the couple die believing that the orator (who, unlike the blind Teiresias who sees all, remains dumb) will speak the message to posterity for the old man, The Chairs mocks rational form through Ionesco's vision of an irrational universe.

Obviously, The Chairs does not move with the relentless logic of Oedipus. The "logic" of Ionesco's play is that no logic exists. "What is needed," Ionesco wrote to the first director of his play, "is plenty of gesture, almost pantomime, light, sound, moving objects, doors that open and close and open again, in order to create [a sense of] emptiness . . . . [A]ll these dynamic objects are the very movement of the play, though this may not as yet be movement as you see it."[42] Structure in The Chairs must be seen in terms of a heightening of tension, and not as suspenseful plot development.

So, our study has come full circle. The structure of Oedipus is a reflection of Sophocles's belief that the world ultimately makes sense even if human beings themselves cannot always understand everything. Ionesco does not share Sophocles's faith. He does not believe that there is a final answer, that there is an explanation for the problem of human misery. Hence his plays can progress towards no Sophoclean resolution. The only catharsis Ionesco will permit the human beings who make up his audience is sad laughter.

Notes

[1] Halvdan Koht, The Life of Ibsen (New York: Blom, 1971), p. 117.

[2] William Archer, Playmaking: A Manual of Craftsmanship (New York: Dover, 1960), p. 139.

[3] Stephen S. Stanton, "Introduction: The Well-Made Play and the Modern Theater," ed. Stanton, in Camille and Other Plays (New York: Hill and Wang, 1957), pp. xii-xiii.

[4] For works by these writers, see my bibliography.

[5]Henrik Ibsen, From Ibsen's Workshop, trans. A. G. Chater (New York: Scribner's, 1911), p. 91.

[6]Robert Brustein, The Theater of Revolt (Boston: Little, Brown & Co., 1964), p. 68.

[7]Bernard Shaw, The Quintessence of Ibsenism (New York: Hill and Wang, 1957), p. 175.

[8]"Ghosts has two endings, not one," declares Jan Kott. "In the manifest tragic ending the mother holds a vial filled with poison beside her dying son's head. At the end of the play's hidden comedy, Regina, Captain Alving's illegitimate daughter, leaves the stricken household." The comedy in Ghosts is not quite so concealed as Kott suggests, but as a subplot, it is indeed "hidden." An analysis of Ibsen's play—as well as our experience of it in the theater—would not seem to support the assertion that there are "two endings." See Jan Kott, The Theater of Essence and Other Essays (Evanston, Ind.: Northwestern University Press, 1984), p. 37.

[9]Ernest J. Simmons, Chekhov: A Biography (Chicago: University of Chicago Press, 1970), pp. 504 and 624.

[10]Anton Chekhov, Letters on the Short Story, the Drama, and Other Literary Topics (New York: Dover, 1966), p. 202.

[11]David Magarshack, Chekhov the Dramatist (New York: Hill and Wang, 1960), pp. 53 and 49.

[12]Ibid, pp. 159-173.

[13]George R. Kernodle, "The Symphonic Form of King Lear," in King Lear: Text, Sources, Criticism, ed. G. B. Harrison and Robert F. McDonnell (New York: Harcourt, Brace, & World, 1962), pp. 142-146.

[14]Cleanth Brooks and Robert B. Heilman, Understanding Drama (New York: Holt, 1945), p. 499.

[15]See Magarshack, p. 187 and Maurice Valency, The Breaking String: The Plays of Anton Chekhov (New York: Oxford, 1966), p. 158.

[16]Maxim Gorky, Reminiscences of Tolstoy, Chekhov, and Andreyev (New York: Viking, 1959), pp. 70-71.

[17]With good reason, Ronald Hayman has remarked that Mother Courage is "the most Shakespearean of Brecht's plays." See Ronald Hayman, Bertolt Brecht: The Plays (London: Heinemann, 1984), p. 63.

[18]See Brecht on Theater, ed. John Willett (New York: Hill and Wang, 1964), p. 201.

[19]Ibid, pp. 43-44.

[20]See Chapter V, The Poetics, in S. H. Butcher, Aristotle's Theory of Poetry and Fine Art (New York: Dover, 1951), pp. 21-23.

[21]Martin Esslin, Brecht: The Man and His Work (New York: Norton, 1974), p. 132.

[22]Ronald Gray, Bertolt Brecht (New York: Grove, 1961), p. 60.

[23]Esslin, Brecht: The Man and His Work, p. 231.

[24]Arnold Hauser, The Social History of Art: Naturalism, Impression, The Film Age, vol. 4 (New York: Vintage, 1962), pp. 226-259.

[25]Both essays can be found in Brecht on Theater. See pp. 47-51 and pp. 77-81.

[26]Brustein, p. 272.

[27]Frederic Ewen, Bertolt Brecht (New York: Citadel, 1967), p. 354.

[28]Norbert Mennemeier, "Mother Courage and Her Children," in Brecht: A Collection of Critical Essays, ed. Peter Demetz (Englewood Cliffs, N.J.: Prentice-Hall, 1962), p. 148.

[29]Herbert Blau, The Impossible Theater: A Manifesto (New York: Collier, 1965), pp. 194-196.

[30]John Willett observes that Mr. Puntila and His Man Matti "has the progression and balance" lacking in Mother Courage. There is no Verfremdung in Mr. Puntila, either. It is, therefore, "smoother and offers less resistance to the audience"; it possesses "a firm logical shape." Apparently, Willett feels that this is all for the good. Although he admits that Mother Courage "has a size and sweep" Mr. Puntila has not, Willett asks whether Brecht "gains or loses" by his epic form. Myths die hard. See Brecht in Context: Comparative Approaches (London: Methuen, 1983), pp. 228-229.

[31]See, for instance, Martin Esslin, The Theater of the Absurd (New York: Anchor, 1961), pp. 229-289.

[32]For Ionesco's view of Brecht, see Notes and Counternotes: Writings on the Theater, trans. Donald Watson (New York: Grove Press, 1964), p. 91.

[33]Ibid, p. 91.

[34]Ibid, p. 27.

[35]Ibid, p. 158.

[36]Quoted in Esslin, The Theater of the Absurd, p. 131.

[37]Ionesco, Notes and Counternotes, p. 159.

[38]Richard Schechner, "The Bald Soprano and The Lesson: An Inquiry into Play Structure," in Ionesco: A Collection of Critical Essays, ed. Rosette C. Lamont (Englewood Cliffs, N.J.: Prentice-Hall, 1973), p. 37.

[39]Ionesco, Notes and Counternotes, p. 244.

[40]Ionesco, "The Chairs," in Playwrights on Playwriting, ed. Toby Cole (New York: Hill and Wang, 1962), p. 284.

[41]Ibid, p. 284.

[42]Ionesco, _Notes and Counternotes_, p. 189.

Epilogue

In this study I have tried to show that theories of dramatic structure rarely square with the practice of great playwrights. By comparing theories and plays instead of merely viewing plays through the spectacles of theories, we discover for ourselves a variety of play structures, unique creations which resist being reduced to our preconceived ideas about dramatic form.

Unfortunately, we have been so influenced by what Aristotle, Freytag, and others have had to say about form--so conditioned by generations of commentators and teachers--that, deep down, we really believe dramatic structure and plot structure are equivalent terms, that Sophocles's _Oedipus_ represents the norm, and that even Shakespeare somehow manages to succeed in spite of his departures from the structure of the drama, in spite of his--one almost hesitates to say it--structural clumsiness and ineptness. Certainly, Aeschylus and Euripides are often compared unfavorably to Sophocles.

Consider, for example, the following paragraph taken from a recent textbook on the drama:

> The plays of Aeschylus, powerful though they are, do not have the same delicacy of construction as do Sophocles's. They are forceful but, in terms of structure, somewhat rude. The structure of the plays of Euripides, Sophocles's successor, was never as fully worked out, and when Aristotle came to discuss the nature of tragedy in his _Poetics_, it was to Sophocles he turned for a model, not to the other two master playwrights of the genre.[1]

123

VARIETIES OF DRAMATIC STRUCTURE

If these remarks come as a jolt, it is simply because the author here says bluntly what others often merely imply.

Now, as we have seen, it is only in Oedipus and Electra that Sophocles shows that "delicacy of construction" praised by the author just quoted. And even Oedipus and Electra are not identical in structure. Where Oedipus looks backward to the past, Electra looks ahead to the future; where Oedipus ends in bad fortune for the hero, Electra concludes in good fortune. Ajax, Antigone, and The Trachiniae are diptychs. Oedipus at Coloneus is episodic and static. As for Philoctetes, it likewise is every bit as "rude" structurally as Aeschylus's plays are supposed to be. The Suppliants, The Persions, The Seven Against Thebes, Prometheus Bound—these Aeschylean dramas reveal little progression. The lyrical element in them is predominant, and the playwright achieves his effects mainly through intensification of mood. Although The Oresteia is both dramatic and lyrical in structure, Aeschylus's overall approach to form—even in this celebrated trilogy—remains chiefly thematic. Similarly, Euripidean form is different from that displayed in Oedipus and inclines towards thematic development of a tragic situation. There is a great variety of structure in the plays of Euripides. The Trojan Women, for instance, is much more lyrical than either Medea or Hippolytus; indeed, The Trojan Women has no beginning, middle, or end in any sense even remotely approaching what Aristotle meant by those terms. Every Greek tragedy (pace Aristotle) does not fall into two parts, and most of the plays do not have any reversal and/or recognition.

Samuel Johnson, A. C. Bradley, and T. S. Eliot all find problems with the structure of Hamlet. Why? Because these great critics—and they are great critics—view the structure of Hamlet in terms of what they believe dramatic form should look like, and on the basis of their perception of what Shakespeare's thematic focus should be. As we have observed, Bradley is unhappy with the structure of all Shakespeare's major tragedies.

But it is clear that Shakespeare did not write for a five-act structure. By imposing this "classical" external form on his plays, however, we imply that they were constructed with such a model in view, which is patently false. The external structure of Greek tragedy--prologue, parodos, episode (on the average five in number), choral ode, and exodus--suggests a uniformity in the dramaturgy of Aeschylus, Sophocles, and Euripides which likewise is not true. If there is no "typical" structure for Greek tragedy, there is also no "typical" structure for Shakespearean tragedy.

Shakespeare's structures--since they begin at the beginning and not <u>in</u> <u>medias</u> <u>res</u>--are non-Aristotelian and are not akin to <u>Oedipus</u>. This is true even of <u>Macbeth</u>, which alone among the five great tragedies has a single-action structure. To one degree or another, the other four plays have multiple-action structures. <u>Hamlet</u> and <u>Othello</u> have a mirror structure; <u>King Lear</u>, in addition to mirroring actions, has a fully developed subplot; and <u>Antony and Cleopatra</u> is extremely diffused and episodic in structural development.

If there is much variety of form in the work of the Greek tragedians and Shakespeare, the same is also true of playwrights in modern drama. Having fashioned a single-action structure for himself, Ibsen stayed with it throughout his major plays. Nevertheless, as we have discovered, Ibsenian structure is no clone of Sophoclean, much less Scribean, dramaturgy. Although Ibsen wrote in the closed form, for example, his expositions are much more extensive and involved than those of the Greeks. Like Ibsen, Chekhov found a form for him-self and repeated it in <u>The Sea Gull</u>, <u>Uncle Vanya</u>, <u>The Three Sisters</u>, and <u>The Cherry Orchard</u>. Unlike Ibsen's, however, Chekhov's plays are in the open form; yet, unlike Shakespeare's, Chekhov's plays are fragmented scenically and produce a contrapun-tal, or polyphonic, effect. Unlike Ibsen's, Chekhov's plays have no plot; and unlike Shakespeare's, no central character.

VARIETIES OF DRAMATIC STRUCTURE

Brecht uses a central character, but he throws out plot in favor of narrative. Like Chekhov--but to a lesser degree--Brecht also uses counterpoint, his plays moving both horizontally and vertically. Unlike Shakespeare, Brecht does not want the audience to identify with the central character, or with any character, or to get carried away by the flow of action. Because he aimed for the "A-Effect," Brecht's individual scenes, by conscious design, stand out more than do those of other great playwrights. If Brecht's plays are both anti-Aristotelian and anti-Ibsenian, so are Ionesco's. Like Chekhov and Brecht, Ionesco works with a tragi-comic form; but unlike them, his structure mimics a surreal world. Rejecting Brecht's narrative structure, Ionesco stitches together a structure of dreamlike images. As we have seen by looking at The Chairs, Ionesco comically imitates the kind of play structure idealized by Aristotle in the Poetics.

Structure is the way a particular dramatist shapes reality in order to present it on the stage. If style is the man, so is structure. Every dramatic form expresses a view of life, a metaphysic, an ontology. So there is no norm for dramatic construction.

Although historical modes of thought and the physical conditions of a theater both influence dramatic structure, we occasionally find plays of different periods and different conventions which seem to have more in common with each other than with plays of their own age. The greater the dramatist, the more variety of structure is normally evident in his work. Compare, for example, Shakespeare in this connection with Ibsen and Chekhov. The fact that Greek plays are written in a common language often blinds us to what is unique in them; the structural differences between Oedipus and The Trojan Women are more important--or, at the very least, just as important--as the similarities. The idiosyncratic nature of the individual dramatist makes it impossible to expect that all plays will be shaped in the same way. There are no "rules," "laws," or "necessary forms."

126

Since there is no one tradition of structure in the drama, it follows that Aristotelian, Hegelian, Freytagian, and similar reductive methods of analysis are not universally pertinent. The terms "open" and "closed" can be useful descriptions of structure, provided we resist turning them into rigid categories. Some plays are open in one way and closed in another. Greek tragedy tends toward a single-action structure; Shakespearean tragedy tends toward a multiple-action structure. Between the polar extremes, however, there are many gradations.

No one dramatic structure is necessarily higher on the scale of perfection than another. The structure of <u>Oedipus</u>, for example, is not better than the structure of <u>Hamlet</u>; the structure of <u>Mother Courage</u> or <u>The Chairs</u> does not represent an improvement over the structure of <u>Medea</u> or <u>Othello</u> or <u>The Sea Gull</u>. We may prefer one kind of structure to another—that is a matter of taste. As Henry James, speaking in another context, once remarked: "As people feel life, so they will feel the art that is most closely related to it."[2] Objectively considered, however, one kind of structure cannot be judged inherently superior to another.

There is no archetypal dramatic form, no "usual scheme," against which all play structures are to be measured and evaluated. If structure is the man, structure is also the idea. Form and content are one. A dramatic structure is to be assessed, not in reference to some outside standard or model, but on how well it contributes to the artistic whole created by the playwright.

Aeschylus, Sophocles, Euripides, Shakespeare, Ibsen, Chekhov, Brecht, Ionesco—each one of these dramatists has shown that masterpieces can be written without regard for a single "ideal" structure.

127

VARIETIES OF DRAMATIC STRUCTURE

Notes

[1]Lee A. Jacobus, <u>The Bedford Introduction to Drama</u> (New York: St. Martin's Press, 1989), p. 41.

[2]Henry James, "The Art of Fiction," in <u>Theory of Fiction: Henry James</u>, ed. James E. Miller, Jr. (Lincoln, Nebr.: University of Nebraska Press, 1972), p. 39.

Bibliography

Archer, William. Playmaking: A Manual of Craftsmanship. New York: Dover, 1960.

Baker, Howard. Induction to Tragedy: A Study in a Development of Form in Gorboduc, The Spanish Tragedy, and Titus Andronicus. Baton Rouge: Louisiana State University Press, 1939.

Baldwin, T. W. William Shakespeare's Five-Act Structure. Urbana: University of Illinois Press, 1947.

Barry, Jackson G. Dramatic Structure: The Shaping of Experience. Berkeley: University of California Press, 1970.

Bateson, F. W. "Catharsis," in Tragedy: Modern Essays in Criticism, ed. Laurence Michel and Richard B. Sewall. Englewood Cliffs, N.J.: Prentice-Hall, 1963.

Beckerman, Bernard. Shakespeare at the Globe. New York: Collier Books, 1966.

Blau, Herbert. The Impossible Theater: A Manifesto. New York: Collier Books, 1965.

Bradley, A. C. Shakespearean Tragedy. Cleveland: Meridian, 1955.

Brooks, Cleanth and Robert B. Heilman. Understanding Drama. New York: Holt, 1945.

Brustein, Robert. The Theater of Revolt. Boston: Little, Brown & Co., 1964.

VARIETIES OF DRAMATIC STRUCTURE

Burke, Kenneth. _Counter-Statement_. Los Altos, Calif.: Hermes, 1953.

Butcher, S. H. _Aristotle's Theory of Poetry and the Fine Arts: With a Critical Text and Translation of the Poetics_. New York: Dover, 1951.

Campbell, Lily B. _Shakespeare's Tragic Heroes_. New York: Barnes and Noble, 1963.

Cargill, Oscar. _Drama and Liturgy_. New York: Octagon Books, 1969.

Chekhov, Anton. _Letters on the Short Story, the Drama, and Other Literary Topics_. New York: Dover, 1966.

Doran, Madeleine. _Endeavors of Art: A Study of Form in Elizabethan Drama_. Madison: University of Wisconsin Press, 1964.

Downer, Alan S. _The Art of the Play_. New York: Holt, 1955.

Dryden, John. "An Essay of Dramatic Poesy," in _The Works of John Dryden_. Vol. XVII. Ed. Samuel Holt Monk. Berkeley: University of California Press, 1971.

_____. "Preface," _All for Love_. New York: Appleton-Century-Crofts, 1966.

Egri, Lajos. _The Art of Dramatic Writing_. New York: Simon and Schuster, 1946.

Eliot, T. S. "Hamlet and His Problems," in _Selected Essays_. New York: Harcourt, Brace and World, 1932.

Else, Gerald F. _The Origin and Early Form of Greek Tragedy_. New York: Norton, 1972.

Esslin, Martin. _The Theater of the Absurd_. New York: Anchor, 1961.

_____. _Brecht: The Man and His Work_. New York: Norton, 1971.

Fergusson, Francis. <u>The Idea of a Theater</u>. New York: Anchor, n.d.

_____. "<u>Macbeth</u> as the Imitation of an Action," in <u>Essays in Shakespearean Criticism</u>. Ed. James L. Calderwood and Harold E. Toliver. Englewood Cliffs, N.J.: Prentice-Hall, 1970.

Forker, Charles. "Shakespeare's Theatrical Symbolism and Its Function in <u>Hamlet</u>," in same as above.

Freytag, Gustav. <u>Technique of the Drama</u>. Trans. Elias J. MacEwan. Chicago: Scott, Foresman, 1904.

Gardiner, H. C. <u>Mysteries End: An Investigation of the Last Days of the Medieval Religious Stage</u>. New Haven: Yale University Press, 1946.

Gassner, John. <u>Masters of the Drama</u>. New York: Dover, 1940.

_____, ed. <u>Medieval and Tudor Drama</u>. New York: Bantam, 1963.

Gorky, Maxim. <u>Reminiscences of Tolstoy, Chekhov, and Andreyev</u>. New York: Viking, 1959.

Granville-Barker, Harley. "Prefaces to Shakespeare," in <u>King Lear: Texts, Sources, Criticism</u>. Ed. G. B. Harrison and Robert F. McDonnell. New York: Harcourt, Brace, and World, 1962.

Gray, Ronald. <u>Bertolt Brecht</u>. New York: Grove Press, 1961.

Grube, G. M. A. <u>The Drama of Euripides</u>. New York: Barnes & Noble, 1961.

Harbage, Alfred. <u>William Shakespeare: A Reader's Guide</u>. New York: Farrar, Straus & Giroux, 1963.

Hardison, O. B., Jr. _Aristotle's Poetics: A Translation and Commentary_. Trans. Leon Golden. Englewood Cliffs, N.J.: Prentice-Hall, 1968.

Hauser, Arnold. _The Social History of Art: Naturalism, Impressionism, The Film Age_. Vol. 4. New York: Vintage Books, 1962.

Hayman, Ronald. _Bertolt Brecht: The Plays_. London: Heinemann, 1984.

Hegel, George Wilhelm Friedrich. _Hegel on Tragedy_. Ed. Anne Paolucci and Henry Paolucci. New York: Anchor, 1962.

Hirsh, James E. _The Structure of Shakespearean Scenes_. New Haven: Yale University Press, 1981.

Hogan, Robert and Sven Eric Molin, ed. _Drama: The Major Genres_. New York: Dodd, Mead & Co., 1966.

Horace. "The Art of Poetry," trans. C. Smart. _European Theories of the Drama_. Ed. Barrett H. Clark. New York: Crown, 1947.

Ibsen, Henrik. _From Ibsen's Workshop_. Trans. A. G. Chater. New York: Scribner's, 1911.

Ionesco, Eugene. "_The Chairs_," in _Playwrights on Playwriting_, ed. Toby Cole. New York: Hill and Wang, 1962.

_____. _Notes and Counternotes: Writings on the Theater_. Trans. Donald Watson. New York: Grove Press, 1964.

Jacobus, Lee A. _The Bedford Introduction to Drama_. New York: St. Martin's Press, 1989.

James, Henry. "The Art of Fiction," in _Theory of Fiction: Henry James_. Ed. James E. Miller, Jr. Lincoln, Nebr.: University of Nebraska Press, 1972.

Jewkes, Wilfred T. _Act Division in Elizabethan and Jacobean Plays, 1583-1616_. Hamden, Conn.: Shoe String Press, 1958.

Johnson, Samuel. _Johnson on Shakespeare_, in _The Yale Edition of the Works of Samuel Johnson_. Vols. VII and VIII. Ed. Arthur Sherbo. New Haven: Yale University Press, 1968.

Jones, Ernest. _Hamlet and Oedipus_. New York: Anchor, 1949.

Kaufmann, Walter. _Tragedy and Philosophy_. New York: Anchor, 1969.

Kernodle, George R. "The Symphonic Form of _King Lear_," in _King Lear: Text, Sources, Criticism_ Ed. G. B. Harrison and Robert F. McDonnell. New York: Harcourt, Brace, and World, 1962.

Kitto, H. D. F. _Greek Tragedy_. New York: Anchor, 1954.

Knight, G. Wilson. _The Wheel of Fire_. Cleveland: Meridian, 1957.

Koht, Halvdan. _The Life of Ibsen_. New York: Blom, 1971.

Kott, Jan. _The Theater of Essence and Other Essays_. Evanston, Ind.: Northwestern University Press, 1984.

Kuala, David. "The Time Sense of _Antony and Cleopatra_," in _Essays in Shakespearean Criticism_. Ed. James L. Calderwood and Harold E. Toliver. Englewood Cliffs, N.J.: Prentice-Hall, 1970.

Mack, Maynard. "The Jacobean Shakespeare: Some Observations on the Construction of the Tragedies," in same as above.

Magarshack, David. _Chekhov the Dramatist_. New York: Hill & Wang, 1960.

VARIETIES OF DRAMATIC STRUCTURE

Mennemeier, Norbert. "Mother Courage and Her Children," in Brecht: A Collection of Critical Essays. Ed. Peter Demetz. Englewood Cliffs, N.J.: Prentice-Hall, 1962.

Moulton, Richard G. Shakespeare as a Dramatic Artist. New York: Dover, 1966.

Muller, Herbert. The Spirit of Tragedy. New York: Washington Square Press, 1966.

Murray, Gilbert. The Classical Tradition in Poetry. New York: Vintage, 1957.

Oates, Whitney J. The Complete Drama. Vol. 1. Ed. Oates and Eugene O'Neill, Jr. New York: Random House, 1938.

Olson, Elder. Tragedy and the Theory of Drama. Detroit: Wayne State University Press, 1966.

O'Neill, Eugene. "Working Notes and Extracts from a Fragmentary Work Diary," in American Playwrights on Drama. Ed. Horst Frenz. New York: Hill & Wang, 1965.

Nietzche, Friedrich. The Birth of Tragedy. New York: Random House, 1967.

Pickard-Cambridge, A. W. Dithyramb, Tragedy, and Comedy. Oxford: Oxford University Press, 1927.

Rosenberg, Marvin. "A Metaphor for Dramatic Form." Journal of Aesthetics and Art Criticism, 17 (1958): 174-180.

Rosenmeyer, Thomas G. The Art of Aeschylus. Berkeley: University of California, 1982.

Rowe, Kenneth Thorpe. Write That Play. New York: Funk & Wagnalls, 1939.

_____. A Theater in Your Head. New York: Funk & Wagnalls, 1960.

Salter, F. M. Medieval Drama in Chester. Toronto: University of Toronto Press, 1955.

Schechner, Richard. "Approaches to Theory/ Criticism." <u>Tulane Drama Review</u>, 10 (Summer 1966): 20-53.

_____. "<u>The Bald Soprano</u> and <u>The Lesson</u>: An Inquiry into Play Structure," in <u>Ionesco: A Collection of Critical Essays</u>. Ed. Rosette C. Lamont. Englewood Cliffs, N.J.: Prentice-Hall, 1973.

Seale, David. <u>Vision and Stagecraft in Sophocles</u>. Chicago: University of Chicago Press, 1982.

Shaw, Bernard. <u>The Quintessence of Ibsenism</u>. New York: Hill & Wang, 1957.

Simmons, Ernest J. <u>Chekhov: A Biography</u>. Chicago: University of Chicago Press, 1970.

Stanton, Stephen S. "Introduction: The Well-Made Play and the Modern Theater," in <u>Camille and Other Plays</u>. Ed. Stanton. New York: Hill & Wang, 1957.

Stoll, Elmer Edgar. <u>Art and Artifice in Shakespeare</u>. New York: Barnes & Noble, 1962.

Stuart, Donald Clive. <u>The Development of Dramatic Art</u>. New York: Dover, 1960.

Tennyson, G. B. <u>An Introduction to Drama</u>. New York: Holt, Rinehart & Winston, 1967.

Valency, Maurice. <u>The Breaking String: The Plays of Anton Chekhov</u>. New York: Oxford, 1966.

Waldock, A. J. A. <u>Sophocles the Dramatist</u>. London: Cambridge University Press, 1951.

Willett, John, ed. <u>Brecht on Theater</u>. New York: Hill & Wang, 1964.

_____. <u>Brecht in Context: Comparative Approaches</u>. London: Methuen, 1983.

Wolfflin, Heinrich. <u>Principles of Art History</u>. New York: Dover, n.d.

Index

About the Author

Edward Murray was born in New York City. He took his B.A. from Youngstown State University where he majored in philosophy and English; he took his Ph.D. in English with a concentration in drama from the University of Southern California. Murray has published six previous books, among them <u>Arthur Miller Dramatist</u> and <u>Clifford Odets: The Thirties and After</u>. His <u>Fellini the Artist</u> has been reprinted in England and chapters from it and other books have appeared in a number of anthologies, the most recent being <u>Modern Critical Interpretations of The Crucible</u>, edited by Harold Bloom. For over twenty years Murray has taught drama and film at the State University of New York at Brockport. He has also been a Visiting Professor at Loughborough University in England and has lectured on Fellini at the University of Jyvaskyla in Finland.